Sanctifying the Name of God

Sanctifying the Name of God

Jewish Martyrs and Jewish Memories of the First Crusade

Jeremy Cohen

PENN

University of Pennsylvania Press
Philadelphia

Copyright © 2004 University of Pennsylvania Press
Printed in the United States of America on acid-free paper

10   9   8   7   6   5   4   3   2   1

Published by
University of Pennsylvania Press
Philadelphia, Pennsylvania 19104-4011

Library of Congress Cataloging-in-Publication Data

Cohen, Jeremy, 1953–
   Santifying the name of God : Jewish martyrs and Jewish memories of the First Crusade /
Jeremy Cohen.
      p.   cm. — (Jewish culture and contexts)
   Includes bibliographical references and index.
   ISBN 0-8122-3780-3 (cloth : alk. paper)
   1. Jews—Germany—History—1096–1147.   2. Jews—Persecutions—Germany.
3. Crusades—First, 1096–1099.   4. Germany—Ethnic relations.   I. Title.   II. Series.
DS135.G31C64   2004
943'.004924—dc22

2003069063

Contents

Preface

Students of literature, anthropology, and psychology have long taken for granted that a "historical" story does not reflect the world of the (historical) characters who function within it but the world of the people who tell it. Some consider this truth so self-evident that they refer to it as a "banal fact."[1] Yet, for some reason, we continue to expect more from the field of history and from the historian. We naively hope and assume that they can penetrate the impenetrable, break through the stories recording the past, and accurately reconstruct the events of their narratives—objectively, as it were, free of all editorial interpretation and distortion. Paraphrasing one of the doyens of historical research during the heyday of nineteenth-century positivism, we expect historians and their craft to tell us how it actually happened, not much more, and certainly nothing less. Most nineteenth- and twentieth-century historians promoted this notion of their mission, and they confidently turned their energies toward pursuing it.

Historians of the last generations, however, have gradually acknowledged the futility of attempting to isolate the events of history from the many layers of their subsequent memories, especially as we realize the magnitude of our investment in the past. Paradoxically, the more we need to reconstruct our history, the more the goal of filtering facts out of their interpretation eludes us. Human nature does not allow for transmitting information entirely objectively, and it never did. A reported event by its very nature has always been an interpreted event. No matter how close to an event historical sources might be, they still convey human memories of what transpired, memories that derive from very much more than that past event itself. One can never travel the entire distance between text and event, a distance compounded at every stage of the transmission of historical information, for its transmitters inevitably reinterpret as they convey it onward.

With such considerations in mind, this book struggles with tales of Jewish martyrdom from the First Crusade, when Jews of northern Europe,

attacked by bands of crusaders, met a violent death to avoid conversion to Christianity. These anti-Jewish persecutions of 1096—or *Gezerot Tatnu* as Jews remember them in Hebrew[2]—have long been enshrined in Jewish historical memory, and, during the past two decades, they have stimulated intense, often highly charged debate among Jewish historians. Surprisingly, only one historian has previously devoted a book-length study entirely to *Gezerot Tatnu*,[3] and the present investigation will seek to make this critical chapter in medieval Jewish history more accessible to a broader readership, at the same time as it offers a different perspective on the events and their memories.

In the first instance, this book will investigate the reactions of the Jews attacked by the crusaders in 1096 and, most directly, the memories of those reactions that lived on among the survivors. Our interest lies primarily with stories told by the survivors and with the role, the significance, of these stories in the Jewish society that produced them. How did Jews in twelfth-century Germany remember and memorialize those who preferred death as a Jew to life as a Christian? What historical and cultural circumstances gave rise to these memories of martyrdom, as opposed to the events that they narrate?

Additionally, this book will read tales of medieval Jewish martyrdom in a manner that few have tried and developed. As the opening years of the twenty-first century have reinforced upon us, communities remember their martyrs—and choose to identify them as martyrs in their memories—because they died for ideals that these communities of the living cherish. When we label past victims of violence and persecution *martyrs*, we give expression to heavy emotional baggage that we presently carry with us. While tales of martyrdom, then, perhaps can teach us something about the martyrs themselves, their ideas, and their deaths, they communicate considerably more about the *martyrologists*, those who remember the martyrs and tell their stories because they find them meaningful. Applying these principles to the extant Hebrew narratives of the 1096 persecutions, we shall see how the martyrs' stories teach us above all else about the survivors who told them. These twelfth-century accounts of the violence and victims of 1096 demonstrate how those living made sense of the self-sacrifice of the dead, and how their memories gave expression to the needs and circumstances of European Jews during the decades that followed.

During the years I have worked on this book, many have found its ideas unsettling; some have even responded to them out of fear or anger. As we shall see, the example of the Jewish martyrs of 1096 nourished the

idealism of Ashkenazic Jews ever since, and the greatest of twentieth-century Jewish historians drew direct connections between Jewish martyrdom during the Crusades and the extermination of Jews during the Holocaust. Cherished memories surely heighten the sensitivity and zeal with which we react to Holocaust deniers, particularly after historians have justly triumphed over deniers in courts of law. Suggesting that tales of martyrdom in our Crusade chronicles might not amount to totally accurate, factual reporting, that they express an ideology of martyrdom that belonged to the living survivor, not the slain martyr, I have appeared to some as treading dangerously close to the borders of "revisionism."

Let me, then, clarify my stance in this book, as succinctly as I can: Revisionist in the traditional, scholarly sense of proposing a fundamentally new interpretation? Invoking Yale historian Donald Kagan's statement that by revisionist "we refer to a writer who tries to change the reader's mind about events in the past in a major way,"[4] I readily confess my revisionist aspirations. Must our conclusions and our method undermine the historical truth of the events of martyrdom, during the Crusades, the Holocaust, or at any other time? Absolutely not. Nevertheless, they demonstrate that the historian must recognize and struggle with the complex relationship between event and text. The attacks of terrorist "martyrs" on the World Trade Center and the Pentagon just several years ago—suicides who died resisting what many Muslims identify as a new, modern-day Western crusade—underscore the critical importance of the historian's task: to understand how cultures endow events with their meaning. Watching the news media daily, particularly in the Middle Eastern setting where I have written my book, we see how one person's martyr is another person's villain. Now more than ever, we must distinguish between martyrs and their memories as responsibly as we can.

Donald Kagan has suggested that the very first revisionist among historians was Thucydides, author of the monumental *Peloponnesian War*, which recounts that fateful conflict between classical Athens and Sparta.[5] Although they may never have heard of Thucydides, the Jews who survived the First Crusade and told of the martyrs of 1096 emulated aspects of his historiographical method. Thucydides explained that in reporting the speeches of his historical characters, he recorded what *he* believed they *should have* said in their particular situations, not necessarily what they did say. So, too, the voices in the extant Hebrew narratives of *Gezerot Tatnu* portrayed Jews sanctifying the name of God in a manner that made sense *to them*. In so doing, they might well have looked favorably on the rationale

that Thucydides offered for his method: "Whoever shall wish to have a clear view both of the events which have happened and of those which will some day, in all human probability, happen again in the same or similar way—for these to adjudge my history profitable will be enough for me." Perhaps those who compiled our sources would even have shared in Thucydides' ultimate hope: "My history . . . has been composed, not as a prize-essay to be heard for the moment, but as a possession for all times."[6] Ashkenazic Jewry's narratives of the First Crusade never enjoyed the popularity of the *Peloponnesian War*; for centuries, at least two of the three surviving prose texts remained virtually unknown. Still, memories of persecutions of 1096 have persistently touched the hearts and souls of Jews concerned with their past, from medieval times until our own.

As the ideas presented in this book took shape over the course of the last decade, I drew from the reactions, suggestions, and criticisms that members of my family, colleagues, students, and friends kindly shared with me. Robert Chazan, Deborah Cohen, Joseph Hacker, Jan Willem van Henten, Ivan Marcus, Michael Signer, Gabrielle Spiegel, and Israel Yuval generously gave of their time in conversation, in correspondence, and in reading all or part of various drafts of the book; to them, among others too numerous to single out, I remain deeply indebted. Among the various institutions and organizations that invited me to air my ideas, I am especially grateful to the Oxford Centre for Hebrew and Jewish Studies for the opportunity to deliver the Louis Jacobs Lectures in 1996, when I presented several chapters of the book in an earlier form and benefited considerably from the responses to them. The Divinity School of the University of Chicago, where I served as Regenstein Visiting Professor of Jewish Studies in 1999, provided me the supportive framework where I completed the bulk of my research and also where I tested my ideas in a graduate seminar on Jewish history and Jewish memory in the Middle Ages. I finished the first draft of the entire book in 2000–2001 while a fellow of the Institute for Advanced Studies at the Hebrew University of Jerusalem, the congeniality of whose staff and supportive atmosphere proved second to none. The College of Humanities of The Ohio State University and the Goldstein-Goren Diaspora Research Center of Tel Aviv University helped to subvent the costs of my research over the many years that it ensued; and a grant from the Chaim Rosenberg School of Jewish Studies of Tel Aviv University offset the costs of preparing the manuscript for publication.

Abbreviations for Primary Sources

ACW	Ancient Christian Writers. New York.
ANF	Ante-Nicene Fathers. Ed. Alexander Roberts et al. 8 vols. Buffalo, N.Y., 1886–88.
ARN	*Aboth de Rabbi Nathan* (in Hebrew). Ed. Solomon Schechter. Corr. ed. New York, 1967.
Aronius	Julius Aronius, ed. *Regesten zur Geschichte der Juden im fränkischen und deutschen Reiche bis zum Jahre 1273.* Berlin, 1902.
'Avodat Yisra'el	*Seder 'Avodat Yisra'el.* Ed. Seligman Baer. Rev. ed. Berlin, 1937.
Benton	John F. Benton, ed. *Self and Society in Medieval France: The Memoirs of Abbot Guibert of Nogent.* New York, 1970.
Bernard	Bernard of Clairvaux. *Opera.* Ed. Jean Leclercq et al. Rome, 1957–77.
Bet ha-Midrash	Adolph Jellinek, ed. *Beth ha-Midrash* (in Hebrew). 3rd ed. 6 pts. in 2 vols. Jerusalem, 1967.
Bible mor. 2554	*Bible moralisée: Codex Vindobonensis 2554.* Ed. Gerald B. Guest. London, 1995.
Carmi	T. Carmi, ed. *The Penguin Book of Hebrew Verse.* Harmondsworth, Eng., 1981.
CCCM	Corpus Christianorum, Continuatio mediaevalis. Turnhout, Belgium.
CCSL	Corpus Christianorum, Series latina. Turnhout, Belgium.
CSEL	Corpus scriptorum ecclesiasticorum latinorum. Vienna.
Dinur	Benzion Dinur, ed. *Israel in the Diaspora* (in Hebrew). 2 vols. in 10 pts. Tel Aviv, 1958–72.
Eidelberg	Shlomo Eidelberg, ed. *The Jews and the Crusaders.* Madison, 1977.
Eliyahu Rabbah	*Seder Eliahu Rabba und Seder Eliahu Zuta* (in Hebrew). Ed. M. Friedmann (Ish-Shalom). Vienna, 1902.
Eusebius	Eusebius. *Ecclesiastical History.* Ed. Kirsopp Lake et al. Loeb Classical Library. 2 vols. Cambridge, Mass., 1926–32.

Exodus Rabbah   *Midrash Shemot Rabbah: Chapters I–XIV* (in Hebrew). Ed.
Avigdor Shinan. Jerusalem, 1984.

FC   Fathers of the Church. New York and Washington.

GCS   Die griechische christlichen Schriftsteller.

Gellis   Jacob Gellis, ed. *Sefer Tosafot Hashalem: Commentary on
the Bible* (in Hebrew). 9 vols. Jerusalem, 1982–93.

Genesis Rabbah *Midrash Bereshit Rabba: Critical Edition with Notes and
Commentary* (in Hebrew). Ed. J. Theodor and Ch. Albeck.
3 vols. 1903–36; repr., Jerusalem, 1965.

Glossa   *Biblia Latina cum glossa ordinaria: Facsimile Reprint of the
Editio Princeps.* 4 vols. Turnhout, 1992.

Guibert   Guibert of Nogent. *Autobiographie.* Ed. Edmond-René La-
bande. Les Classiques de l'histoire de France au Moyen
Age 34. Paris, 1981.

H   A. M. Habermann, ed. *Sefer Gezerot Ashkenaz ve-Tzarefat.*
Jerusalem, 1945.

Hermann   Hermann of Cologne. *Opusculum de conversione sua.* Ed.
Gerlinde Niemeyer. MGH Quellen zur Geistesgeschichte
des Mittelalters 4. Weimar, 1963.

Ibn Daud   Abraham ibn Daud. *Sefer ha-Qabbalah: The Book of Tradition.* Ed. Gerson D. Cohen. Philadelphia, 1967.

Ibn Ezra   Abraham ibn Ezra. *The Religious Poems* (in Hebrew). Ed.
Israel Levine. 2 vols. Jerusalem, 1975.

Josephus   Josephus. *Works.* Ed. and tr. H. St. J. Thackeray et al. Loeb
Classical Library. 9 vols. Cambridge, Mass., 1926–65.

Josippon   *The Josippon* (in Hebrew). Ed. David Flusser. 2 vols. Jerusalem, 1978–80.

Judah, *Diwan* Judah ben Samuel ha-Levi. *Dîwân.* Ed. A. M. Habermann.
4 vols. Farnborough, Eng., 1971.

Kinot   *Seder ha-Kinot le-Tish'ah be-Av.* Ed. E. D. Goldschmidt.
Jerusalem, 1968.

Lam. Rabbah *Midrasch Echah Rabbati* (in Hebrew). Ed. Salomon Buber.
Vilna, 1899.

Lev. Rabbah *Midrash Wayyikra Rabbah* (in Hebrew). Ed. Mordecai
Margulies. 5 vols. Jerusalem, 1953–60.

MGH   Monumenta Germaniae historica.

McGinn   Bernard McGinn, ed. *Apocalyptic Spirituality.* London,
1979.

Meir b. Baruch	Meir ben Baruch of Rothenburg. *She'elot u-Teshuvot: Defus Prag.* Ed. M. Bloch. Budapest, 1895.
Mekh. Rashbi	*Mechilta de-Rabbi Simon b. Jochai* (in Hebrew). Ed. D. Hoffmann. Frankfurt am Main, 1905.
Mekhilta	*Mechilta d'Rabbi Ismael* (in Hebrew). Ed. H. S. Horowitz and I. A. Rabin. 2nd ed. Jerusalem, 1960.
Melito	Melito of Sardis. *On Pascha and Fragments.* Ed. and tr. Stuart George Hall. Oxford, 1979.
Memorbuch	Siegmund Salfeld, ed. *Das Martyrologium des Nürnberger Memorbuches.* Quellen zur Geschichte der Juden in Deutschland 3. Berlin, 1898.
Mid. Mishle	*Midrash Mishle.* Ed. Burton L. Visotzky. New York, 1990.
Mid. Shemu'el	*Midrasch Samuel (in Hebrew).* Ed. Salomon Buber. Krakow, 1893.
Mid. Tana'im	*Midrasch Tannaïm zum Deuteronomium* (in Hebrew). Ed. D. Hoffmann. 2 vols. Berlin, 1909.
Mid. Tehillim	*Midrash Tehillim.* Ed. Salomon Buber. 1891; repr., Jerusalem, 1966.
Mid. Zuta	*Midrash Suta: Hagadische Abhandlungen über Schir ha-Schirim, Ruth, Echah, und Koheleth* (in Hebrew). Ed. Salomon Buber. Berlin, 1894.
Musurillo	*Acts of the Christian Martyrs.* Ed. Herbert Musurillo. Oxford, 1972.
N/S	Adolf Neubauer and Moritz Stern, eds. *Hebräische Berichte über die Judenverfolgungen während der Kreuzzüge.* Quellen der Geschichte der Juden in Deutschland 2. Berlin, 1892.
OTP	*The Old Testament Pseudepigrapha.* Ed. James H. Charlesworth. 2 vols. Garden City, N.Y., 1983–85.
Otzar Mid.	J. D. Eisenstein, ed. *Ozar Midrashim: A Library of Two Hundred Minor Midrashim* (in Hebrew). 2 vols. New York, 1915.
Oz, 'Ad Mavet	Oz, Amos. *'Ad Mavet.* Tel Aviv, 1971.
Oz, Crusade	Oz, Amos. *Unto Death.* Tr. Nicholas de Lange. London, 1975.
PDRE	"*Pirke de-Rabbi Eli'ezer.*" Ed. Michael Higger. *Horeb* 8 (1944): 82–119; 9 (1946): 94–166; 10 (1948): 185–294.
Pesikta Rab.	*Pesikta Rabbati: Midrasch für ein Fest-Cyclus und die aus-*

gezeichneten Sabbathe (in Hebrew). Ed. M. Friedmann (Ish-Shalom). 1880; repr., Tel Aviv, 1963.

Pesikta Rav K.   *Pesikta de-Rav Kahana.* Ed. Bernard Mandelbaum. 2 vols. New York, 1962.

Peter, *Letters*   Peter the Venerable. *Letters.* Ed. Giles Constable. 2 vols. Cambridge, Mass., 1967.

Peter, Sermons   Peter the Venerable. "Sermones tres." Ed. Giles Constable. *Revue Bénédictine* 64 (1954): 224–72.

Peters   Edward Peters, ed. *The First Crusade: The Chronicle of Fulcher of Chartres and Other Source Materials.* Philadelphia, 1971.

Philo   Philo. *Works.* Ed. F. H. Colson et al. 10 vols. and 2 suppl. vols. Cambridge, Mass., 1929–53.

PL   Patrologia latina. Ed. J. P. Migne et al. 221 vols. Paris, 1861–64.

Poetics   Aristotle. *Poetics.* Ed. Stephen Halliwell. Cambridge, Mass., 1995.

Raymond/Hill   Raymond of Aguilers. *Historia Francorum qui ceperunt Iherusalem.* Tr. John Hugh Hill and Laurita L. Hill. Memoirs of the American Philosophical Society 71. Philadelphia, 1968.

RHC   *Recueil des historiens des croisades: Historiens occidentaux.* 5 vols. Paris, 1844–95.

Rosenfeld   Abraham Rosenfeld, ed. *The Authorised Kinot for the Ninth of Av.* London, 1965.

Ruth Rabbah   Myron Bialik Lerner. "The Book of Ruth in Aggadic Literature and Midrash Ruth Rabba" (in Hebrew). Ph.D. dissertation. 3 vols. Hebrew University of Jerusalem, 1971.

Sefer Ḥasidim   Judah ben Samuel the Pious. *Seser Ḥasidim: Das Buch der Frommen* (in Hebrew). Ed. Jehuda Wistinetzki and J. Freimann. 2nd ed. Frankfurt am Main, 1924.

She'iltot   *Sheeltot de Rab Ahai Gaon* (in Hebrew). Ed. Samuel K. Mirsky. 5 vols. Jerusalem, 1959–77.

Sifre Deut.   *Sifre on Deuteronomy* (in Hebrew). Ed. Louis Finkelstein. Corpus tannaiticum 3,3,2. 1939; repr., New York, 1969.

Sifre Num.   *Siphre ad Numeros adjecto Siphre zutta* (in Hebrew). Ed. H. S. Horowitz. Corpus tannaiticum 3,3,1. 1917; repr., Jerusalem, 1966.

Soferim   *Masekhet Soferim.* Ed. Michael Higger. New York, 1937.

Song Rabbah	*Midrash Rabbah: Shir ha-Shirim.* Ed. Shimshon Dunski. Jerusalem, 1980.
Tanakh	*Tanakh: A New Translation of the Holy Scriptures according to the Traditional Hebrew Text.* Philadelphia, 1985.
TB	Babylonian Talmud.
Tchernichowsky	Saul Tchernichowsky. *Shirim.* 5th ed. Jerusalem, 1947.
Thucydides	Thucydides. *History of the Peloponnesian War.* Loeb Classical Library. Ed. and tr. Charles Forster Smith. 4 vols. Rev. ed. Cambridge, Mass., 1928–33.
TJ	Palestinian (Jerusalem) Talmud.
Tosefta	*The Tosefta* (in Hebrew). Ed. Saul Lieberman. 5 vols. New York, 1955–88.

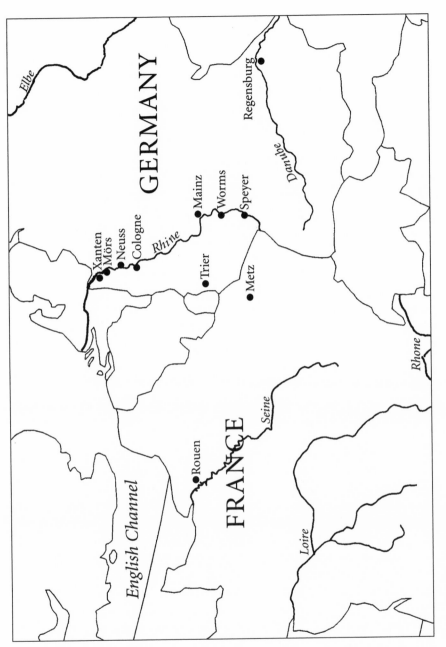

The persecutions of 1096.

Introduction
The Persecutions of 1096

I shall speak out in the grief of my spirit before my small congregation.
I shall wail and lament; for the Almighty has dealt bitterly with me.
Be silent, hear my words and my prayer.
If only he would hear me.

The crusaders massed at the gateway
To blot out the name of his remnants.
Small children cried out to him with one voice:
"Hear, O Israel, the Lord is our God; the Lord is one."[1]

Thus the *payyetan*, the Jewish liturgical poet of the Middle Ages, recalled the massacres of the spring and summer of 1096, when, during the earliest months of the First Crusade, bands of armed crusaders attacked Jewish communities in western and central Germany. The crusaders converted those Jews whom they could, while others who fell in their path they killed. Jewish settlements of the Rhine valley—in Speyer, Worms, Mainz, Cologne and its suburbs, Metz, and Trier—and others including Regensburg and Prague to the east suffered serious losses in life and property. This marked the first major outbreak of anti-Jewish violence in medieval Christian Europe.[2]

Why did the massacres occur? Some historians have argued that economically grounded jealousies soured the relations between German Jews and their neighbors; perhaps the still ongoing Investiture Conflict between the popes and the kings of Germany further aggravated existing tensions. Yet most of the evidence from both Jewish and Christian sources indicates that religious zeal motivated the attackers above all else.[3] Consider the rationale which one of the Jewish chronicles of the persecutions of 1096, written in Hebrew during the first half of the twelfth century, put in the mouths of the crusaders. "Even as we set out on a long journey, to seek the shrine of the idolatrous deity and to exact revenge from the Muslims, behold, the Jews, whose ancestors gratuitously killed and crucified him, live among us;

let us first take our revenge upon them."⁴ While labeling the Holy Sepulcher the "shrine of the idolatrous deity" clearly reflects the caricature of a Jewish voice, the contemporary French abbot Guibert of Nogent confirmed that this very reasoning inspired attacks upon the Jews, as he described events in Rouen in 1096.

The people who had undertaken to go on that expedition under the badge of the cross began to complain to one another. "After traversing great distances, we desire to attack the enemies of God in the East, although the Jews, of all races the worst foes of God, are before our eyes. That's doing our work backward."⁵

Different explanations for the massacres of 1096 are hardly mutually exclusive, but one must recognize that the motivation for the persecutions—at least insofar as those who wrote chronicles of the Crusade understood it—had much to do with the ideology and conduct of Christian holy war. The pope who launched the First Crusade never instructed his knights to attack the Jews, and the fact that forcibly converted Jews openly returned to Judaism after the violence subsided suggests that the Christian establishment acknowledged the illegitimacy of the violence.⁶ Still, one can well appreciate how various factors contributed to the passion of the attackers: rampant hostility toward the "infidel," the long history of anti-Jewish teaching in the Catholic Church, an intense longing for the end of days that nourished the crusading spirit, and the code of vengeance that medieval knights generally followed. Thus set against the general background of the Crusades, anti-Jewish violence should not be written off too hastily as deviating from the character of the movement and involving only a few, atypical warriors. Count Emicho of Flonheim and others who initiated the hostility enjoyed a degree of aristocratic status, and they seem to have believed firmly that crusaders had a moral obligation to punish the Jews. Such conviction also found an echo in a Latin chronicle of the First Crusade by the French monk Raymond of Aguilers, which recounts how God spoke of the Jews to the crusaders as they neared the Holy Land in 1099: "I entertain hatred against them as unbelievers and rank them the lowest of all races. Therefore, be sure you are not unbelievers, or else you will be with the Jews, and I shall choose other people and carry to fulfillment for them my promises which I made to you."⁷ Even after the crusaders had battled intensely against the Muslims, the Jews exemplified religious unbelief for them; they, and not the Muslims, were the enemies of God par excellence, the greatest threat to God's covenant with his chosen people. Several decades later, the

great Cistercian abbot Bernard of Clairvaux injected basic ideas of Christian anti-Judaism into his call for the Second Crusade, even as he worked hard to prevent violent attacks upon the Jews.[8] His colleague the Benedictine abbot Peter the Venerable of Cluny, in a well-known letter to King Louis VII of France, echoed our Hebrew chronicle's explanation for the pogroms against the Jews.

Why should we pursue the enemies of the Christian faith in far and distant lands while vile blasphemers far worse than any Muslims, namely the Jews, who are not far away from us but who live in our midst, blaspheme, abuse, and trample on Christ and the Christian sacraments so freely and insolently and with impunity?

Peter reiterated that Christians should not kill the Jews, but this, he hastened to explain to King Louis, establishes that "God has no wish to release them through the punishment of death, since he preserves them for a life worse than death."[9]

Peter demonstrates how the ideology of crusading and Christian anti-Judaism went hand in hand; we see such linkage both in this letter of 1146 to King Louis and in a sermon "In Praise of the Lord's Grave," which Peter preached in the presence of the pope in 1146 or 1147. As he praised the holiness and importance of the Holy Sepulcher in Jerusalem, Peter designated Jesus' grave the chief reason for a Christian to rejoice in Christ, that which truly facilitates Christian victory over the enemies of God. Today, he declared, the Holy Sepulcher embodies the Christian hope for final salvation, hope that has now spread throughout the entire world; only a few remaining Jews and the wicked sect of Muhammad still resist it. God has confirmed this status of Jesus' grave and the hope that it fuels in numerous ways, but above all in a miraculous fire that kindles the lamps in the Holy Sepulcher every Easter—a miracle that Peter's sermon discusses at length. Here, then, lies the route to salvation: Giving up the pleasures of this world, a Christian must cultivate the holiness, the memories, and the miracles enshrined in the grave of Christ, joining the universal assembly of faithful souls that it has attracted, and liberating it from the pollution of non-Christians. In this context, Peter depicted the Jews and their way of life as demonstrating by counterexample all that the crusader should strive for. While Peter's letter to King Louis associates the Jews with the sinful pursuit of financial profit, his sermon on the Holy Sepulcher develops the opposition more thoroughly. The Jews do not interpret Scripture properly, so as to comprehend the grandeur of Jerusalem and its holy sites and see the way

toward eternal life. The Jews murdered the body of Christ that gave the Holy Sepulcher its sanctity. And thus the annual miracle of the fire there, recalling the flame with which God showed that he preferred the biblical Abel's sacrifice to Cain's and the prophet Elijah's to that of the prophets of Baal, carries another urgent message.

At the present time, O Lord . . . you differentiate clearly between us and the Jews or pagans; thus do you spurn their vows, their prayers, and their offerings; thus do you show that these are repugnant to you. . . . In this way do you proclaim that the sacrifices, prayers, and vows of your Christians are pleasing to you. You direct a fire to proceed from heaven to the grave of your son, which only they respect and revere; with that same fire you set their hearts on fire with love for you; with its splendor you enlighten them, now and forever. And since the perfidious enemies of your Christ disparage his death more than his other acts of humility, in adorning the monument of his death with a miracle of such light you demonstrate how great is the darkness of error in which they are confined. While they despise his death above all, you honor the monument of his death above all; what they consider particularly shameful you prove to be especially glorious by means of so wonderful a sign. You reject the Jews like the hateful Cain, the Muslims like the worshippers of Baal, and you do not light a fire on their offerings.[10]

The miracle of fire at Jesus' grave proves that God has rejected the Jews, like Cain, and the Muslims, like the idolatrous prophets of Baal. Jews and Muslims, in Peter's eyes, together embodied the threat of unbelief which endangered the Christian world and which therefore, paradoxically, held out the promise of salvation for those who would join the Crusade and overcome it. Texts like these surely demonstrate how crusading and its ideology gave unprecedented forms of expression to Christian anti-Judaism in all its depth and complexity. Modern historians have still not uttered the final word as they attempt to define the importance of the 1096 persecutions in the history of Jewish-Christian relations.

Typically compelled by their attackers to choose between conversion to Christianity and death, the Ashkenazic Jews of northern Germany broke with historical precedent in no less striking a fashion. To be sure, some of them attempted to bribe the crusaders, to seek refuge with the local author- ities, to flee altogether, and even to take up arms; but it appears that one of two outcomes awaited most of those Jews attacked. First, many opted for baptism, although Jewish and Christian sources testify that they generally did so under duress, "more for fear of death than for love of Christian doctrine."[11] Over the protests of the Catholic clergy but with the approval of the German emperor Henry IV, most of the converts probably returned

to Jewish life within several years of the violence.[12] Still, one should not underestimate the extent or the significance of the conversions. Large numbers in some Jewish communities—Trier, Metz, and Regensburg, for example—evidently were baptized, as were smaller but sizable numbers of the Jews of Mainz and elsewhere, and the shock of these conversions haunted the self-consciousness of Ashkenazic Jewry throughout the decades that followed.[13] For their part, most of the crusaders and local townspeople who attacked the Jews apparently deemed their baptism an acceptable, if not a preferable, alternative to their death.[14] As one Hebrew source recounts, in rationalizing their attacks on the Jews the crusaders resolved, "Let us first take revenge on them and wipe them out as a nation, and Israel's name will be mentioned no more, or let them become like us and confess their faith in the 'offspring of whoredom'"—a hostile Jewish caricature of Jesus.[15] Significantly, no evidence suggests that Jews who accepted baptism suffered any physical harm. On the contrary, some accounts portray Christians preventing Jews from harming themselves so as to baptize them in good health, while others relate that Christians used torture to induce Jews to convert. We read, for example, of a Jew of Cologne named Isaac the Levite whom the Christian mob apprehended in the nearby town of Neuss.

They inflicted heavy tortures upon him. And when they beheld his suffering, they defiled [baptized] him against his will, since the blows with which they had beaten him left him unconscious. Having regained consciousness, he returned three days later to Cologne. He entered his house and, after waiting but an hour, went to the Rhine and drowned himself in the river. About him and others like him Scripture states [Psalm 68:23], "I will bring back from the depths of the sea."[16]

The story of Isaac the Levite—which opposes the waters of baptism to those of the Rhine, each inducing both death and life of sorts[17]—openly contrasts baptism with the second end that commonly awaited Ashkenazic Jews attacked in 1096, the death of the martyr. Here, too, Latin and Hebrew sources agree. Many of those attacked elected to die a martyr's death; and of these, very many took their own lives and those of their loved ones in order to avoid capture, torture, forced conversion, and death at the hands of the enemy. Christian writers recoiled at accounts of such behavior, as did the Latin chronicler Albert of Aachen when relating Count Emicho's attack on the Jews of Mainz:

The Jews, seeing that their Christian enemies were attacking them and their children, and that they were sparing no age, likewise fell upon one another, brothers,

children, wives, and sisters, and thus they perished at each other's hands. Horrible to say, mothers cut the throats of nursing children with knives and stabbed others, preferring them to perish thus by their own hands rather than to be killed by the weapons of the uncircumcised.[18]

In such sacrifice of life *'al kiddush ha-Shem* (in sanctification of God's name), as medieval Jews put it, and, perhaps, in violation of rabbinic rules against suicide, many students of Jewish history have beheld one of the distinctive hallmarks of Ashkenazic Jewish culture. Some have contrasted it sharply with the frequent preference of medieval Sefardic, or Spanish, Jewry for conversion (to Christianity or Islam) in the face of religious persecution.[19]

Alongside the anti-Jewish violence and the readiness of many Jews to kill themselves as martyrs, yet a third dimension of the persecutions of 1096 compounds the novelty of this critical experience in Jewish history. For centuries the ancestors of these Ashkenazic Jews had recalled moments of national tragedy in liturgical poetry (*piyyut*), and an impressive number of *piyyutim* bemoan the suffering and casualties of 1096.[20] Beside poetic laments of this sort, however, stand three Hebrew chronicles of the Crusade, among the first works of local Jewish historical writing in medieval Europe. The chronicles include a relatively long text attributed to one Solomon bar Samson of Mainz, a somewhat briefer and entirely anonymous "Account of the Persecutions of Old" (often dubbed the "Mainz Anonymous"), and a more abbreviated report by Eliezer bar Nathan, a well-known Ashkenazic rabbi of the twelfth century. These Hebrew Crusade chronicles have fascinated historians over the past century and more, and among the numerous published studies of these texts one can isolate several major avenues of inquiry.[21]

First, some investigators have used the chronicles as windows to the actual events of 1096. Mined for information in this way, the Hebrew narratives have revealed the causes of the pogroms, the motivations and behavior of the Christian attackers, and the reactions of the afflicted Jews. The worth of these studies depends directly on the chronicles' factual accuracy, what some have called their "facticity"—a term I find grating and try to avoid. Such use of the chronicles to establish exactly what transpired during the Crusade rests on several basic assumptions concerning the close relationship between historical events and the historical texts reporting them. Historians of all fields have hotly debated these assumptions in recent decades, and, while prominent scholars continue to write the narrative history that

the Hebrew Crusade chronicles appear to document, more and more skeptical voices have joined the conversation in recent years.[22]

Second, other scholars have moved from the history of the events of 1096 to a history of the three chronicles themselves: their authors; the date, nature, and whereabouts of their composition; the relationship between them; and their varying degrees of reliability. Most readers have considered the two longer and more detailed of the three chronicles—the narrative attributed to Solomon bar Samson and the "Mainz Anonymous"—more valuable; yet investigators have still not reached a consensus concerning their chronological order and accuracy. For years some may have "favored" the longer Solomon bar Samson text as the oldest and best record of the violence and martyrdom; but votes had always been cast for the Mainz Anonymous, which now appears to have overtaken its rival. Here one must also consider the specific relationship between these chronicles and other Jewish and Christian texts of the period, both prose and poetry, just as one must identify criteria for determining which source should take precedence.[23]

Finally, still other investigators have evaluated the importance of the Hebrew Crusade chronicles in the development of Jewish historical writing. Since the publication of the long-forgotten Solomon bar Samson text and the Mainz Anonymous alongside the better-known chronicle of Eliezer bar Nathan at the end of the nineteenth century, these texts have ranked among the first and the most important genuinely historical works produced by medieval Jews.[24] Yet our own generation has called this view into question, too. In his groundbreaking book *Zakhor: Jewish History and Jewish Memory*, historian Yosef Yerushalmi altogether denied that medieval Jews had a penchant for historical writing. Writing under the influence of the German sociologist Maurice Halbwachs and other students of collective memory, Yerushalmi argued that medieval Jews enshrined their communal memories above all in liturgy and in ritual, which bore no connection to the study or recording of history as such. These liturgies and rituals, he maintained, "are all like musical notations which, in themselves, cannot convey the nuances and textures of live performance," and thus "what was 'remembered' had little or nothing to do with historical knowledge in any sense that we would assign to such a phrase." Although Professor Yerushalmi reckoned our Crusade chronicles exceptional, since they take a genuine interest in the events of 1096 that had just transpired, their constant use of ancient models and symbols to endow these events with permanent value means that "ultimately even they . . . pour new wine into old vessels."[25] In response, histo-

rian Amos Funkenstein rejected Yerushalmi's sharp distinction between collective memory, laden with cultural baggage, and more authentic historical concern; he proposed that we discern signs of real "historical consciousness" even in texts that are not specifically historical.[26] From such a perspective, in spite of Yerushalmi's claim, the Hebrew chronicles of 1096 might number among sincere attempts on the part of medieval Jews to pinpoint the place of recent events in God's unfolding plan for the history of the world. In any event, as the study of traditional Jewish texts matures in our "postmodern" age, evaluations of our chronicles and their stories of Jewish martyrdom must grapple with the role that the writing of history plays in any society and culture. We must apply to the chronicles all those critical methods appropriate for interpreting a historical text, however radical or unwelcome the results might be.

As we have noted, this book addresses a somewhat different, though hardly unrelated, question: How have the persecutions of 1096 assumed meaning in Jewish historical memory and literature, both in medieval and in modern times? I hope to demonstrate how, just as with other momentous occurrences in the Jewish past—the crucifixion of Jesus and the Nazi Holocaust of European Jewry offer instructive examples—the historian cannot root an understanding of the events of 1096 in any untainted, original, and therefore entirely reliable memory. Rather, the character and meaning of the persecutions as historical events have derived from a continuous process of collective memory and of historical writing. Within these processes, the more meaningful a culture deems an event in its past—that is, the more interest it expresses in interpreting those events—the more elusive the raw data of that event become. Put differently, we must recognize that the most accessible, provable event in question is not reported in the historical record standing before us but *is* the very composition of that record, an event which the very existence of the text corroborates. The text provides better evidence of the historical setting in which it was composed than of the characters, circumstances, and developments in the story that it tells.

I have written this book in the hope that it will demonstrate how the historian must approach the relationship or distance between historical writings and the events they recount. Part 1 presents a selective review of the vast historical scholarship on crusading, martyrdom, and the persecutions of 1096, hoping to supply the reader with an instructive "map" of the issues involved. Chapter 1 reviews the place of martyrdom in Jewish tradition and in crusader Europe generally; it seeks to portray the Jews' perplex-

ing zeal for inflicting death on themselves against a more informed background. Chapter 2 then considers several highlights in the modern study of the persecutions of 1096: from their treatment by those who initiated the academic field of "Jewish studies" in nineteenth-century Germany, to their reevaluation by present-day historians in Israel and the Diaspora. Having shown how the historical meaning of these medieval persecutions has varied widely in response to changes in modern sensitivities, Chapter 2 continues with a discussion of medieval historical writing, Christian as well as Jewish. We shall explore several models for assessing the value of medieval historical texts, models that require us to investigate the specific cultural climate of the Crusade chronicles, to understand how the communities that recorded their stories had an impact on the meaning of the stories themselves. Based on this assessment of current research, Part 1 concludes by proposing guidelines for a rereading of the martyrs' stories, guidelines outlined and demonstrated in Chapter 3. Part 2 then applies these guidelines to five episodes of Jewish self-sacrifice related in the Hebrew Crusade chronicles. While my Aristotelian education has led me to elaborate a framework for my study before dissecting the martyrs' tales themselves—that is, to explore my points of departure before attempting to reach my destination—some readers might prefer to begin with the analysis of the stories in Part 2 and only then return to the more theoretical issues discussed in Part 1.

However one proceeds, the reader will hopefully leave this book convinced that the ideology—and graphic tales—of sanctifying God's name that the chronicles relate about the martyrs of 1096 teach us more about the twelfth-century Jewish communities which survived the persecutions than about the martyrs who did not. As historical sources, these chronicles pertain most directly to the context of their composition. Regarding the persecutions of 1096 that they recount, they are works of literature and martyrology as well as history, texts whose questions and answers still weigh heavily on us all.

PART I

Problems and Solutions

Chapter 1
To Sanctify the Name of God

Unquestionably the most striking aspect of the 1096 persecutions and their Hebrew chronicles is the slaughter of Ashkenazic Jews by their own hands.

Not wishing to deny their beliefs and to give up the fear of our king . . . , they held out their necks to be slaughtered and offered their untainted souls to their father in heaven. . . . Each one in turn sacrificed and was sacrificed, until the blood of one touched the blood of another: The blood of husbands mixed with that of their wives, the blood of fathers and their children, the blood of brothers and their sisters, the blood of rabbis and their disciples, the blood of bridegrooms and their brides . . . , the blood of children and nursing infants and their mothers. They were killed and slaughtered for the unity of God's glorious and awesome name.[1]

The three Hebrew chronicles of the First Crusade and most subsequent Jewish memories have considered such martyrdom awe-inspiring, the ultimate expression of religious self-sacrifice, outstripping in its piety even a willingness to undergo a violent death at the hands of one's enemy.

From the perspective of traditional Judaism, however, this phenomenon proves no less problematic than impressive. The law of the Talmud indeed considered the obligation to sanctify God's name in martyrdom—especially to avoid engaging in idolatry, and above all in times of violent anti-Jewish persecution—a divine commandment. Nevertheless, *submitting to death* to avoid transgression was one thing; *inflicting death*, upon oneself or upon someone else, was very much another. Biblical law condemned homicide; acknowledging the Torah's affirmation of the value of life, talmudic rabbis included suicide in this prohibition. Even if one could find precedents for justifying suicide in extenuating circumstances, how could one condone the presumption involved in slaying another person?

And yet, here were not the excessive reactions of extremists or marginal types in the Jewish community, nor can one write off this pattern of Jewish behavior, which Christian sources document as well, as a fantasy of

those who remembered 1096. Self-wrought acts of *kiddush ha-Shem*, as Jews traditionally have referred to Jewish martyrdom, loom large in the collective memory of scrupulously observant German-Jewish communities as the dominant, most praiseworthy response to the violence. How could they idealize such patently sinful behavior? How can we best seek to understand the cultural logic and significance of Ashkenazic *kiddush ha-Shem* during the First Crusade?

Modern scholars have generally approached this problem with one of two strategies, which are hardly mutually exclusive. One strategy explains the behavior of the martyrs as expressing the distinguishing characteristics of early medieval German Jewry. Ashkenazic Jews attributed considerable authority to *aggadah*, rabbinic lore, including the tale of the suicide pact at Masada found in the tenth-century Hebrew history book *Josippon*, and they gave weight to such stories in defining *halakhah*, or legal norms, too. Ashkenazic Jews, some have claimed, had inherited rabbinic traditions of the land of Israel that cherished memories of ancient Jewish martyrdom but did not generate active involvement in messianic and political movements. Messianic expectations ran high among Jews and Christians alike late in the eleventh century, but northern European Jewry looked forward to an otherworldly redemption, outside the realm of history as we know it; an act of sanctifying God's name might secure salvation for the martyr not in this world but in the next. (By contrast, the Marranos of Spain, runs this argument, drew inspiration from Babylonian rabbinic traditions that placed higher value on redemption in this world, such that one might endeavor to remain alive at all costs.) These Jewish communities hated the church intensely, and such hatred militated against conversion—however insincere or temporary—to Christianity. No less important, some have claimed, German Jews nurtured a collective self-image of piety. Again, Jewish traditions of the land of Israel and Italy bequeathed to them an ideal of righteousness that emphasized the exemplary morality and spirituality of their communities at large, not the grandeur of a small rabbinic elite. Early Italian-Ashkenazic tradition hallowed the memories of voluntary Jewish martyrs before the First Crusade. Ashkenazic Jews displayed remarkable self-confidence as to the validity of their local ritual customs; intuition may thus have led them to identify their own inclinations with the mandates of the law, such that they even modified the codified law, or halakhah, to reflect their local customs. While debate on this supposition ensues, many would agree that the distinctive Ashkenazic ideology of *kiddush ha-Shem* was firmly in place before the violence began. Our chroniclers surely wrote for specific didactic

purposes, but they pursued those objectives by faithfully recording the beliefs and behavior of those who sacrificed themselves.[2]

An alternative, though not incompatible, strategy for making sense of self-inflicted Jewish martyrdom in 1096 focuses on the ideological climate of the First Crusade. The Crusade undertook to mobilize the forces of Christian Europe under the banner of the church, to redeem the beleaguered Byzantine Empire from Turkish attack, to liberate the Holy Land in which Jesus lived and died from the rule of the infidel—and all this to avenge the wrong that was done to Jesus, the most exemplary martyr of all. Those who attacked the Jews found their mandate within this general understanding of the Crusade. Here were the most accessible enemies of Christ, those who had forfeited their covenant with God in their overt hostility toward his son. What more noble an undertaking than to baptize or destroy them! In his renowned call to engage in holy war, Pope Urban II promised crusaders a heavenly reward. Popular opinion, in turn, assigned those who fell in battle against the infidel the most direct access to paradise; they achieved the status of martyr in a genuine act of *imitatio Christi*, the imitation of Christ.

Attacked on these terms, it appears, the Jews of the Rhineland tried unsuccessfully to defend themselves, to bribe the local potentates, usually the bishops, to defend them, and to secure immediate divine assistance. When all else failed, there remained only the options offered by the crusaders: Christianity or death. Within such a context, self-inflicted martyrdom perhaps offered a different, more meaningful alternative. For the Jew thereby took the initiative in his or her own hands, actively determining his or her own destiny, not permitting the enemy to seal his or her fate. Moreover, in acts of self-determined martyrdom, the Jews challenged the very hostile ideology of the Crusade that precipitated their woes: The ultimate self-sacrifice was not that of the crusaders or of Jesus before them but that of the Ashkenazic Jew.[3]

To understand Jewish reactions to the persecutions of 1096 we must surely acknowledge the unique Ashkenazic Jewish experience as well as the climate of the Crusade, and we have much to learn from both these interpretive strategies. Perhaps a social and religious profile that predisposed Jews to martyrdom, coupled with the external stimulus of the Crusade and its hostile ideology, contributes the only sensible explanation for the acts of suicide and homicide committed by the Jewish martyrs. Nonetheless, when they ground the martyrs' behavior in the perspective on martyrdom that infuses the three Hebrew chronicles of 1096, I believe that both scholarly

approaches stand in need of correction. As I shall explain in Chapter 3 and seek to demonstrate in Part 2 of this book, we must evaluate the written records of *kiddush ha-Shem* in 1096 on a qualitatively different basis. Laying the groundwork for such a reassessment of the Hebrew chronicles, this chapter offers a brief overview of Jewish and Christian traditions of martyrdom and self-sacrifice as they developed in late antiquity, were transmitted to the early Middle Ages, and resonated during the period of the Crusades.

"I Shall Be Sanctified in the Midst of the Israelite People"

The painfully rich history of martyrdom in Jewish experience, from the biblical period and into modernity, merits thorough investigation unto itself.[4] Here we can offer only a general picture of early developments, highlighting landmarks that may inform the events of 1096 and/or the memories of these events among their survivors.

The willingness of heroic Israelites to offer their own lives and those of their loved ones out of devotion to God or for the greater good of their people appears in the earliest layers of Jewish tradition: from Abraham's binding of Isaac to the suicide of Samson and the self-induced slaying of King Saul; and from the attempted executions of Daniel and his three friends to the self-endangering refusal of Mordecai and Esther to yield before the evil designs of Haman. Yet martyrdom and the figure of the martyr assumed especial significance in Jewish society and religion beginning with the persecution of Judaism by the Hellenistic emperor Antiochus Epiphanes in the second century B.C.E. The Second Book of the Maccabees recounts the fate of those Jews who refused to violate their ancestral laws. "For instance, two women who had had their children circumcised were brought to trial; then, with their babies hanging at their breasts, they were paraded through the city and hurled headlong from the ramparts" (6:9–10). An elderly Jew named Eleazar was "forced to open his mouth and eat pork; but preferring death with honor to life with impiety, he spat it out and voluntarily submitted to the torture" (6:18–19). Even when his captors suggested that he publicly taste of kosher meat simply to give the impression to others that he was eating pork, he refused, fearing that "many of the young might believe that at the age of ninety Eleazar had turned apostate. If I practiced deceit for the sake of a brief moment of life, I should lead them astray and stain my old age with dishonor. I might, for the present,

avoid man's punishment, but alive or dead I should never escape the hand of the Almighty" (6:24–26).

Tortured to the brink of death, Eleazar exclaimed: "To the Lord belongs all holy knowledge; he knows what terrible agony I endure in my body from this flogging, though I could have escaped death; yet he knows also that in my soul I suffer gladly, because I stand in awe of him" (6:30). More horrifically still, 2 Maccabees relates that the king brutally tortured a mother and her seven sons, killing them in succession as the others watched, once again for not eating pork. Refusing even to address the king in Greek, the brothers gave no heed to his entreaties and threats and suffered most terribly as a result. Yet

the mother was the most remarkable of all, and she deserves to be remembered with special honor. She watched her seven sons perish within the space of a single day; yet she bore it bravely, for she trusted in the Lord. She encouraged each in turn in her native language; filled with noble resolution, her woman's thoughts fired by a manly spirit, she said to them: "You appeared in my womb, I know not how; it was not I who gave you life and breath, not I who set in order the elements of your being. The creator of the universe, who designed the beginning of mankind and devised the origin of all, will in his mercy give you back again breath and life, since now you put his laws above every thought of self." (7:20–23)

Identifying mother and sons with the ever-victorious goodness of reason—and transforming 2 Maccabees' tale of a single chapter into an epic of twelve chapters—the pseudepigraphic Fourth Book of the Maccabees added lavishly to this ode of praise.

O mother with the seven sons, who broke down the violence of the tyrant and thwarted his wicked devices and exhibited the nobility of faith! Nobly set like a roof upon the pillars of your children, you sustained, without yielding, the earthquake of your tortures. Be of good cheer, therefore, mother of holy soul, whose hope of endurance is secure with God. Not so majestic stands the moon in heaven as you stand, lighting the way to piety for your seven starlike sons, honored by God and firmly set with them in heaven. For your childbearing was from our father Abraham. (17:2–6)[5]

Other Judaic texts of late antiquity resound with similar themes. According to Philo the Jew of Alexandria in the first century C.E., the Jews who protested when the Roman Emperor Caligula sought to erect a statue of himself in their temple stood ready to die—and kill themselves—rather than have their shrine violated.

We gladly put our throats at your disposal. Let them slaughter, butcher, carve our flesh without a blow struck or blood drawn by us and do all the deeds that conquerors commit. But what need of an army! Our selves will conduct the sacrifices, priests of a noble order: wives will be brought to the altar by wife-slayers, brothers and sisters by fratricides, boys and girls in the innocence of their years by child-murderers. . . . Then, standing in the midst of our kinsfolk after bathing ourselves in their blood . . . , we mingle our blood with theirs by the crowning slaughter of ourselves.[6]

The first-century Jewish historian Josephus likewise left us his well-known account of the suicide pact of the Jewish zealots at Masada, urged upon them by their leader, Eleazar ben Yair, following the Romans' destruction of Jerusalem and the temple.

Unenslaved by the foe let us die, as free men with our children and wives let us quit this life together! This our laws enjoin, this our wives and children implore of us. The need for this is of God's sending, the reverse of this is the Romans' desire, and their fear is lest a single one of us should die before capture.[7]

Josephus recounted yet another Jewish suicide pact at Yodfat, from which only he and one comrade escaped with their lives; yet not only did he fail to explain the justification for such suicide in Jewish law, but he reportedly sought to convince his comrades that God opposed it.[8]

The destruction of the temple, the Bar Kokhba rebellion of the 130s, and the anti-Jewish decrees of the Roman emperor Hadrian also gave rise to numerous tales of martyrdom and self-sacrifice in the Talmud and midrash. These tales relate how four hundred young Jewish captives en route to Rome threw themselves into the sea rather than submit to sexual slavery. They retell the story of the mother and her seven sons.[9] And they recount the willingness of individual sages—Rabbi Akiba and Rabbi Chaninah ben Teradyon perhaps the best known among them—to martyr themselves for God and the Torah. As the period of the Talmud drew to a close, the acclaimed story of ten martyrs wove various traditions concerning such heroes into an ornate narrative that still fills an important place in Jewish liturgy today.[10]

Yet the talmudic sages' concern for martyrdom did not rest with memories and tales of specific martyrs. As with virtually every other aspect of human experience, these rabbis strove to define the particulars of a Jew's obligation to sacrifice his or her life under the law. Several factors bore directly on their conclusions. On the one hand, the rabbis accorded fundamental value to human life, and they had no doubt that their God con-

curred. In the divine commandment of Leviticus 18:5, "You shall keep my laws and my rules, by which one shall live," the rabbinic preacher emphasized *"by which one shall live,* not by which one shall die," and reasoned that "the commandments were given only to Israel for the purpose of living by them," not for leading Jews to their deaths.[11] On the other hand, believing the fulfillment of divine law the purpose of human life, the rabbis demanded that the Jew submit to death sooner than violate three of the most cardinal *mitzvot,* or commandments, of the Torah. The Talmud reports the consensus of a second-century deliberation that reportedly transpired in an attic in the Judean town of Lod. "Regarding all the transgressions enumerated in the Torah, if they [presumably idolatrous pagans] say to a person, 'transgress and you shall not be killed,' he should transgress rather than be killed—except those of idolatry, incest, and homicide." Subsequent rabbis added important qualifications to these basic guidelines: During an outright persecution of Judaism, one must forfeit one's life sooner than violate what seems the most trivial of regulations. In any event, never may a Jew sin in public to save his or her life, only in private, except if the Jew's oppressor clearly has only his own personal gain in mind and intends no public disparagement of Judaism.[12] Furthermore, although the martyrs remembered in the ancient Jewish sources that we have mentioned include both suicides and those killed—or willing to be killed—by their oppressors, the rabbis of the Talmud eventually began to distinguish between the two types. In those instances where the halakhah mandated that one "should be killed rather than transgress," the rabbinic formulation always employs the passive "should be killed," never an active voice that might suggest a self-inflicted death. And when Rabbi Chanina ben Teradyon, wrapped in a Torah scroll and bundles of vine-shoots (to prolong his immolation and suffering) and then set afire by the Romans, was prompted by his students to open his mouth and thereby die more quickly, he replied: "Better that he who gave life should take it away, and one should not bring physical harm upon oneself."[13] Still, outright rabbinic prohibition of suicide took quite some time to crystallize.[14]

Beyond spelling out these guidelines for self-sacrifice on behalf of the faith, classical rabbinic texts eventually defined such martyrdom as the optimal fulfillment of God's command in Leviticus 22:32: "You shall not profane my holy name, that I may be sanctified (*ve-nikdashti*) amidst the Israelite people—I the Lord who sanctify you." While the rabbis like Akiba and Chanina who reportedly suffered during the second-century Hadrianic persecutions evidently did not draw a connection between this verse and

martyrdom, later tradition attributed it to them, and they served in subsequent Jewish memory as exemplars of *kiddush ha-Shem*, the sanctification of the name of God. In its new martyr-oriented conception, the injunction of the Torah not to profane the divine name, thus facilitating the sanctification of God, gave a rationale to the laws of self-sacrifice that we have just considered, especially those requiring martyrdom of a Jew, even when homicide, incest, and idolatry did not come into play.[15] The *Sifra* (a legal midrash on the Book of Leviticus) and the Babylonian Talmud attribute such an association to Rabbi Ishmael, also one of the famed ten martyrs, despite his disagreement with the consensus that his colleagues reached concerning one of the three cardinal transgressions in the attic in Lod.

Rabbi Ishmael used to say: How do you establish that if they tell a man in private, "Engage in idolatry and you will not be killed," he should transgress and not be killed? Scripture states: "by which one shall live," not by which one shall die. Would this mean that he should obey them even in public? Scripture states: "You shall not profane my holy name, that I may be sanctified." If you sanctify my name, I too will sanctify my name by your agency.[16]

Although Ishmael ruled that one might perform an idolatrous act (in private) to save one's life, his understanding that the commandment of *kiddush ha-Shem* mandated martyrdom to avoid any public transgression of the law lived on in rabbinic traditions. Other sources confirm the linkage of sanctification with martyrdom and with martyrdom's decisively public nature—as in the case of Daniel's friends Hananiah, Mishael, and Azariah, who "delivered themselves to the furnace in sanctification of the [divine] name." The Talmud explained:

They drew an *a fortiori* [*kal va-ḥomer*] inference from the frogs [of the ten plagues in Egypt]. Of these frogs, who were not bound by the commandment of sanctifying God's name, it is written in Scripture that "they shall enter your house . . . , your ovens, and your kneading bowls." And when are kneading bowls next to the oven? When the oven is hot [so as to result in the frogs' death]. Therefore, [if the frogs were willing to risk death in the service of God,] how much the more so should we, who are bound by the commandment of sanctifying God's name [suffer the fire]!?[17]

Acknowledging the heroic motivations of the biblical Daniel's three friends, rabbinic midrash ruled that the prohibition against suicide did not apply to Hananiah, Mishael, and Azariah, just as it did not apply to King Saul, who ordered his own squire to kill him rather than fall captive to the Philistines.[18] Early in the post-talmudic, geonic period, the Babylonian *She'iltot*

reviewed the laws of *kiddush ha-Shem* binding the Jew as its author understood them.

In cases of idolatry, incest, and homicide, even in private he must be killed and not transgress; in the case of other prohibitions [committed] in public he must likewise be killed and not transgress; if it is for the [oppressor's] personal gain [rather than the humiliation of Judaism], even in public and even in case of an idolatrous act he must transgress and not be killed; in time of persecution, even in the case of prohibitions other [than idolatry, incest, and homicide] and even in private he must be killed and not transgress.[19]

Incidents and written records of medieval Jewish martyrdom prior to the Crusades do not abound, but the little evidence that remains suggests that the biblical and rabbinic sources we have considered made their mark on both the lore and the law of early medieval Jews. On the one hand, rabbinic homilies and other popular traditions continued to offer precedents for the distinctive behavior attributed to Ashkenazic Jews in 1096 by the Hebrew Crusade chronicles.[20] Several late midrashim lavish praise on suicides with indisputably noble intentions.[21] *Josippon*, the tenth-century Hebrew adaptation of the histories of Josephus by an anonymous Italian Jew, recounts the collective suicides of Jews at Gamla and Masada during the rebellion against Rome.[22] A document from the Cairo genizah nearly contemporaneous with *Josippon* reports that three Jewish sages in Italy took their own lives at a time of persecution, one of them "slaughtered like a lamb sacrificed in the courtyard of the temple."[23] And a handful of additional Jewish and Christian documents, whose reliability and authenticity might be questionable, relate instances of self-inflicted martyrdom among French and German Jews late in the tenth and early in the eleventh century.[24]

On the other hand, Jewish legal sources composed within several generations of our Hebrew Crusade chronicles cast a different picture on the records of 1096. In summarizing the basic guidelines for compliance with the commandment of *kiddush ha-Shem*, the dean of medieval rabbinic jurists, the Spanish-born Moses Maimonides, unhesitatingly condemned acts of martyrdom beyond the limits of these stipulations. "Anyone of whom it is stated that he should transgress and not be killed, and who then lets himself be killed without having transgressed—such a person is culpable for having taken his own life."[25] Yet some Ashkenazic rabbis, perhaps with the martyrs of 1096 in mind, displayed greater understanding for those who exceeded the demands of the law. The northern European Tosafists of the

twelfth and thirteenth centuries permitted Jews to sacrifice their lives rather than violate any of the commandments, even when not in public or at a time of persecution.[26] Reacting to Rabbi Chanina ben Teradyon's principle that "one should not bring physical harm upon oneself," some defended the actions of the four hundred captive youths who drowned themselves, arguing that "when people fear that idolaters will use unbearable torture to make them commit a [heinous] sin, then it is obligatory to bring physical harm upon oneself."[27] In this view, one understood the same midrash that excluded King Saul and Daniel's three friends from the ban of suicide to mean that "at a time of persecution, one can deliver oneself to death and even kill oneself," particularly if one fears irresistible tortures. So, too, did those Jews of Ashkenaz in 1096 "who slaughtered the children at the time of forced conversion find their justification."[28]

When crusaders offered Ashkenazic Jews a choice between conversion and death in 1096, those Jews who submitted to martyrdom certainly acted in compliance with rabbinic understandings of *kiddush ha-Shem*: Christianity in their eyes constituted an idolatrous religion; this was a time of persecution; and most of those martyred met their deaths in public. Moreover, the Hebrew Crusade chronicles accentuate patterns of behavior that assumed prominence in earlier tales of Jewish martyrdom: a zealous commitment to the faith, the valor of men and women alike, concern for the punishment that they would suffer were they to live—not to mention the motif of self-inflicted death itself. Still, those Jews who killed themselves and their loved ones during the period of the Crusades had acted outside the strictly defined limits of halakhah as it was generally understood in their day. Though absolutely confident that these martyrs had sanctified God's name in the optimal fashion, the Tosafists recognized the need retroactively to provide justification for their behavior, and they responded accordingly.[29]

Christian Martyrdom and Crusading

Common wisdom has it that when given a choice between conversion and death, medieval Sefardic and Near Eastern Jews typically opted for conversion, while many more of their Ashkenazic coreligionists in northern Europe chose martyrdom. Although challenged on a variety of grounds, this generalization does have some truth to it, and a number of historians have linked these opposite tendencies to differences in belief and culture between

Muslim and Christian worlds. Medieval Christendom, they have suggested, produced more Jewish martyrs than the world of Islam because martyrdom as an ideal had greater prominence in Christianity than in mainstream Muslim tradition.[30] As earlier studies have established, Christian ideas of martyrdom influenced Jewish patterns of thought and behavior from the earliest stages of Christian history, just as Christian martyrs and stories of martyrdom drew on earlier Jewish models for inspiration.[31] These Christian traditions, too, must therefore figure in an understanding of the martyrs of 1096 as well as the Hebrew Crusade chronicles that memorialize them.

From Jesus to some of his disciples to the numerous Christian victims of Roman persecution, early Christianity presented its adherents with an array of esteemed and idealized martyrs.[32] In his Epistle to the Galatians, the apostle Paul had called upon Christians to participate, albeit metaphorically, in the crucifixion of Jesus; Jesus' disciples Stephen and Peter, as recounted in the Acts of the Apostles, offered additional models of readiness to submit to violent death on behalf of the new faith; and there is no question that the zeal of Christian martyrs contributed to the remarkable speed with which the church grew and flourished in the Roman Empire. "Acts," or accounts, of such martyrdom quickly assumed a place in the liturgy of Christian communities, inspiring the living as they commemorated the slain, usually on the anniversaries of their deaths.[33]

A willingness to suffer became a hallmark of Christian devotion, and apologists like the second-century church father Tertullian downplayed the loss of bodily life in the greater scheme of things.

Certainly, we are willing to suffer, but in the way that a soldier endures war. No one actually has a liking for suffering, since that inevitably involves anxiety and danger. However, a man fights a battle with all his strength and, though he complain about there being a battle, he finds delight in conquering in battle, because he is attaining glory and reward. There is a battle for us, because we are called to trial in court so that we may fight there for the truth while our life hangs in the balance. And the victory is to hold fast to that for which we have fought. This victory has attached to it the glory of pleasing God and the reward of eternal life.

Tertullian here redefined the notions of victory and defeat so that the former, which entails the reward of eternal life, depends not on overcoming the enemy in armed combat but on holding fast to the faith in the face of his violence. Accordingly, a martyr's death serves as prima facie evidence of triumphant success and, by extension, of everlasting reward. "We have

won the victory when we are killed; we escape at last when we are led forth. So you may call us 'faggot fellows' and 'half-axle men,' because we are bound to a half-axle post and burned in a circle of faggots. This is the garb of our victory . . . ; in such a chariot do we celebrate our triumph."[34]

Early Christian literature offers numerous examples of the martyr's victory over God's enemies, of the martyr's spiritual reward, and of the solidarity of the martyr's community. While Tertullian may have disavowed any outright desire to suffer, his words help to explain the enthusiasm with which many Christians of the Roman Empire hastened to sacrifice their lives, seeking—and perhaps provoking—opportunities to prove themselves in such a fashion. The acts of the martyrs record several accounts of actual suicides,[35] and many more of those who actively volunteered to die a martyr's death, even if they did not inflict the fatal blow upon themselves. Such voluntary martyrs played an important role in the imperial persecutions, as we learn from the vociferous protests against their behavior on the part of various church fathers, both before and after Tertullian.[36] Significantly, their objections hint at no meaningful distinction between these two kinds of voluntary death: suicide versus slaughter actively provoked by the martyr but not self-inflicted. In the second century, for instance, Clement of Alexandria contended that "those who have rushed on death (for there are some, not belonging to us, but sharing the name [of Christians] merely, who are in haste to give themselves up, the poor wretches dying through hatred to the Creator)—these, we say, banish themselves without being martyrs, even though they are punished publicly."[37] Though he eventually died a martyr's death, the third-century Cyprian of Carthage likewise admonished his followers, "Let no one among you . . . offer himself up to the pagans of his own volition."[38] Several generations later, his successor Mensurius forbade the veneration of Christians who "gave themselves up of their own accord and [knowing that this would result in their execution] volunteered the information that they possessed Scriptures which they would not hand over, when no one had asked them to do so."[39] Not only did Augustine of Hippo prohibit suicide in all cases except those when God explicitly commands it; he also did not distinguish between suicide and other expressions of voluntary martyrdom—"willful death," "rushing toward death," and "willful demise"—when condemning the excessively eager Donatist martyrs of his own generation.[40]

Even without direct reference to the acts of the Christian martyrs themselves, one can discern a zealous inclination to martyrdom in the early church that shares much with the outlook and actions attributed to the

Jewish martyrs of 1096. The Hebrew Crusade chronicles portray death in sanctification of God's name as ideal proof of one's faith in God. Though routed and slaughtered by the crusaders, the Jewish martyrs of Ashkenaz emerge victorious in this contest. Their faith is vindicated; they, not their attackers, merit the ultimate reward of eternal life after death. The Hebrew chronicles lavish praise on the valorous self-sacrifice of women with no less enthusiasm than they muster for men, just as women figured prominently in Christian martyrology.[41] The poems and chronicles lamenting the persecutions of 1096 draw no qualitative distinction between a Jewish martyr's wholehearted submission to death in sanctification of God's name and death actively inflicted by the martyr on himself or his loved ones.

Interesting confirmation of this parity appears in *Sefer Hasidim* (The Book of the Pious), a collection of Jewish pietistic teachings composed in Germany during the century after our chronicles.

There were two who slaughtered themselves but were not able to end their lives, and the Gentiles thought that they were dead even though they were not. Years later they died, and a certain Jew dreamt that those who were actually slain said to them [in paradise], "You shall not enter our company, since you were not killed in sanctification of the name as we were." They proceeded to show that their necks were cut, but the others responded, "Still, you did not die." Then an elderly man approached and said: "Because you wounded yourselves with intention to kill and because you were not baptized in their water, it is appropriate for us to be with you." And they brought them into their company.[42]

The crux of this pietistic tale is not whether Jewish martyrs were killed by themselves or by others but whether they in fact were killed, just as the acts of the Christian martyrs blur the distinction between acts of suicide and other examples of self-sacrifice more broadly construed.

Significantly, recent investigators of religious martyrdom in late antiquity have similarly—and consciously—refrained from such a categorical distinction. Avoiding the term "suicide" altogether, one pair of scholars has chosen to study the phenomenon of "voluntary death": "the act resulting from an individual's intentional decision to die, either by his own agency, by another's, or by contriving the circumstances in which death is the known, ineluctable result."[43] In a similar vein, others have broadened their definition of suicide to include, as Emile Durkheim proposed, "any case of death which results, directly or indirectly, from an act, positive or negative, accomplished by the victim himself and in the knowledge that it would necessarily produce this result."[44]

Augustine of Hippo's condemnations of suicide may well have become the norm in Christian law and doctrine, but their vehemence testifies no less to the strength of the popular sentiment that they seek to overcome. An inclination to martyrdom remained rooted in Christianity, as evidenced in two chapters in early medieval European history that also shed light on our own investigation. The first of these transpired during the 850s, when some fifty Christians in Muslim Cordoba sacrificed their lives in testimony to their faith. Remarkably, these "martyrs of Cordoba" precipitated their own demise, deliberately insulting Muhammad and Islam precisely with the intention of provoking their Muslim overlords. Modern scholarship has proposed a variety of explanations for their behavior, recorded by two contemporary Christian writers: a bishop named Eulogius, himself one of those slain, and Paulus Alvarus.[45] Yet the fact remains, as one historian has observed, that this episode was unique in the history of the church. These martyrs died at the hands of monotheists, not pagans; their deaths did not result from the persecution of Christianity but may have caused it; and, unlike the Christian martyrs of late antiquity, they worked no miracles.[46]

Again, one finds that the German Jews slain by the crusaders in 1096 shared much with these Christian martyrs of Cordoba, at least insofar as the two groups were portrayed by their respective martyrologists. In both instances, martyrdom and its memories served to assert a distinctive identity, that of the individual victim as well as that of the entire minority community, defiantly resisting any tendency—or temptation—to assimilate gradually or to convert outright to the culture of the majority. In either case, the narratives that memorialize the martyrs draw heavily on exemplary martyrs of old, biblical and postbiblical, in testifying to the glory of their subjects. Like their ancient Christian predecessors and the Jewish martyrs portrayed in the Hebrew Crusade chronicles, the martyrs of Cordoba viewed their public declaration of faith as guaranteeing them everlasting life in the next world immediately upon their deaths.

Most telling of all, however, the indisputably voluntary nature of their martyrdom as a group surpassed that of ancient martyrs. In the debate that they sparked in the Christian communities of southern Spain, any distinction between their actions (which stopped short of physically taking their own lives) and suicide figured little, if at all. Both Eulogius and Paulus Alvarus felt impelled to respond repeatedly to the challenges of their contemporaries that "this was not a time of persecution"; how, then, could those slain truly qualify as martyrs?[47] The martyrs' critics said, moreover, that "those who are not drawn violently to their death but proceed of their

own free will should not rank as martyrs nor be considered like them."[48] The question was not, technically speaking, whose hands actually wielded the fatal weapon at the moment of death. The problem lay in the claim of some Christians, including members of the local clergy, that official violence neither compelled those slain to deny their faith nor removed them from the practice of their holy, pious religion. Rather, they died of their own free choice, submitting themselves to harm on account of their pride, which constitutes the source of all sin. In a word, they became the murderers of their own souls.[49] *Mutatis mutandis*, one could conceivably make the same argument with regard to some of the Jewish martyrs of the First Crusade.

The second chapter of medieval Christian history shedding light on the Jewish martyrs and martyrologies of 1096 is that of the First Crusade itself. Jewish scholars of the last several generations already acknowledged its importance in this regard, citing such groundbreaking studies as Carl Erdmann's *Origin of the Idea of Crusade* to shed light on the Jewish zeal for martyrdom in 1096. First published in German in 1935, Erdmann's work has determined the agenda for most discussion of the roots, substance, and evolution of the crusading ideal ever since. In brief, Erdmann contended that the idea of the crusade stemmed from an age-old Christian concept of holy war; mid-eleventh-century popes had recently revitalized this concept in the spirit of the Cluniac monastic reform movement, articulated most forcefully by Pope Gregory VII. When Pope Urban II delivered his fateful address to the Council of Clermont in November 1095, launching the First Crusade, the essential crusading idea had already taken shape. Although Urban successfully blended this concept with popular notions of the soldier of Christ (*miles Christi*), his guiding idea was basically a notion of world order; the crusade comprised a means for establishing a thoroughly Christian society subject to the authority of the papacy. According to Erdmann, Urban's primary goal lay not in the redemption of Jerusalem but the defense of the Byzantine Empire from attack by the Muslims. The pope displayed little interest in promoting popular piety in general or pilgrimage among laypersons in particular. Contrary to what many subsequently understood, the "indulgence" that he granted crusaders offered them only a reduction in the penance due for their sins, hardly a blanket remission of guilt.[50]

Although Yitzhak Baer and other Jewish scholars may have looked to Erdmann's foundational thesis for support in rationalizing the responses of Ashkenazic Jews to the First Crusade,[51] it seems that critical responses to

Erdmann among Crusade historians of the last decades might prove even more helpful. If Erdmann specified ideas of holy war and the army of Christ as the core of crusading ideology, others have stressed the value that it placed on pilgrimage and penance. Where Erdmann identified Byzantium and the defense of eastern Christendom as the chief objective of the Crusade, others have focused on the sanctity of Jerusalem and the attraction of its holy places. While Erdmann viewed the Crusade as a papal power play of sorts, others have discerned its foundations in popular piety, in mystically grounded calls for repentance, and in heightened anticipation of the last days.[52] Finally, some scholars have challenged Erdmann's insistence that the ideology of crusading antedated the Crusade itself. Perhaps it materialized only as the crusaders made their way eastward, or, perhaps, it jelled in the formulations of Christian chroniclers who looked backward after the fact, especially writers who gave accounts of the Crusade from a distinctly monastic point of view. For our present purposes, this last issue of chronology assumes particular importance insofar as it concerns the crusading ideal of martyrdom, the widespread popular belief that death in battle guaranteed the crusader's soul entry into paradise: Did this promise induce the Christian combatants of the First Crusade to take up the cross, or did it begin to circulate only later?[53] More generally, this issue also sharpens the question of the distance between the events of the Crusade and Christendom's discourse of crusading. Without recognizing such a gap, how, for example, might one rationalize the title of Crusade historian Jonathan Riley-Smith's valuable article "Crusading as an Act of Love"?[54]

We shall see below that precisely these dimensions of the crusading ideal highlighted by Erdmann's critics inform the mentality of the Hebrew chronicles of 1096: Jerusalem and its sacred sites, collective popular piety, atonement for sin, expectations of the end of days, and the like. Granted, one might logically expect a degree of similarity between Christian and Jewish ideals of religious martyrdom at the time of the Crusade. Still, we cannot justify postulating a direct line from the ideology of monastic and papal reform in the tenth and eleventh centuries to that of the Crusade, as Carl Erdmann would have it, and from crusading ideology to the mentality of the Jewish martyrs, as proposed by Yitzhak Baer. Moreover, although Baer and his school have sought to minimize the distance or gap— chronological and otherwise—between the events of 1096 and the descriptions of Jewish martyrdom recorded in the chronicles, this too is hardly self-evident.

Jonathan Riley-Smith has argued cogently that, in the wake of partici-

pants' and eyewitnesses' narratives of the First Crusade, monastic writers in Europe composed a "second generation" of more stylized, "finished" chronicles; only in these later texts, he maintains, did the full-blown idea of the Crusade take shape for the first time. Crusading ideology of the early twelfth century, therefore, was far more developed and nuanced than that which had existed on the eve of the First Crusade. According to Riley-Smith, the monastic origin of these second-generation chronicles resulted in their perception of the crusaders as temporary members of monastic orders, "professed into what looked to them like a military monastery on the move."[55] These monastic chronicles bequeathed to posterity the classic Christian ideals of crusading: (1) a holy war of untold cosmic and historical significance; (2) a Christian society of the elect, imbued with the values of monastic reform (penance, prayer, and desire to find favor in the eyes of God); (3) the emulation of biblical models by that very elect group, especially in the conquest of the promised land; and (4) a commitment to martyrdom as a preferred means for the imitation of Christ. Reacting to Riley-Smith, French scholar Jean Flori has since compiled statistical tabulations of references to martyrdom and death in combat in both eyewitness accounts and the later, monastic chronicles of the First Crusade. A pronounced hope for a martyr's death, he has concluded, must have pervaded the ranks of the crusaders from the very outset of their expeditions eastward.[56] Though ostensibly contradictory, the findings of Riley-Smith and Flori naturally militate toward a middle ground. No doubt the martyr's zeal imbued the crusading spirit from the outset, but a more mature, refined expression of the crusading ideal of martyrdom awaited the monastic chronicles (and calls for additional Crusades) of the twelfth century.

What, then, might the prior history of Christian martyrdom contribute to our appreciation of the Hebrew chronicles of the First Crusade? First, helpful examples of the manner in which martyrs and their idealization by their survivors serve to fortify a religious community in crisis. Second, precedents for the zeal that could lead prospective martyrs not only to provoke their demise but even to commit suicide. (To be sure, ancient Jewish martyrs must have inspired Ashkenazic Jewry during the Crusade and its aftermath; yet, owing to the physical and ideological threat with which the Crusade confronted the Jews, Christian models might well have offered a standard for emulation and competition.) Third, as Shmuel Shepkaru has noted insightfully, a basis for the Hebrew chronicles' confidence that those who sanctified God's name made their way, immediately

and directly, to heavenly paradise. Against the background of medieval Christian tradition,

voluntary death [now] served medieval Jews as an avenue through which to ascend to God and personally benefit from their altruism. These new characteristics were added to the martyrological narrative because of the new living reality [of crusading] in the Latin West and the veneration of martyrdom and its blissful reward. The Christian leaders of the crusades ensured the appeal of the crusades through martyrdom and by granting a subsequent celestial reward in heavenly Jerusalem. Ashkenazic Jews could not fall behind and produced their own system of reward. The new characteristics of this celestial system were thus uniquely Ashkenazic, yet not exclusively Jewish.[57]

Finally, the Christian narratives of the First Crusade offer a model for appreciating how, inspired by memories of self-sacrifice that surely occurred, our Hebrew texts gave a mature formulation to their own brand of crusading ideal—that of death in the sanctification of God's name (*'al kiddush ha-Shem*)—only during the decades that followed the Crusade. In the first instance, therefore, they serve as testimony to the historical experience of that later generation. We shall see not only that the processes and products of Jewish collective memory in twelfth-century Ashkenaz mirrored those of Christian records of the Crusade, but that they utilized symbols, traditions, and literary devices similarly shared by the two religious communities. And this they did to an astounding extent.

The First Crusade and Its Historians

The anti-Jewish violence of 1096 has received little attention in general works on the history of the Crusades. Most such histories make do with passing mention of the persecutions; several offer brief reviews of the major events; but, apart from occasional consideration of the attackers' motives, few undertake any extensive investigation or analysis.[1]

All this is understandable. The attacks on Jewish communities were a diversion for the crusaders rather than a primary objective; in relation to other anti-Jewish hostilities of the Christian Middle Ages, they inflicted relatively little physical damage of lasting consequence, despite the tragic loss of life that they entailed. The size, economic prosperity, and cultural achievement of northern European Jewish communities typically rose throughout the twelfth century, notwithstanding the pogroms. If anything, one should wonder at the prominence accorded the persecutions of 1096 in Jewish memory and historical writing, compared, for example, with the relatively unknown "Rintfleisch" and "Armleder" massacres in Germany in 1298 and 1336–38, bloodshed sparked by anti-Jewish slander and social stasis that claimed thousands more casualties.[2] Nevertheless, twelfth-century Hebrew chroniclers of the First Crusade committed their stories to writing out of the conviction that Jews of the Diaspora had never before suffered nor valiantly withstood the trials of suffering as the Jews of the Rhineland did in 1096. For the chronicle attributed to Solomon bar Samson, not only did the Jewish martyrs of 1096 outshine those who had preceded them, but never "has there been anyone like them again."[3]

Following the lead of their medieval predecessors, modern historians of medieval Jews have commonly viewed the persecutions of 1096 as a critical turning point in medieval Jewish history. Until the First Crusade, runs this argument, Jews fared relatively well in the Latin West. They lived alongside their Christian neighbors with minimal interference from church or state, and they suffered physical persecution in only a few, isolated instances. After the violence of 1096, however, the status of medieval Jews

declined steadily. Massacres of Jews in the name of Christian piety revealed how existing safeguards for the life and property of the Jewish minority did not suffice. The Jews' need for greater protection enhanced their dependence on, and weakness before, Christian princes, without whose goodwill they remained at the mercy of an increasingly hostile European society. At the same time, the physical persecution of the Jews, albeit technically illegal, awakened medieval Christendom to their anomalous situation. Why did Christians permit the enemies of Christ to remain and to thrive within the domains of Christianity, far beyond the limits set by legislators and theologians of old? Christian theologians and jurists responded by repeatedly reevaluating the Jews, their Judaism, and their contemporary situation during the twelfth and thirteenth centuries; then a constellation of principled and practical considerations led the political rulers of medieval Europe to begin expelling Jews from their lands.[4]

In the wake of 1096, Israeli historian Haim Hillel Ben-Sasson concluded, "the Jews now realized that charters alone could not provide absolute security against mob fury. Christian religious fervor had kindled a fire in the tents of Jacob and had led to slaughter in his habitations. The blood of the Jews had, as it were, been made free for the Christian masses. In respect to legal formulations, security, and possibilities of livelihood, the First Crusade inaugurated a new and harsh epoch for Jews in Christian lands."[5] Writing in 1936—before the Holocaust, the State of Israel, and Ben-Sasson—Cecil Roth had offered a still more definitive appraisal:

The effects of the Crusades upon the Jew . . . continued to dominate his history for at least four centuries, and left traces upon it which are discernible even today. They influenced his political position, his geographical distribution, his economic activity, his forms of literary expression, even his spiritual life. It may be added that, in almost every direction, the influence was for the bad. Take any realistic description of the position of world Jewry down to the close of the last century; take any indictment drawn up by an anti-Semite in our own times; take any contemporary analysis of the weakness of the Jewish position or the alleged shortcomings of the Jewish character; and in almost every instance it will be possible to trace the origin, if not actually to the Crusades, to the currents which they stirred.[6]

Various investigators have endeavored to modify or to refute this notion that the persecutions of 1096 constituted a virtual crossroads in medieval European Jewish history, but only a few have sought to understand the basis for the theory and its popularity in modern scholarship. We have before us a tradition among Jewish writers that has repeatedly, since 1096,

reformulated current memories of the persecutions in response to the changing needs and temperament of the Jewish culture prevailing when they wrote. We know not all the links in this tradition; especially in the medieval period, many agents of historical memory—or "phantoms of re-membrance" as medievalist Patrick Geary has designated them[7]—remain highly elusive.

Postponing our own treatment of the Hebrew chronicles to Part 2, we turn in this chapter to aspects of both modern and medieval historical scholarship that inform the development of this historical tradition. I have deliberately chosen to move backwards, as it were, from modern to medie-val historical scholarship. For while historians today generally agree that they themselves participate in the cultural dynamic that shapes the record-ing of past events, they have shied away from stating as much about their medieval Jewish counterparts. But surely, if memories of the persecutions have nourished the ideologies of nineteenth-, twentieth-, and now twenty-first-century scholars—and these ideologies have an impact on their histor-ical scholarship—why should one expect otherwise of Jews who preserved and recorded such memories in the twelfth century? Ultimately, we cannot appreciate the meaning of the memories of 1096 without exploring their place in the history of historical writing.

A 1096 Complex?

The persecutions of 1096 received scant attention in Jewish historical litera-ture of the late medieval and early modern periods, and the period of their interest for modern writers begins with the publication of the three Hebrew chronicles in the nineteenth century. Arguing that reliable historical evi-dence does not justify the portrayal of 1096 as a critical junction in Jewish history, Israeli scholar Simon Schwarzfuchs has recently characterized that portrayal as the creature of Jewish historians in nineteenth-century Ger-many. Romanticism then conditioned European historical thought, and the "charms of the East and the birth of colonialism" sparked renewed interest in the Crusades. Products of the modern Jewish enlightenment (or *Haska-lah*) and proponents of the movement of the Science of Judaism (*Wissen-schaft des Judentums*) for "rehabilitating" Judaism—that is, making it more acceptable to Gentiles—in modern European society, Jewish historians of the time confronted a serious problem: Precious little evidence documented Jewish life in medieval Europe, such that the history of medieval Jewry

became chiefly a literary history, a history of archaic texts rather than real people, texts that seemed to predominate over any other aspect of experience. Nonliterary evidence was scanty and largely non-Jewish, so that one had trouble discerning continuity between ancient Jewish history and the subsequent reappearance of the Jewish people in the history of Europe. The rediscovery and publication of the Hebrew Crusade chronicles in the nineteenth century, reasoned Schwarzfuchs,

> allowed for relating the annals of the Jews in Western Europe in the terms of Jewish historical experience. . . . These stories became history; they allowed for explaining the decline of the condition of European Jews, for which they cast blame on the rabble and thus [still] allowed for fruitful dialogue with the heads of the church and with political rulers. They also testified to the antiquity of Jewish settlement in Europe and transformed the Jews of the Rhine valley into Europeans. Overnight, the tragedy of the Crusades became one of the high points in the entirety of Jewish history.[8]

Schwarzfuchs rightly concluded that nineteenth-century Jewish historians passed their perspective on to their successors, but the recent history of its impact, both among its progenitors in the nineteenth century and among its more recent proponents in the twentieth, warrants more attention. Renowned Jewish scholars of the nineteenth century like Heinrich Graetz, Moritz Güdemann, and Simon Dubnow attributed extensive significance to the persecutions of 1096.[9] In one respect, the Hebrew chronicles of the events made the Jewish experience in early medieval Germany an authentic one, and it shed light on the predicament of the modern German Jew as well. For the massacres demonstrated that along with Jews themselves, the unjustified hatred for them also had a long history in Germany. Frightful though the accounts of martyrdom might be, one could understand—and these historians even applauded—the staunch resistance of Ashkenazic Jews to Christianity, their vehement protest against the moral bankruptcy of the Christian church.

In a different vein, however, the events of 1096 demonstrated how, for better and for worse, the destiny of Germany's Jews hinged upon that of the German civilization in which they lived. Their tragic results notwithstanding, declared Graetz, the Crusades ultimately brought positive changes to Western society that benefit Jews of the present day too. As for modern Jews' medieval ancestors, Graetz, Güdemann, and Dubnow all linked their enthusiasm for martyrdom to the pernicious influence of religious mysticism and Christian monasticism. Such influence persisted among Ashke-

nazic Jews, resulting in a truly dark, primitive age that suppressed their healthy cultural creativity. It stifled their poetic spirit and serious investigation of the Bible and Talmud; it substituted backward inflexibility for the well-reasoned, natural curiosities of medieval Sefardic Jews; and, as Güdemann argued in 1880, it effectively postponed the onset of Jewish enlightenment in Germany. "Everything that we now see and encounter among our people—the flight from the world, dejection of the spirit, anxiety, pettymindedness in matters of religion, superstition, and esotericism—all these are products of that terrible time, which, with repeated, periodic recurrences, has become deeply ensconced in their [the Jews'] memory, never to be forgotten."[10]

While the impressive contributions of these early giants of modern Jewish scholarship endure, succeeding generations produced a new approach to Jewish history that has altered the meaning found in the persecutions of 1096. More than to Graetz and company, twentieth-century students of Jewish history generally turned to the voluminous writings of Yitzhak Baer, Benzion Dinur, Bernhard Blumenkranz, Cecil Roth, Salo Wittmayer Baron, Haim Hillel Ben-Sasson, Jacob Katz, and others for their basic understanding of the medieval Jewish experience. To be sure, the intervening decades of research had unearthed new documentary sources to illuminate the events and impact of the Crusades, and these historians benefited from new theories and interpretations that refined their analysis of this data. No less important, these authors lived through two momentous transitions in Jewish history that nineteenth-century Jewish scholars could never have anticipated: the Nazi Holocaust and the reestablishment of a Jewish state in the land of Israel. Surely, one must shy away from simplistic connections between their personal experiences and their understanding of 1096. But one would err no less naively in supposing that they remained aloof to what transpired around them as they pursued their investigations. How have the giants of postwar Jewish historical research related to the anti-Jewish violence of 1096?

In the footsteps of their nineteenth-century predecessors, most Jewish historians of the twentieth century still deemed the 1096 massacres a fateful turning point in the medieval Jewish experience.[11] Reacting against a "lachrymose" conception of Jewish history—one that perceives the Jewish past as an uninterrupted series of tragedies and persecutions—some historians avowedly ceased to characterize the First Crusade as the beginning of the gradual decline and disappearance of most of European Jewry by the end of the Middle Ages. Yet that characterization has remained prevalent, and

even Salo Baron, first to crusade against the lachrymose conception of Jewish history, retained the notion of 1096 as a critical watershed.[12] Twentieth-century Jewish scholars remained responsive to the centrality of Crusade-related research among non-Jewish medieval historians. Whether one considers the Crusades a congenial or deplorable by-product of medieval civilization, the judgment of American scholar Sidney Painter (who himself believed the Crusades' impact overrated) remains typical. "They are at once the chief proof of the tremendous vitality and expansive power of medieval civilization and the most concrete illustration of the meaning of the common expression 'an Age of Faith.'"[13]

Just as the Crusades have exemplified the Middle Ages for many general medievalists, so did the persecutions of 1096 and their aftermath embody much that is special about medieval Jewish history for its twentieth-century investigators. Like their nineteenth-century forerunners in Germany, these historians continued to read the Hebrew Crusade chronicles primarily as accurate documentary evidence of what occurred in 1096, and only secondarily as noteworthy developments in Jewish literary history. Furthermore, they too perceived in the new Ashkenazic penchant for sanctifying the name of God—often with one's own sword—both a conscious repudiation and an unconscious adaptation of Christian ideals and behavior.

This point needs elaboration. Preference for a martyr's death over forced conversion clearly signifies a wholesale rejection of the values of the oppressor, and, in the case of the Jewish martyrs of 1096, sanctifying the name of God represents an expression of ultimate commitment to the norms of the minority. As Israeli historian Yitzhak Baer wrote in the epilogue to the English translation of *Galut* (the Hebrew term for "exile"), published in 1947,

We taught the world the idea of martyrdom, and in the third great age of our history—the real age of the Galut—this idea was realized in the very body of the people [namely, in 1096]. For two thousand years we suffered for the sake of the redemption of mankind; we were driven forth and scattered over every part of the earth because of the fateful interaction of the religious and political factors determining our history.[14]

Yet, while Baer highlighted the exclusivism and idealism in the worldview of the Jewish martyr, he also developed an argument that his nineteenth-century predecessors suggested but did not pursue: The extreme to which Ashkenazic Jews took their idealism in 1096 derived, at least in part, from

the influence of the Christian world around them. What induced Jews of the Rhineland to martyr themselves as they did? As we noted in the previous chapter, Baer drew upon historian Carl Erdmann's groundbreaking work *The Origin of the Idea of Crusade*, along with other research on Christian monasticism of the tenth and eleventh centuries, to argue that just as foreign cultures regularly triggered the appearance of new institutions and ideas among Ashkenazic Jewish communities, so

did such influences bear on their inner life and the collective religious spirit itself. The tradition of martyrdom in sanctification of God's name reappeared among the Jews in France and western Germany from the beginning of the eleventh century, and it was infused with an exceptional enthusiasm in the face of widespread persecution. The parallel with the religious movement that was then awakening among the Christians and that emerged from the French monastery of Cluny should be evident.[15]

No matter that violent persecution and martyrdom naturally aggravated the distance between rival religious communities struggling for exclusive recognition as God's chosen people, a common environment yielded parallel sets of ideas and behaviors.[16]

So, too, with the written records of the persecutions. Baer argued that the three Hebrew chronicles derive from a (lost) common source, composed in the immediate aftermath of the violence of 1096. They therefore embody reliable, eyewitness accounts of what took place. In support of his claim, he cited an array of similarities between the surviving Hebrew chronicles and contemporary Christian accounts of the First Crusade. Information as to what had transpired traveled freely between Jewish and Christian communities, he concluded, and in strikingly similar media—letters, stories, and, finally, more extensive, more carefully edited chronicles.[17]

Despite these various avenues along which Baer and his mid-twentieth-century colleagues pursued the lead of nineteenth-century Jewish scholarship, they took issue with their predecessors on vital aspects of the persecutions of 1096. The influences of the surrounding Christian environment notwithstanding, Jewish historians of the last century rarely viewed the events of the First Crusade as serving to blend Jewish and German-Christian experiences. To be sure, they depicted the Jewish minority as skilled at adaptation from the majority culture in which they lived; but such influence or adaptation did not threaten the national distinctiveness of the Jewish minority or the steadfastness of its Judaism. The persecutions of 1096 did not render the annals of the Ashkenazic Jewish experience a subset

of German or Christian history. They did not inaugurate a period during which Ashkenazic Judaism succumbed to backward, pernicious cultural influences from the larger, Christian world around it. Rather, they demonstrated the reciprocal, healthy interactions of medieval Jewish and Christian communities, even as each side preserved its independence and hostility vis-à-vis the other. Indeed, most historians had already read the violence of 1096 as an expression of the anti-Judaism deeply ingrained in Latin Christendom. And many since accepted the judgment of Israeli scholar Jacob Katz that "the attitude of the Jewish martyrs, perhaps more than any other factor, bears out the assertion that the Jewish community at this time conceived its position and religious mission in terms of its own antagonism to Christianity."[18]

Katz's statement hints at the application of the new scholarly consensus to the specific issue of Jewish martyrdom. Not only did medieval Ashkenazic Judaism continue to grow independently in spite of what it assimilated from Christian civilization, but intercultural exchange stopped short of tainting the essential, distinguishing religious principles of northern European Jewry. Unlike the Jews of medieval Spain, praised by earlier scholars like Graetz and Dubnow for their urbaneness, their rationalism, and their involvement in the scientific endeavors of the non-Jewish culture around them, Ashkenazic Jews zealously defined and maintained limits to such cross-cultural interaction. The very aloofness that their nineteenth-century predecessors had deemed primitive, Baer, Dinur, Ben-Sasson, Katz, and others now hailed as that which guaranteed the continued survival of traditional rabbinic Judaism through the ages. Ashkenazic Jewish martyrs rejected the behavior of the Marranos of Spain who converted to Christianity in the face of religious violence but sought to remain faithful to Judaism in secret. The German Jews who chose death over baptism epitomized the remarkable achievement of medieval European Jewish civilization: its steadfast commitment to its spiritual ideals even under the threat of physical destruction. Thus, Yitzhak Baer: "The persecution of 1096 was no passing incident, but a momentous catastrophic event, the finale to the first and classic movement in the history of rabbinic Judaism and liturgy in the Rhineland."[19] Benzion Dinur: Ashkenazic Jews who "died in this manner, bequeathed to future generations the belief that Israel is indeed the nation of God and that the generation of self-inflicted martyrdom is a generation of the elect."[20] And Haim Hillel Ben-Sasson: "This hallowing of the Holy Name by martyrdom strengthened Jewry from within, enriched it spiritu-

ally, crystallized the concepts of honour and heroism among the Jews and gave them the strength to face later trials."[21]

One can rightly appreciate that these twentieth-century scholars attempted to correct prejudicial judgments of nineteenth-century scholarship: Historians of the twentieth century construed the interaction between Ashkenazic Judaism and the surrounding Christian civilization a natural, wholesome one, which did not violate the true, unique spirit of Judaism but actually perpetuated it. At the same time, they beheld this interaction as limited, and they thus accentuated the glorious singularity of self-inflicted Jewish martyrdom in 1096. From the perspective of the generation of the Holocaust and the struggle for Israeli independence, this might appear perfectly sensible. But might one not detect an inconsistency here, fueled, perhaps, by ideological concerns no less overbearing than those of Graetz and his colleagues? The horrors of the Holocaust notwithstanding, what justified the glorification of Ashkenazic Jewish culture any more than its disparagement by earlier scholars, in their preference for a Sefardic sort of Jewish rationalism? Why should Jewish martyrdom, passive or self-inflicted, not be subjected to the same literary, historical, and cultural analysis typically applied in the study of any community's normative religious practice?

The last quarter-century has yielded a surprisingly large number of new investigations of the persecutions of 1096 and their Hebrew chronicles. As this book goes to press, I can think of four scholarly monographs,[22] at least half a dozen collections of essays,[23] and scores of articles published during the last twenty years devoted in large measure, if not entirely, to the persecutions of 1096 and their aftermath. Against the background of a sharpened historical self-consciousness, exemplified in books like David Myers's *Re-Inventing the Jewish Past*,[24] and alongside the enrichment of Jewish studies with a "postmodernist" critical perspective, some scholars have begun to challenge the prevalent view of the Hebrew Crusade chronicles' basic reliability (a view that still enjoys considerable support among American, Israeli, and European scholars[25]). Admittedly, many a reader of the Jewish Crusade chronicles had already acknowledged their apologetic, ideologically grounded agenda, and even before World War II the French scholar Isaiah Sonne had discerned "fruits of fabrication" in passages from Solomon bar Samson's Hebrew narrative.[26] Yet modern research on the persecutions of 1096 turned a new leaf, when in 1982 American medievalist Ivan Marcus proposed to apply anthropologist Victor Turner's "paradigm theory" to an analysis of that same chronicle. Marcus called for approach-

ing the Hebrew chronicles primarily as "fictions: imaginative reorderings of experience within a cultural framework and system of symbols."[27]

Furthermore, writers of the last several decades have taken issue with the long-hallowed contrast between the active involvement of medieval Sefardic Jews in the surrounding Gentile culture and Ashkenazic Jews' self-imposed isolation from it. Some have argued that mutual awareness, dynamic intellectual exchange, and shared traditions and symbols characterized medieval Jewish-Christian relations in northern Europe much more than had been acknowledged, and that this must inform our appreciation of the persecutions of 1096.[28] Israeli scholar Israel Yuval has linked Jewish martyrdom during the First Crusade to a partial responsibility that Jews bore for subsequent Christian blood libels against them;[29] he quickly prompted heated responses from those who labeled such studies methodologically misguided, "consciously post-Zionist," and liable to promote anti-Semitic slander.[30] Thus accused, Yuval lashed out at the double standard, "the ahistorical method," and "the excessively positivistic interpretations" of his detractors, arguing that at the root of one critic's charges against him lies his fear,

"what will the Gentiles say?" This fear has led him completely to disqualify accepted models for research, and to view him that uses them in the present context a dangerous person. . . . Ought we to convert our historical studies into a broadsheet for propaganda because of the distortions of anti-Semites? Shall we destroy our world on account of fools?[31]

The emotional stakes in this academic debate might appear surprisingly high, and they reveal once again just how profoundly our own frame of reference conditions the way we remember the past. Nonetheless, recent receptiveness to greater cultural exchange between medieval Christians and Ashkenazic Jews can prove fruitful for our study of the persecutions of 1096 and their written records. Yuval has proposed that the new paradigm of Jewish martyrdom derived from a messianic hope for revenge upon the enemies of Israel: God would bring the redemption once Jews had suffered enough at the hands of their enemies to warrant divinely wrought revenge. Thus expressed in acts and stories of sanctifying God's name, such messianic hope fueled new suspicions among Christians concerning Jews: If yearning for their redemption and our punishment led them to kill their own children, how can we expect them to behave toward our children? Perhaps, some have suggested, one can find reactions to self-inflicted Jewish

martyrdom in Christian literature and art of late medieval England and Germany.[32] Ivan Marcus has suggested that the Christian willingness to dedicate one's life to the Crusade and Ashkenazic enthusiasm for martyrdom manifest essentially the same phenomenon. Jewish pietists of twelfth-century Germany echoed crusaders' conviction that, the perils of their endeavor notwithstanding, "God wills it—*Deus vult*," in their own striving to fulfill *retzon ha-bore'*, the will of the creator.[33] And, as the remainder of this book proposes to demonstrate, I believe that the new style and stories of Ashkenazic martyrdom reveal twelfth-century Jews expressing themselves in the idiom of Christian culture. The ideology and narratives of *kiddush ha-Shem* fit squarely into that cultural milieu, and their significance relates directly to the history of the Christian idea of the Crusade and its literature.

Before moving on, I would venture the unorthodox suggestion that the modern scholarly treatment of the 1096 persecutions resembles the interpretation of the fall of Masada in contemporary Israeli culture. In the summer of 1971, *Newsweek* columnist Stewart Alsop criticized the State of Israel and Prime Minister Golda Meir for their intransigence in Middle East peace negotiations. Alsop argued that this lack of flexibility derived from a "Masada complex," a challenge to which Prime Minister Meir subsequently retorted at a Washington press corps luncheon: "It is true, we do have a Masada complex; we have a pogrom complex; we have a Hitler complex."[34] As Israeli sociologist Nachman Ben-Yehuda explained, the Masada myth treasured by modern Israelis (and Diaspora Jews, too)

revolves around the idea of proud and self-conscious Jews fighting for their own cultural identity and freedom, in their own land, to the bitter end. It is a narrative of the few against the powerful many, struggling against tremendous odds. It is the story of preference for a liberating and violent death as opposed to a despicable life.[35]

The elements of Jews fighting and of waging their struggle in their own land are critical here. For the Masada complex hinges on a twentieth-century secular Zionist mentality that negates the value of a religiously defined Jewish civilization in *galut*, in the exile, a mentality that looks to the modern independent State of Israel as the fulfillment of Jewish history. From such a perspective, literary critic Yael Zerubavel has elaborated, "exile displays the Jews' choice to prove their devotion to the Jewish faith through a martyr's death. Kiddush ha-Shem . . . , the traditional Jewish concept of martyrdom, represents the Jews' failure to offer armed resistance to their

persecutors and actively defend themselves."[36] In this Zionist spirit, the tank corps of the Israel Defense Forces for years conducted its swearing-in ceremony on the top of Masada. Israeli schools and youth movements regularly have made pilgrimages to the ancient fortress. And the synagogue discovered within Masada's ruins long functioned as a favorite site among tourists for bar and bat mitzvah celebrations.[37]

Although the persecutions of 1096 have hardly evoked a similar popular concern among Israelis, I believe that the Masada complex and myth can enrich our grasp of their significance in Jewish historical memory. We remember both 1096 and Masada as singular expressions of Jewish heroism, when outnumbered bands of Jews slaughtered themselves rather than surrender to their enemies. In either case, those responsible for our memories of these events—the survivors of the pogroms, on the one hand, the first-century Jewish historian Josephus, on the other—themselves capitulated before their attackers and undoubtedly used their chronicles to explain their own behavior as much as to record historical information. For centuries, Jewish readers neglected both Josephus and the Hebrew Crusade chronicles, until they awakened a new, intense interest in recent decades. In the case of Masada, as Ben-Yehuda and Zerubavel have demonstrated, the narrative has been consciously edited, redefined, and exploited in Israeli society in order to breed commitment to national ideals. Popular concern and debate in turn generated alternative or "counternarratives," even concerted efforts at "myth-wrecking," which compete for acceptance in Israeli collective memory.[38]

We have observed a similar pattern in the case of modern historical interpretation of the persecutions of 1096. The first generations of modern Jewish scholars used the plight of Ashkenazic Jewry during the Crusade to highlight both noble and deplorable aspects of the German Jewish experience, and thus to promote their own quasi-messianic vision of a symbiosis of German and Jewish cultures. During and after the Holocaust, Jewish historians presented an opposing interpretation of these events, which transformed the self-sacrificing piety of the martyrs and their heirs from primitive barbarism into a glorious achievement. In Yitzhak Baer's words, it bespoke that "which was, ultimately, most formative and decisive in the development of the character of the Jewish people throughout history."[39] Baer and scholars like him, we might suggest, not only revised their predecessors' evaluation of 1096 but also defended the exemplary character of the martyrs against the disparaging challenge of the Masada myth. And, finally, our own generation has reexamined these and other milestones of Jewish

history, challenging prevailing assumptions, rethinking the relationship between the historical event and the texts that record it, perhaps contributing to what the social scientist would term "myth-wrecking." After presenting some of my arguments to a meeting of Israeli schoolteachers some years ago, some in my audience, in fact, begged me to substitute new myths for the ones I seemed to undermine. I replied—and still do believe—that contemporary historians should not permit themselves to mythologize. But that hardly means that one ought to remain insensitive to the culturally destructive—and constructive—reverberations of historical scholarship.

Historicity and "Facticity"

Whether one accepts the argument of Yosef Yerushalmi's *Zakhor* that medieval Jews took little interest in recording history, agrees with Amos Funkenstein that they nevertheless evidenced a genuine "historical consciousness" in other genres of writing, or maintains more generously that they did pursue historical scholarship,[40] the Hebrew Crusade chronicles mark an important milestone in the cultural history of European Jews. Yerushalmi, Funkenstein, and other, more traditional scholars all concur that our chronicles view the persecutions of 1096 as events of cosmic significance for northern European Jewry, and therefore as events that future generations of readers should remember. I have encountered no scholarly opinion that the persecutions did not occur or that Jews of the Rhineland did not martyr themselves in the manner recounted. Modern investigators likewise agree that, in their twelfth-century context, the Hebrew Crusade chronicles served a rhetorical, educational, perhaps even inspirational purpose far exceeding the mere documentation of what had transpired.

What value, then, have these medieval martyrs' tales for modern students of history? How accurately do they document what actually happened in 1096? Until recently, most historians simply assumed that the narratives of persecution and martyrdom filling the chronicles are largely factual, that they offer accurate, graphic descriptions of real events; and, as we have noted, distinguished scholars still subscribe to this view. Over the past two decades, Robert Chazan has elaborated and upheld this approach more extensively than anyone else, in three books and numerous essays, only several of which shall we mention here. In his *European Jewry and the First Crusade* (1987), Chazan reiterated the consensus that the chronicles drew on earlier, no longer extant eyewitness accounts of the persecutions, and he

defended the reliability of the surviving Hebrew narratives and their sources on a number of grounds. Of these sources, now lost, Chazan wrote:

These sources are surely rooted in eyewitness observation, but this is in itself no guarantee of accuracy. The most striking characteristic of these sources, it seems to me, is their commitment to detail and diversity. Rather than portraying a stereotyped and repetitive set of behaviors, both Christian and Jewish, they focus on a variety of actions and reactions. The uniqueness of specific circumstances, groups, and individuals is highlighted. . . . Christian behaviors . . . are not depicted as uniform. . . . The variety of Jewish behaviors portrayed is even wider. . . . The diversity of behavior depicted is the best index available of the reliability of the original sources. . . . While there may have been exaggeration of some aspects of Christian or Jewish behavior, both wholesale suppression of key tendencies and widespread fabrication of actions and attitudes are unlikely.

As for the surviving chronicles themselves, Chazan readily granted their biased character, but he argued that they "seem to have retained the strong sense of the specific, the unique, and the diverse that is the hallmark of their sources." Chazan linked their "respect for historical reality" to their deep appreciation of the martyrs' self-sacrifice and its cosmic significance, as well as to an increasing concern for accuracy and detail in twelfth-century Christian historical writing.[41] Additionally, while diversity within the three Hebrew narratives testified to their reliability in Chazan's eyes, so did the correspondences between them, as well as the correspondence between them and Christian records of the First Crusade. Explaining how the chronicles documented the events of 1096, Chazan also used the texts to understand the impact of the persecutions on the generation of the chroniclers, and he proceeded to reconstruct both the events and their legacy at length.

Reviewers of *European Jewry and the First Crusade* challenged its method and its conclusions, but Chazan has continued to defend and to refine this reasoning ever since. In an essay entitled "The Facticity of Medieval Narrative: A Case Study of the Hebrew First Crusade Narratives" (1991), Chazan claimed that "the lack of identifiable stereotypes for the behavior and thinking of the Jewish martyrs suggests that the narratives are grounded in direct observation rather than in preexistent models."[42] So too, he argued, may one conclude from the absence of any consistent organizational framework in the chronicles. Moreover, even if specific details in particular scenes of martyrdom might leave their readers skeptical, one can safely draw conclusions concerning typical patterns of thought and behavior among Christians and Jews in 1096. Chazan has thus remained firm in

his conviction that the chronicles reliably reflect the experiences both of the martyrs and of those who survived to memorialize them. He subsequently explored the phenomenon of such dual significance in his essay "The Time-bound and the Timeless: Medieval Jewish Narration of Events" (1994). Here he distinguished between texts rich in the detail of their reporting and therefore of more limited, "timebound" interest, on the one hand, and liturgical poetry rich in "timeless" symbolism but unlikely to document particular events, on the other hand. Albeit with reference to a twelfth-century text composed later than our chronicles, Chazan also discerned "a middle course, affirming both the importance of the specific events and the profound meaning which those details embody and reveal."[43] And, in the latest of his three books on the persecutions of 1096, *God, Humanity, and History: The Hebrew First Crusade Narratives*, Chazan has identified this dual character as the key to a proper reading of our chronicles and the tales of persecution and martyrdom which they transmit.

Noteworthy opposition to Chazan's treatment of the Hebrew Crusade chronicles—from his underlying assumptions regarding their "truth value" as works of twelfth-century historical writing to his distinctive interpretation of their contents—has emerged from various quarters. One of his more outspoken critics has been Ivan Marcus, who, grouping Chazan with other contemporary "historical positivists," has argued that his *European Jewry and the First Crusade* in particular and his reflections on medieval Jewish historical writing in general focus almost exclusively on the "facticity" of narratives that are not in reality documentary "sources." Not that events and "facts" do not exist out there "behind" these texts, but they are not "in" them. The persistent—and misguided—assumption that they *are* not only leads to few positive results but, more significantly, stands in the way of a more appropriate analysis that would make better historical sense of what the sources can tell us.[44]

Instead, Marcus has advocated an approach that he terms "anthropological history." Citing recent analyses of other medieval Jewish historical texts—those of Abraham ibn Daud's *Sefer ha-Qabbalah* (The Book of Tradition) by his teacher Gerson Cohen,[45] and *Megillat Ahima'atz* (The Chronicle of Achimaaz) by Israeli historian Robert Bonfil[46]—Marcus has proposed that the historian's objective when interpreting texts like our chronicles should be not facts "but something I would call 'historiographical creativity.'"[47] Through the eleventh century at least, Bonfil has beheld much in common between such creativity and that of midrash. For both historical writing of the early Middle Ages and midrash tend more to "rhet-

oric than logic, inconsistency more than cogent argumentation . . . , education more than critical search for knowledge."[48] Or, as Marcus would have it, the anthropological historian "assumes that the narrative presents a set of symbolic expressions of experiences or events that can be known only as mediated through the narrative." Such a historian thus "assumes that the text as written preserves an expression of an actual historical extra-textual reality," but that this "historical reality is not reducible to an event or fact but exists in the mind of those who wrote, edited, copied, owned, read and reread the narrative." The text thereby testifies both to the events of "historical experience" and to an "imagined literary world formally constructed" within it. Experience might provide the building blocks—or story line—for the narrative that gives expression to this literary world, but the structure of this imagined world governs the narrative's inclusion and portrayal of historical events.[49]

We shall find the appreciation of medieval historical texts advocated by Bonfil and Marcus especially helpful in rereading the Hebrew chronicles of the First Crusade, but there remains yet another approach that warrants our consideration—and, at least in part, our adoption. Developments in literary and cultural criticism over the last decades have helped to blur traditional boundaries between the academic disciplines of history, literature, and hermeneutics. Just as the school of New Historicism has risen to prominence in literary studies, so have historians recognized the need to reappraise their primary sources using tools borrowed from the scholar of literature. Particularly in the case of tales transmitted orally before their inscription in written records, folklorists have focused instructively on the historical career of the stories as such, as well as the specifics of their contents, their structures, and their symbolic codes. Here the folklorist, the literature specialist, and the cultural (or "anthropological") historian share a good deal, although it helps to keep in mind that the literary scholar seeks above all to reconstruct the history of the story rather than to document historical events external to it. Insofar as postmodern criticism has seriously curtailed—and, in some cases, entirely eliminated—our ability to understand a concrete reality that existed prior to and independently of the text, so has such criticism obscured the distinction between history and "mere" fiction or legend. I often have my students read Israeli author Amos Oz's novella *Crusade* before introducing them to the texts of the Hebrew Crusade chronicles, because it offers a wonderful case in point.[50] "Mere fiction," it nevertheless captures and conveys much of the crusading experi-

ence no less instructively than many of the twelfth- and thirteenth-century sources.

No longer can the cultural historian ignore the agenda and the methods of the folklorist, as Israeli scholar Eli Yassif has recently reminded students of medieval Jewish history. "As regards the historical perception of the Middle Ages, it has come to be understood that 'facts' and 'truth' are not necessarily one and the same. History is no longer construed as 'what actually took place,' but as 'that which was believed to have taken place.'" Literary sensitivity can teach the historian that "the point where *fabula* (the historical legend) meets society's perception of its past (its collective memory and consciousness) contains the historical 'truth' of the Middle Ages." This truth, in turn "can be defined as the tale's accord with the values, the system of norms, the collective memory, and the consciousness of the society" to which its tellers belonged.[51]

Still, a measure of distinction between the disciplines of literary and historical studies remains helpful. Contrasted simplistically, the literary scholar views the narrative text both as point of a departure and as an ultimate goal—so that understanding the text's cultural-historical context serves merely as a means to that end—while the historian typically treats the narrative text as a window to the values, norms, memory, and consciousness in the society under study. In the spirit of Dominick LaCapra's cogent argument that historiography necessarily blends a documentary reconstruction of the past with an interpretative dialogue between the past and the historian, this book attempts to make room for both approaches.[52]

History, Memory, and Interpretation in Twelfth-Century Christian Europe

No less than the modern investigations of the crusading ideal that we have already discussed (in Chapter 1), recent studies of Christian historical writing of the Middle Ages can prove helpful in our interpretation of the Hebrew Crusade narratives. As present-day medievalists have grown increasingly self-conscious in light of postmodernist critiques of their historian's craft, they, too, have expressed more sophisticated interest in medieval historical writing. Twelfth-century Christendom's cultural renewal included an awakening of historical interest among intellectuals throughout Europe, and their writings evidenced a more sensitive, more nuanced respect for the past and its written record.

Modern investigation of these phenomena holds out numerous possibilities for an enriched understanding of medieval historical narratives in general and our Hebrew chronicles of 1096 in particular. Some have elaborated the educational purposes that historical investigation could serve during the Middle Ages, from its applications within the pietistic world of the monastery to its moral utility for a more general public. Some have related historical writing to an increase in literacy in medieval Christendom, weighing just how the transition from oral to written communication affected the collective memory of European societies. Others have scrutinized the distinctive style and language of historical texts, the literary devices, motifs, and symbols that they employed to convey their messages effectively. Still others have sought to define the limits of medieval historiography, differentiating it from the literature of *exempla* (brief stories employed by preachers for educational, inspirational purposes), from liturgical texts, and from lives of the saints. With an eye on our present subject, one might note how these concerns have enhanced our appreciation of the Latin chronicles of the First Crusade. Their didactic, theological, ideological purpose resounds incessantly. They make distinctive use of biblical (especially Old Testament) language and imagery—which itself reflects new trends in twelfth-century Christian scholarship—and scholars have called attention to their distinctive language of persecution, as well as to their interweaving of blatantly legendary material with eyewitness accounts of the Crusade.

From among a bounty of impressive investigations of medieval historical writing and the narrative representation of events, I would spotlight three works of the past several decades that strike me as especially promising for our ensuing analysis of the Hebrew Crusade narratives. These are not necessarily the most acclaimed or most accepted contributions to the field. Yet each offers insights that allow us to read the records of the persecutions of 1096 afresh.

Few theoretically oriented considerations of historical writing have stimulated as much discussion as the groundbreaking essay "The Value of Narrativity in the Representation of Reality," by the American historian of ideas Hayden White. Here White set out from the premise that "narrative is a metacode, a human universal on the basis of which transcultural messages about the nature of a shared reality can be transmitted."[53] In simpler terms, narrative is a universal dimension of human culture, one that articulates basic truths of human experience as people in various societies and ages perceive them.

But precisely what kind of meaning do representations of reality in

narrative form convey? To explore this question, White compared three
varieties of texts recording historical events, selecting specifically medieval
European examples. Although the three genres seem to reflect an evolution-
ary trend from the more primitive to the more refined, White sought primarily to distinguish between the different views of the world to which
each genre gave expression. He first pondered early medieval *annals*, lists
of dates and occurrences with no narrative structure, no thematic sequence,
no moral messages, no ranked order of the events' importance, and no
narrator's voice. Human initiative, human morality and law, the political
and social order of the surrounding community receive no attention in
annals. One fails to find in such lists of events "a notion of a social center
by which to locate them with respect to one another and to charge them
with ethical or moral significance."[54]

From annals White moved on to the *chronicle*, which he deemed superior on account of "its greater comprehensiveness, its organization of materials by 'topics and reigns,' and its greater narrative coherency." The theme
of authority—divine authority and human authority—assumes prominence in the text of the chronicle and in the world outside the text that the
chronicle reflects. For "the truth claims of the narrative and indeed the very
right to narrate" depend on legitimate authority. Nonetheless, overarching
moral principles and the sense of community in which such principles tend
to bind narrator and reader together are still missing in the chronicle. The
chronicle may have a story, but, like the annals, it has no moral, and, as
such, it comes to no implicitly logical, clear-cut conclusion; its reader still
bears "the burden of retrospectively reflecting on the linkages between the
beginning of the account and its ending."[55]

What, then, singles out White's third textual genre, *narrative*, that
which modern readers typically consider genuinely historical writing? "Interest in the social system, which is nothing other than a system of human
relationships governed by law, creates the possibility of conceiving the kinds
of tensions, conflicts, struggles, and their various kinds of resolutions that
we are accustomed to find" in any coherent, truly meaningful account of
the past.[56] The historical narrative derives its integrity neither from the
overwhelming sense of rootlessness that characterizes annals nor from the
authority of a specific sponsor, the loyalties of prospective readers, or the
bias of a particular faction typical of the chronicle. Rather, the story itself—
its literary structure, the internal coherence of its plot, the dynamics and the
symbolism of its language—renders the events of the narrative intrinsically
meaningful. Morality and an impulse to teach morality are ever present in

narrative histories; for, more than the mere actuality of past occurrences, they convey the truth of the story within the community that creates it. Such truth, White concluded, is not the truth of "facticity," but a spiritual or ideological truth, a conviction of ideals or values *that is a product of the human imagination.* It "arises out of a desire to have real events display the coherence, fullness, and closure of an image of life that is and can only be imaginary."[57]

From White's general assessment of narrative history we turn to a more detailed investigation of the workings of historical memory in medieval culture, in British historian Janet Coleman's *Ancient and Medieval Memories.* As Coleman has related, the nature of medieval recollections of the past were grounded in classical tradition and above all in the tradition of Aristotle, who accorded greater importance to the orator, the rhetorician, and the poet in his society than to the historian.

An orator does something more than present a chaotic record of lived life. He provides a more general account of the probable and, therefore, more universal lessons to be drawn from past experiences. The orator unites a community of individual rememberers by integrating them into the collectively accepted plausible fictions of their common past. His job is effectively to edit out the uniqueness of past experiences remembered and to forge in its place a general truth in which all men share. The rhetorician-cum-poet, a creator of such credible fictions, is a moraliser who draws a timeless and universal message from a plausible past. The historian, a recorder of sensually experienced events, has no such message.[58]

Simply put, the classical tradition valued collective memory for the moral truths that it bespeaks; while these surely depend on the plausibility of such memory, they have little stake in its factual accuracy.

This outlook eventually nourished the works of the church fathers, who readily accepted the events of biblical history as fact, while they invested most of their energies to explain the metaphoric and allegorical meaning of the narrative history in the Bible. As Augustine (354–430) explained in his best-known discussions of biblical interpretation—in his *On Christian Doctrine* and *Confessions*—these narratives of salvation history have multiple layers of meaning; and these allow for different simultaneous interpretations of the Bible's symbolic truth. So long as none violate the principles of Catholic faith, virtually any worthwhile symbolic interpretation is "fair game." Once more the significance of the specific events of the past paled before that of the eternal truths which it demonstrated, a judgment expressed more emphatically still by early medieval theologians like Gregory the Great (ca. 540–604) and Isidore of Seville (ca. 560–636).

The nearly exclusive concentration of early medieval intellectual life in the monastery added further to the devaluation and disregard for the actual events of the past. The ideals and daily routine of the monk's life suggested a lifestyle of self-belittlement, and they spawned a society in which the ultimate value of the community's spirituality overshadowed the particular experiences and memories of each individual. Monastic recollections of the past, like the biblical commentaries of Gregory the Great, were overwhelmingly figurative and associative. The English Venerable Bede (673–735) valued classical texts not so much for their record of the past as for their Latin, which, rooted in divine wisdom, allowed the monk access to heavenly truths. The theological writings of Anselm of Canterbury (1033–1109), who had little use for historical scholarship, typified what Coleman terms the prevailing notion of "monastic memory in service of oblivion." And the mystical asceticism espoused by Bernard of Clairvaux (1090–1153) likewise provided "methods by which the practitioner might transcend the memory of sacred text and the memory of lived life, to achieve the forgetfulness of self in the contemplation of God."[59]

Admittedly, not all twelfth-century scholars ignored the particular, denying—or at least minimizing—the worth of remembering past events. Logicians like Peter Abelard (1079–1142) extended their "discretionary, rational attention to words and propositions" in all of their particularity; and historical writers began to appreciate history "as a succession of discrete, exemplary anecdotes to be understood literally as the primary significations of experience."[60] But these relatively few voices hardly overturned the prevailing value judgment. Much like Hayden White's "narrative" history and Robert Bonfil's history as midrash, historical remembering in twelfth-century Christendom remained

an exercise in constructing harmonies between the past as recorded in texts and the present for use in the present. . . . What we refer to as the history written by medieval "historians" was for them largely an exercise in oratory just as Cicero and other Roman models taught them it was, but now set within the overarching exemplary theme of God's design for man's salvation, the meaning of which had no historical dimension—

beyond that of the present spiritual moment. For the medieval Christian, if the meaning of salvation "had no historical dimension" as such, why struggle to recollect the past in all its particulars?[61]

To these perspectives on the imaginative character of medieval historical writing one might add the intriguing framework developed by the

American scholar Karl Morrison in his *History as a Visual Art in the Twelfth-Century Renaissance*. This book has not been widely quoted, perhaps because it makes for unusually difficult reading, and it has not consistently elicited praise from its reviewers. Yet it does prove unusually suggestive for our discussion of the Hebrew Crusade chronicles, and I feel that it warrants our attention here. Rejecting many attempts to impose our own present-day sensitivities on medieval texts, *History as a Visual Art* highlights the discrepancies between a medieval sense of literary beauty and our own expectations as modern readers. While literary criticism today places the highest value on the written text and the ability of its language to generate meaning, medieval narratives convey much of their meaning through silences. These silences were not simply empty, devoid of significance, but they served as "containers" of meaning—and one could unlock them only with recourse to the *visual* powers of the imagination.

According to Morrison, twelfth-century historical writing typically confronted its readers with what seemed to be a disjointed series of dense narrative reports, beckoning readers to unravel their symbolic codes in search of spiritual renewal. The Christian ideology and world of religious experience that historical writers shared with their readers generated an array of powerful, provocative images lying behind the fragmentary veneer of twelfth-century history books. These shared images enabled readers to decipher the silence, to rise to the challenge of interpretation—in Morrison's terms, to bridge the "hermeneutical gap" between themselves and the texts—and to appreciate the narratives as by-products ("artifacts") of Christianity and its ritual. In a difficult but pithy passage, Morrison had proposed that twelfth-century historical narratives, in turn, are characterized by

the transmutation of experience through criticism into information, and . . . the further passage from information in the words of the text to epiphany between the lines. . . . The imaginative, synesthetic [multisensory] multiplication of images, especially visual and verbal ones (enhanced by the powerful psychological discipline of psalmody), was essential to this way of thinking, and indeed . . . through a fusion of violence and beauty it established an interplay among the arts of imagination, including historical writing.[62]

Let us try to paraphrase. Criticism (that is, the interpretation of the historical text) allows for bridging the gap between tidbits of historical information and the reader's yearning for spiritual release and renewal. Visual and verbal images rooted in the community's religious life and shared by

text and reader allow for such interpretation. The discipline of the liturgy predisposes the individual reader to make the desired connections. And the violence in the church's symbolic code—as reflected in the blood of Christ and his martyrs—contributes to a jarring literary aesthetic of silence and loose ends which typically runs against our modern sensitivities. Not everything "hangs together" or "falls into place" as we might hope and expect.

Interestingly, those silences which Morrison has considered most central to the interests of twelfth-century Christian chroniclers—silences concerning the kingdom of God, women, and the passage and nature of time—find parallel emphases in the Hebrew Crusade chronicles. Equally noteworthy, Morrison has accorded the theme of martyrdom a key role in promoting the desired interaction between texts and readers of history in the twelfth century. With reference to works like the English John of Salisbury's life of St. Thomas Becket, Morrison has observed:

It was no dishonor to be overwhelmed by Antichrists, false prophets, and other ministers of Satan in this world. . . . Imitating Christ in obedience to the shame of the Cross, saintly martyrs offered themselves as sacrifices, none in a more Christ-like fashion than Becket, whose body was slain and whose blood shed at the very altar where he had daily offered the Eucharistic sacrifice. . . . "But who of the faithful," John asked, "may dare doubt that God will either convert or grind into dust the authors and perpetrators of so great a sacrilege?" Who indeed could doubt that the martyrs too would come in glory, heralded by the sound of priestly trumpets, at that moment near at hand when Christ entered in triumph the kingdom gained with his own blood?

Indeed, the subject of martyrdom captured the dynamic whereby twelfth-century historical writing sought to exercise the imagination of its readers, charting their course to release and fulfillment. Tales of martyrdom thus contributed directly to "the power of history to amuse, enlighten, and convert." Ultimately, this power "depended on the ability of readers to see themselves playing roles in the spaces between the lines of the texts, to relive with ardor, pity, and dread the events recounted."[63]

Critical approaches like those of Hayden White, Janet Coleman, and Karl Morrison require us to reevaluate the persecutions of 1096 as recorded in the Hebrew chronicles. They demand that we reread with greater openness to multiple, alternative interpretations (or truths) of a text that need not be mutually exclusive. If medieval historical memory served the spiritual quest of the truly pious rememberer (Coleman), and if the cultural world of the present spawns the truly narrative account of the past (White),

then the tales of the martyrs of 1096 reflect first upon the German Jews of the first half of the twelfth century who told and recorded them, more than upon the Jewish victims of 1096 themselves. Ashkenazic Jewish communities between the First and Second Crusades had survived the persecutions. They remembered the events of 1096; their memories infused our Hebrew chronicles; their experience and collective solidarity underlie the composition of these chronicles. Their stories, we venture to reason, did not terminate suddenly or illogically, but presented the past in a way that would explain the present and prepare for the future. The episodes of martyrdom related in the chronicles give expression to the historical reality—the norms, the morality, the idealized worldview—of the survivors more than that of the martyrs.

Morrison's model, in turn, sheds light on the symbols and strategies employed by our Hebrew texts to transmit meaning to their readers, not the least significant of which was a strategy of omission, disjointedness, and silence. Like Christian historical texts of the twelfth century, the Jewish Crusade chronicles reflect "a method of composition by fascicles, a segmented order."[64] Vignettes of selected scenes of persecution, betrayal, and martyrdom are bundled together with only minimal concern for their overall coherence within the structure of a fully integrated whole. Much of the actual sequence of events remains fair game for the reader's imagination, and the frequent blending of prayer with the play-by-play of events reinforces the need to mine the events for their spiritual and ideological significance. Graphic descriptions of violence, death, and brutal agony abound in these texts, as do the images and aesthetic of the religious cult: the temple in Jerusalem, the altar, the meticulous preparation of the sacrifices, the priest and his vestments, the knife and blessing of ritual slaughter, the flow of sacrificial blood, and God's acceptance of the offerings. As Morrison would have it, all these transform the havoc of violence into a rite of beauty. Reread in this way, the Hebrew chronicles of 1096 seek first to define a "hermeneutical gap" between the historical event and the reader, between violent acts of martyrdom and their survivors. Then they strive to bridge that gap by requiring readers to involve themselves in the text, and thus to determine its truth.

Chapter 3
Points of Departure

One ought not to conclude too hastily that the Jewish martyrs of 1096 subscribed to—and acted upon—the very ideas of *kiddush ha-Shem* expressed in the Hebrew chronicles that took shape only after the persecutions. At the very least, such a conclusion is insufficient unto itself. On the one hand, it proceeds from a questionable assumption: that medieval historical narratives should accurately explain behaviors that they record with a minimum of distortion, such that the skilled reader can distinguish between the motivations of those involved in a prior event and those who remembered that event after the fact. On the other hand, it fails to acknowledge that the events best documented by texts like our chronicles are the moments of their inscription in their own distinctive context, hardly identical with that of the events they narrate. Granting the traumatic impact of 1096 on Ashkenazic Jews, how can one imagine that their worldview before the violence remained unaltered in its aftermath? To the contrary, prevalent ideas about God, history, and their own political situation must have changed drastically. Perhaps most important, those who survived—and remembered—the Crusade viewed martyrdom from a perspective diametrically opposed to that of those who were slain. They had escaped—or deliberately avoided—the martyr's death that our Hebrew chronicles come to memorialize.

Presuppositions

In view of these caveats, I propose to balance prior analyses of Jewish martyrdom in crusader Ashkenaz with a rereading of the martyrs' tales before us.[1] In the preceding chapters, I discussed implications of modern textual criticism for our present-day understanding of works of history in general, medieval historical texts in particular, and narrative accounts of the Crusades above all. Laden with ideological and cultural baggage, texts such as

our Hebrew Crusade chronicles give foremost expression to the experience of those who told, received, and transmitted their stories of martyrdom, and those who committed them to writing. Accordingly, we invoke the suggestion of American medievalist Gabrielle Spiegel that the best means for investigating the "mutuality" between historical events and their written record

is to focus analysis on the moment of inscription, that is, on ways in which the historical world is internalized in the text and its meaning fixed. This process of "inscription" . . . is not to be confused with "written" in the traditional sense of "recorded." Rather, it represents the moment of choice, decision, and action that creates the social reality of the text, a reality existing both "inside" and "outside" the particular performance incorporated in the work, through the latter's inclusions, exclusions, distortions, and stresses. At work in shaping a literary text is a host of unstated desires, beliefs, misunderstandings, and interests which impress themselves upon the work, sometimes consciously, sometimes not, but which arise from pressures that are social.[2]

More simply, we depart from the premise that narrative accounts of past events always incorporate the world and experiences of their narrators, such that they can never supply a pure, unadulterated, or totally objective replica of what transpired. Blending these insights with those of other investigators whom we have already considered, we embark upon a reading of the Hebrew chronicles that considers the character and function of collective memory, especially that which follows upon catastrophe. We shall weigh the unstated as well as the stated, struggling with the symbolic codes through which Ashkenazic Jews who survived the persecutions expressed their deepest feelings. Alongside several other recent historians,[3] we shall argue that Ashkenazic Jews involved themselves in the culture and religious traditions of the non-Jewish world around them more than most earlier scholars recognized (or wanted to recognize). This level of interaction, which the chronicles themselves help to document, must inform our reading of them.

Additionally, we shall afford ample concern to considerations of "intertextuality," itself a term with multiple meanings. In the most familiar sense, "intertextual" concern demands that we recognize the countless allusions to traditional sources in the narratives before us, allusions ranging from the blatantly conscious to the probably unintended. Yet even if our storytellers remained unconscious of or insensitive to many intertextual allusions in the chronicles, they still demand our attention and consider-

ation. For, as Jonathan Culler noted, intertextuality concerns the place of a text within the linguistic and literary discourse that generates meaning and allows for communication within a culture, even more than it designates the conscious borrowing of one text from another. Moreover, as Judaic folklorist Eli Yassif has explained, the intertextuality of medieval Jewish memory and historical legends extends to alternative, even competitive frames of reference in which particular elements of a story can and must be understood.[4] To analyze such tales properly one must allow for simultaneously valid, alternative readings, which take note of their debt to different sorts of texts and cultural perspectives ("intertexts") and the richly layered symbolic codes at work within them.

Finally, we must attend to several aspects of the relationship between the martyrs and the martyrologist of 1096. First, as sociologists Eugene and Anita Weiner recognized in *The Martyr's Conviction: A Sociological Analysis*, narrative governs the function of martyrdom in a society, since the martyrologist confers enduring social significance on the event of the martyr's death. Appraising such a "narrational" theory of martyrdom, the Weiners have reminded us that "martyrdom is essentially a story, a structured transmission of happenings within a body of oral and written traditions. Ultimately, the text is the most important factor in martyrdom."[5] In this spirit, we can helpfully apply to crusader Ashkenaz the conclusion of a recent study of early Christianity, in which the textual representations of martyrology "do not just reflect, in some unproblematic way, reality and social institutions, but, rather, help to create and maintain them." Narrative accounts of a community of sufferers and the persecuted work "not simply to represent a realistic situation so much as to provide a self-definition" for the communities that nurtured these narratives.[6]

Second, building upon the observation that dying to sanctify God's name as portrayed in the Hebrew chronicles constituted a Jewish response to Christian crusading, I incline to agree with Jonathan Riley-Smith that crusading ideology itself matured only during the generations following the First Crusade and above all in a second "generation" of chronicles, not those of eyewitnesses.[7] If our Hebrew texts mark a similar development in Jewish memories of 1096, we might well entertain the possibility that their outlook on *kiddush ha-Shem* paralleled the Latin monastic chronicles' idea of the Crusade. Primarily, these chronicles depict not the events of 1096, but the discourse or meaning of those events as it took shape in Christian and Jewish societies, respectively—the discourse of crusading, on the one hand, the discourse of *kiddush ha-Shem*, on the other.

Third, and most important of all, not even the martyrological agenda of the Hebrew chronicles obscures the fact that many Jews who suffered attack survived the massacres. The percentages of casualties and survivors we simply do not know. Yet one may safely conclude that while some Jews undoubtedly fled to safety, the common means of survival was conversion to Christianity. Various sources, the chronicles included, mention the speedy return of many forced converts to their Jewish communities once the violence had subsided; over and against the protests of the Catholic clergy, the German emperor Henry IV formally permitted the return of forcibly baptized Jews to their Judaism.[8] References to flight, a more "kosher" means of avoiding death than baptism and, in terms of Jewish law, a more acceptable response to persecution than suicide, are scarce. Conversion exposed these Jews to Christianity under varying circumstances and for varying lengths of time; perhaps it intensified their immersion in the Christian culture around them. No doubt, if one will permit the metaphor, conversion left the Jews who later reassumed their Judaism with a difficult cross to bear. Particularly as they memorialized the martyrs, the burden of their lingering guilt must have been immense, a supposition that the chronicles confirm in self-reinforcing passages like this:

Now it is appropriate to praise those who were converted against their will. They were prepared to sacrifice their lives over anything that they ate or drank. They prepared their meat with ritual slaughter, cut out the fat (which the law forbade them to eat), and inspected the meat—all according to the specifications of the sages. They did not drink the wine of the Gentiles, nor did they go to their churches, except on rare occasions; for whenever they did go, they went under duress, very fearful and disgruntled. Even the Gentiles knew that they had not apostasized willingly but for fear of the crusaders, that they did not believe in their religion but still maintained that of the Lord, and that they still were devoted to the supernal God, creator of heaven and earth. As for one who speaks ill of them, it is as if he denounces the countenance of God.[9]

How do these various presuppositions crystallize into a meaningful basis for understanding Hebrew narratives of 1096? Among the converts to Christianity who survived the persecutions and then returned to Judaism and among their children, I maintain, we must seek the impetus for the composition of the chronicles, the mentality that nourished their tales of *kiddush ha-Shem*. And if, from antiquity until the present day, Jews have memorialized their martyrs with symbols, with ideas, and in literary genres shared with the surrounding Gentile culture, how much more might this

be the case with our twelfth-century Hebrew chronicles, which took shape among those who themselves (or whose parents) had once affiliated with that culture.

Previous readers of our Hebrew chronicles have pointed to various aspects of their function, from their role as memorials in communal worship to their polemical and educational purpose: Lavishing praise upon the martyrs, they preach resistance to Christianity at all costs, and they aim to inculcate such a value judgment in the minds and instincts of their readers.[10] Yet we recall Dominick LaCapra's observation that the historical text tends "not only to exemplify discursive practices or ideologies in a relatively straightforward way but also to engage in processes that, whether consciously or not, render them problematic, at times with critical implications."[11] I firmly believe that the Hebrew martyrologies of 1096 testify to greater complexity in the predicament of Ashkenazic Jewry than many have realized. The prospect of another crusade understandably terrified German Jews. Anti-Jewish aspects of the still maturing crusading mentality left them unsettled. Not least important, they remained hard pressed from within, in the wake of the martyrs' self-sacrifice, to rationalize the baptism that had allowed for the continuing survival of their communities. The chronicles surely give expression to the isolation and alienation of medieval Ashkenazic martyrs from the surrounding Christian civilization. Still, at the same time as they call for revenge,[12] they respond to the polemical challenge of the crusading ideology, and, with a deep-seated ambivalence, they contrast the self-sacrifice of the martyrs and the compromise of the survivors. They reveal an Ashkenazic Jewry much more in touch with the culture of the Christian majority than many have been willing to admit. In other words, while the chronicles do not fabricate the persecutions of 1096, their particular tales of Jewish martyrdom derive from the historical consciousness of those who opted for life in Christendom over death in (a presumably Jewish neighborhood of) paradise. Within a mentality emanating at once from rabbinic and Christian influences, they give air to notably conflicted Jewish memories of 1096.[13]

Although the generations-old debate among historians as to the chronological order of the three Hebrew Crusade chronicles and the relationship between them might bear upon our analysis of specific stories appearing in more than one source, we presently have no need to rehash the alternative opinions.[14] Rather, we proceed from the premises that all three chronicles were most likely composed between the First and Second Crusades (1096–1146), that they may well have drawn on other accounts of

the pogroms that have not survived, and that their stories of martyrdom reflect the existing collective memories of Jewish communities in the Rhineland. Albeit in varying degrees, the methodology we have proposed can be applied in principle to all the Hebrew chronicles of 1096. And yet, our discussion will dwell predominantly on the longest, most graphic and detailed, most quoted of the three texts, that attributed to Solomon bar Samson of Mainz. No doubt that the composite nature of this work, along with its compilation some fifty years after 1096, contributed to the intricacy of its contents, which provide fertile ground for testing our methodology. Before we proceed to a detailed analysis of several choice instances of martyrdom in the chronicles, some brief reflection on the complexity of their "message" brings the first part of this book to a close.

Preliminary Applications

One can readily identify motifs in the chronicles which link them to the religious and cultural climate reigning in twelfth-century Europe, and by means of which the chronicles struggled with the hostile crusading ideology permeating that climate. No matter that these motifs may have been well grounded in classical rabbinic tradition, their convergence and prominence in chronicles of the First Crusade illuminate common ground in the language and thought of medieval Judaism and Christianity. Early in the twelfth century, for example, Jews and Christians alike yearned for an imminent final redemption, and they appreciated the Crusades from such a perspective. Bernard of Clairvaux beckoned Christian Europe to participate in the Second Crusade with the admonition that "now is the acceptable time, now is the day of ample salvation," but yet "the earth is shaken and trembles because the God of heaven has begun to lose his land."[15] And so did two of the Jewish chroniclers link the date of the Crusade with biblical messianic prophecy by noting that the persecutions occurred "in the eleventh year of the nineteen-lunar-year cycle *Ranu* [256 in gematria], when we yearned for salvation and consolation, as in the prophecy of Jeremiah [31:6], 'Cry out in joy (*Ronnu*] for Jacob; shout at the crossroads of the nations.'"[16] The chronicles resound with calls for vengeance against those who attacked the Jews of the Rhineland, underscoring the apocalyptic implications of the events of 1096. "The killers are destined for eternal damnation; those killed in sanctification of the holy name of the supernal God are destined for life in the next world, and their souls in paradise will be bound

up in the bundle of life."[17] Needless to say, the Jews prayed that "the Lord, our God, grant us our revenge . . . speedily."[18]

European Christians deemed the Crusades of the utmost historical significance, perhaps equivalent to that of the ancient Israelite conquest of the promised land, perhaps even greater. Using biblical terms that described truly unique events, the Hebrew chronicles clamored in turn that the excellence of the Jewish martyrs of 1096 had virtually no rival throughout all of history. "Who ever heard the like? Who ever witnessed such events? Ask and see: Has there ever been self-sacrifice [*'akedah*] like this since the days of Adam?"[19] These martyrs ranked with Daniel and his friends, with Rabbi Akiba and his colleagues killed during the Hadrianic persecutions, and with the heroes of Betar and the Bar Kokhba rebellion. In 1096, notes the chronicle—evoking an array of eschatological motifs that Israel Yuval has explored at length[20]—Passover, the festival of redemption, fell on the same day of the week (Thursday) as the original Passover, that of the exodus from Egypt. As the festival of Pentecost then approached, Ashkenazic Jews displayed an allegiance to God comparable to that of the Israelites at the foot of Mount Sinai.

On the third of Sivan, a day of sanctification and abstinence for Israel at the time when the Torah was given, on that very day when Moses our teacher, may he rest in peace, said, "Be prepared for the third day"—on that day the community of Mainz, saints of the supernal God, were separated in holiness and purity, and they were designated to ascend to God all together.[21]

Like their Christian contemporaries, the Jewish chroniclers viewed the conflict of 1096 a holy war of epic proportion. At stake was Jerusalem, the site of God's ancient sanctuary, the most sacred of space, and the unrivaled holiness that participation in the sacrificial cult of old entailed. The Hebrew narratives depict martyrs who transformed their self-inflicted deaths into rituals of that cult. They speak of a symbolic altar, a knife suited for the ritual slaughter of animals, a blessing recited over the sacrifice—in these cases by the victims themselves—the flow of the victim's blood onto the ground, and, of course, the favor that would accrue in God's eyes as a result. Thus did Isaac ben David, warden of the Jewish community in Mainz, lead his two children into the synagogue, in front of the holy ark, "and he slaughtered them there, in sanctification of the great name of the high and lofty God. . . . He sprinkled from their blood on the pillars of the holy ark . . . , and he said, 'May this blood be atonement for all my sins.'"[22] As

the crusaders struggled to conquer the earthly Jerusalem, the Jews of Ashkenaz in their acts of *kiddush ha-Shem* recreated a spiritual Jerusalem within the midst of their own communities.

Yet this notion of a spiritual Jerusalem, built on foundations of piety and self-sacrifice and overshadowing the earthly Jerusalem in its sanctity, also reflects the worldview of the twelfth-century monastery, that worldview which brought the idea of the Crusade to its maturity. Despite his central role in the call for the Second Crusade, the Cistercian abbot Bernard of Clairvaux quoted Paul's Epistle to the Galatians and counseled a young Englishman to shun the pleasures of this world. Instead, he should enroll as a citizen of Jerusalem, "not of that earthly Jerusalem to which Mount Sinai in Arabia is joined . . . but of that free Jerusalem which is above and the mother of us all." What did this entail? Bernard diverted the would-be pilgrim from his passage to the Holy Land (the earthly Jerusalem) and convinced him to remain at his Cistercian monastery in Clairvaux (as close as one could approach the heavenly Jerusalem here on earth).[23]

Our Hebrew chronicles display similar confidence in the collective piety of Ashkenazic Jewry. They cast entire communities as saintly—young and old, male and female, learned and simple, those mentioned by name and the mass of others—and they describe the slaughter of the Jews of Mainz, "the precious children of Zion," as comparable to the destruction of Jerusalem.[24] Quoting Lamentations 1:6, "Gone from fair Zion are all that were her glory," the chronicle glosses, "This refers to Mainz."[25] These Jews of the Rhineland, we read in the chronicles, excelled in their prayer, their fasting, their charity. Like Christian monks and nuns, they prized their opportunity for self-sacrifice. "If only our death would be at the hands of the Lord, so that we should not die at the hands of the Lord's enemies."[26] As in popular perception of the Crusades, they considered death on the field of battle against the infidel an immediate entry visa into paradise. For the martyr "a world of darkness is exchanged for a world of light, a world of misery for one of happiness, a passing world for a world that endures forever."[27] Of no less interest, just as women figured conspicuously in Christian martyrology and communities of women assumed new prominence in twelfth-century Christian monasticism,[28] so do the Hebrew chronicles highlight the role of Jewish women in the persecutions. Time and time again, the Hebrew narratives single out female martyrs for special praise. Repeatedly do women take the initiative, calling upon their husbands to react to the desecration of the Torah scroll, hurling stones upon their attackers, resisting the lure of baptism more effectively than their men,

bravely submitting to execution or plunging themselves to their deaths, and, as in the case of one Mistress Rachel of Mainz, sacrificing their own little children.[29]

Moreover, the sacrifice of a child by a parent, particularly as a means of atoning for sin, reminds us that at the center of crusading ideology loomed the figure of Jesus himself. Bearing the sign of the cross on their clothing, crusaders commonly deemed their efforts above all a commitment to Christ—to avenge the wrong done to him, to liberate the holy places where he lived and died, to emulate his own selfless martyrdom. Acknowledging this commitment, the Hebrew chronicles may betray an awareness of the heightened twelfth-century Christian interest in the Jew's role as Christ-killer. So they depict the crusaders, who proclaim to the Jews: "You are the descendants of those who killed our God and hanged him on a tree. He himself said, 'The day will come when my children will come and will avenge my blood.'"[30] In return, the chronicles lash out disparagingly at Jesus, at what they consider the crusaders' misguided devotion to him, and at the sign of the cross. They contrast the Jewish martyrs with the crusaders, and the efficacy of *kiddush ha-Shem* with the futility of the Crusade, declaring that "for naught they have thrown our corpses to the ground, for the sake of an illusion they have killed our saints, for the sake of a vile corpse they have spilled the blood of righteous women, and for the sake of the words of a subversive idolater they have shed the blood of children and nursing infants."[31]

At the same time, however, the Hebrew narratives use motifs linked to the character of Jesus to depict the Jewish martyrs, insinuating that they actualized these images more than Jesus himself. Like Jesus, many of the martyrs had their clothes removed and stolen. Relating incidents of *kiddush ha-Shem*, the chronicles employ imagery of the Passover sacrifice, perhaps suggesting that the Jewish martyr, not Jesus, was the genuine paschal lamb, or *agnus Dei*.[32] And finally, in both Judaism and Christianity, the classic, most powerful biblical prototype for martyrdom and self-sacrifice that atones for sin is the story of the Akedah, Abraham's binding of Isaac, in Genesis 22. Not at all by accident do our chronicles regularly compare the Ashkenazic martyrs of 1096 to the bound Isaac, just as Christian theology reckoned the Akedah a prefiguration of the crucifixion. Yet Christianity found it significant that the biblical Isaac did not die on his father's altar, while Jesus did; the promise of the New Testament thereby completed and surpassed that of the Old.[33] Instructively, the Hebrew chronicles stress that the Jewish martyrs themselves outdid the biblical patriarchs. They num-

bered in the hundreds; Isaac was merely one. More important, they in fact died; and, as Shalom Spiegel has shown and as we shall soon see, they are repeatedly described as suffering execution not once but, owing to the strength of their spirit, twice. Like the crucifixion, acts of martyrdom that fulfilled the message of the Akedah warranted the interruption of nature's most regular cycles.

Were there ever 1,100 Akedahs on one day—all of them like the Akedah of Isaac, son of Abraham?! The earth rumbled over just one Akedah that was bound on Mount Moriah . . . and the heavens grew dark. What did they do now? Why did the heavens not grow dark and the stars not hold back their splendor?[34]

Drawn from ideas and traditions prevalent in early twelfth-century Christianity, these prominent motifs in the Hebrew chronicles conveyed a polemical response to the hostile pressure that the climate of crusading undoubtedly exerted upon Ashkenazic Jewish communities. Quite simply, the message read: Our martyrdom, the atonement it effected, and the salvation it secured were genuine; yours are not. Our martyrs outstrip your martyrs, and even Jesus, your Martyr par excellence. Our holy war, in which we readily died as martyrs, was greater, more meritorious, than yours.

Nonetheless, alongside their response to the Christian idea of Crusade, descriptions of *kiddush ha-Shem* in the Hebrew narratives also bespeak the guilt, misgivings, and doubts that must have preoccupied the Jews of the Rhineland when they contrasted their survival with their compatriots' self-sacrifice. Various scholars have recently elaborated the powerful role played by Christian doubt in the religious and intellectual life of the crusading period and within the context of Christian-Jewish relations in particular.[35] Why should a similar phenomenon among Ashkenazic Jews, many of whom owed their existence to their own baptism or that of their parents in 1096, surprise us?

Even if they were eclipsed by grief over the Jewish martyrs of the First Crusade, expressions of guilt and self-deprecation do sometimes appear in the piyyutim, the liturgical poems, in which German Jewry mourned the tragedy of the persecutions. Rabbi Menachem ben Makhir, a contemporary, surely lamented how "tender-hearted women, with their own hands slaughtered their children born in purity." But he also recounted how the crusaders "sought to mislead me, and they made heavy my yoke; they thwarted their [that is, the Jews'] fear of God, compared signs, and perverted me."[36] Comparing signs may refer not only to the crusaders' sign of

the cross but also to the symbolic exegesis of the Hebrew Bible at the foundation of Christian faith. And the expression for "perverted me" (*oti 'ikkeshu*) evokes associations of a generation of sinners, insincere converts, and Christianity's wicked progenitor Esau as he was described in the Bible and rabbinic midrash.[37]

Another liturgical poet, an otherwise unknown Rabbi Abraham, vividly recalled the glory of the martyrs and then declared on behalf of the survivors:

We must not question the fate of the dead,
since they have been irrevocably destined for eternal life.
Yet we must question ourselves; for we have been found very guilty,
insofar as we have transgressed precepts of the righteous.

The next stanza, however, seems to equivocate.

O everlasting God, we flee to the shadow of your wings.
For we have been left, abandoned and suffering,
rather than bowing our heads and joining the crucified one. . . .
Let all who trust in him be put to shame.[38]

Who are the "we" of this cry, the martyrs or the survivors? The martyrs had not been left, abandoned and suffering; yet the survivors did indeed pay homage to the crucified one, at least temporarily, and thus "have been found very guilty." The poet's admission of guilt notwithstanding, might we have a protestation of innocence on the part of the survivor? The poet has at once condemned and vindicated; his words reject a dogmatic distinction between those who sanctified God's name in their deaths and those who suffer to acknowledge him in their lives.

If the Jewish survivors of 1096 thus sought to assuage their own pangs of conscience, so too could they occasionally even dare to question the legitimacy of the martyrs' behavior. An oft-quoted medieval rabbinic commentary on the law against homicide in Genesis 9:5 tells of

a certain rabbi that slaughtered many young children during a persecution, because he feared that they would be forced to apostasize. With him was another rabbi, who grew most angry with him and called him a murderer. Yet he did not hesitate. And this other rabbi declared: If I am correct, that rabbi will be killed in an unusual fashion. So it happened, that the Gentiles caught him; they then flayed his skin and put sand between his skin and his flesh. Afterward the evil decree was annulled. If he had not slaughtered the children they would have been rescued.[39]

Perhaps with similar misgivings, a thirteenth-century Ashkenazic Jew asked Rabbi Meir of Rothenburg if he needed to do penance for having slaughtered his wife and four sons in sanctification of God's name during a pogrom in Koblenz.[40]

I suggest that the novel impulse that led Ashkenazic Jews to record their memories of the recent past in the Crusade chronicles likewise vented—and somehow aimed to resolve—deep-seated ambivalence toward both martyrs and survivors of the persecutions of 1096. The chronicles depict a Jewish society in which traditional norms of behavior broke down. In the accounts of *kiddush ha-Shem*, for example, children often outshine their parents and wives their husbands. Do such role reversals betray veiled admissions of self-doubt, hints that not the entire community passed muster during this ultimate trial? Like the survivors, did the martyrs themselves somehow fall short of perfection? Repeatedly do the Hebrew chronicles recount how various martyrs, confronted by the crusaders with the choice between baptism or death, wavered in their indecisiveness. Some reacted like Isaac ben David, warden of the community of Mainz, who first accepted baptism, then repented, and finally slaughtered himself—but even then in a narrative sequence riddled with question, doubt, and perhaps a measure of parody.[41]

Others who chose martyrdom over baptism first begged their oppressors for extra time to reach their decision. Regarding David ben Nathaniel the *gabbai*, yet another official of the Mainz Jewish community, the chronicle may be suggesting that he asked for additional time precisely when tempted with the prospect of temporary conversion. For the Catholic priest negotiating with him explained that of the Jews who had taken refuge in the castles of the local bishop and count, "none survived . . . except those few whom they defiled [baptized] and who then returned to their faith [*ve-shavu le-toratam*]."[42] Though no self-respecting priest would have held out the prospect of only temporary conversion to Christianity, and though the published translations of the Hebrew chronicle understandably render *ve-shavu le-toratam* "gone over to their [i.e., the Christians'] belief,"[43] the simplest, literal understanding of these words is that they returned *to their own belief*. And here one encounters precisely the quandary that plagued the memories of the survivors: the choice between conversion in order to maintain Jewish life and death in order to sanctify the name of God. Admittedly, the chronicles at times construe such requests for a stay of execution favorably, assuming that the martyr wished to reject Christianity more dramatically, perhaps before a larger crowd of Christians who gathered to celebrate

his prospective conversion. On other occasions, however, both classical rabbinic lore and medieval Ashkenazic texts considered such hesitation (when
confronted with a choice between forced conversion or death) evidence of
sinful doubt, as in the acclaimed tale of Rabbi Amnon of Mainz, supposed
author of the High Holy Day prayer *U-Netanneh Tokef,* who delayed three
days before refusing the local bishop's demand that he convert.[44]

Curiously, the chronicles link instances of Jewish martyrs suggesting
to their Christian attackers that they might ultimately opt for baptism with
descriptions of Jews, already slaughtered but yet retaining an ounce of life—
Jews submitting to martyrdom, as it were, yet a second time. As noted with
reference to the work of Shalom Spiegel, this motif expressed the polemical
claim that the Jewish martyrs of 1096, not Jesus or the crusaders, best realized the ideal of atoning self-sacrifice expressed in the biblical Akedah story.
Still, in keeping with our allowance for simultaneous, multiple, even contradictory readings of a text, this would not preclude these same episodes'
dramatization of the indecisiveness and self-doubt haunting the Jewish survivors. We read that one Shemariah of Mörs convinced his captors to give
him and his family one last night alone before converting them. During the
night, Shemariah arose, slew his wife and three children, and "afterward he
slaughtered himself and fainted, but he still was not dead."[45] On the mor-
row, Shemariah's captors found him and, upon his refusal to convert, buried him alive; yet the next day they found that he still had not died, and
they buried him alive once more—in all, his third execution! Not only was
Shemariah martyred three times, but, like the survivors who did convert,
he also refused to die.

More suggestively, the Hebrew narrative recounts that after one group
of Jews in Mainz had been slain,

the uncircumcised ones . . . hurled them naked, through the windows down onto
the ground, mounds and mounds, piles and piles, until they were like a tall moun-
tain. Many of them were still alive when they threw them; their souls were still
bound together with their bodies, with a trace of vitality left in them, and they
beckoned to them (their attackers) with their fingers, "Give us a little water so that
we may drink." When the crusaders saw as much, that there was still a trace of life
in them, they asked: "So you wish to pollute yourselves, so that we will give you
water to drink and you can still be saved?" They shook their heads and looked to
their father in heaven, as if to say, "No," and pointed with their fingers to the holy
one, blessed be he; but they could say absolutely nothing because of their wounds.
They [the enemy] continued to strike them, adding greatly to their blows, *until they
slew them a second time.*[46]

The contrived confusion between drinking water and the crusaders' life-saving water of baptism generates the dramatic tension in this scene: What did these once-slain Jews in fact request in their efforts to survive? Up until the last moment of their lives, even after they were slain once, their decision remained unclear. In the Jews' request for water, the crusaders beheld a willingness to embrace Christianity; the Hebrew report highlights their steadfast commitment to God. Might not the survivors have here conflated martyr and forced convert in this narrative representation of their conflicted memories?

Telling and recording the stories preserved in the chronicles, Ashkenazic Jews of the twelfth century struggled with the trauma that their communities had suffered, and I have found psychiatrist Judith Lewis Herman's fascinating investigation *Trauma and Recovery* especially helpful in weighing what this entailed. Probing the impact of trauma on its victims and survivors, Herman has noted insightfully that "to study psychological trauma means bearing witness to horrible events. When the events are natural disasters or 'acts of God' those who bear witness sympathize readily with the victim. But when the traumatic events are of human design, those who bear witness are caught in the conflict between victim and perpetrator."[47] Those who testify to the experience of trauma must accordingly internalize the implications of the traumatic experience for themselves.

In the case of the persecutions of 1096, the Jews who survived to tell the story themselves numbered among the traumatized. Not only did their memories have to take a stand with regard to what had transpired during the Crusade, but they also gave expression to these Jews' post-traumatic suffering, stress, and efforts to heal. "Beyond the issues of shame and doubt, traumatized people struggle to arrive at a fair and reasonable assessment of their conduct, finding a balance between unrealistic guilt and a denial of all moral responsibility."[48] In the case of the survivors of *Gezerot Tatnu*, Dr. Herman's words ring true indeed. Sharing their experiences with others constituted "a precondition for the restitution of a sense of a meaningful world." Like many other victims of trauma, our storytellers engaged in "testimony as a ritual of healing,"[49] and one can well appreciate how their tales helped them work through the various stages of recovery from their communities' collective post-traumatic stress: from educating, to reexperiencing, to integrating their trauma into their current worldview and self-image.

I submit that one cannot fathom the depths of our stories without recognizing their function as therapy for traumatized communities plagued

by guilt over the very fact and the means of their survival. Such recognition hardly depends on the intentions of the individuals who composed the chronicles, "the chroniclers" as we tend to call them, in whom our study has little interest. Rather, we intend to bypass the chroniclers and depart from the stories themselves, probing their meaning for those who told and transmitted them. Such a reading of the Hebrew Crusade chronicles may well appear unconventional, unsettling, perhaps even iconoclastic. Yet it deserves a fair hearing, which Part 2 of this book will attempt to present.

PART II

Martyrs of 1096

Chapter 4
Last Supper at Xanten

The wave of attacks on German Jews highlighted in the Hebrew chronicles of the First Crusade progressed down the Rhine in a northerly direction—from Speyer, Worms, and Mainz in May of 1096, to Cologne and its environs from the last days of May and into July. We read that several hundred Jews fled Cologne and sought refuge in a number of smaller villages in the area, but that the violence caught up with them there as well. On Friday evening, June 27, the crusaders reportedly fell upon a band of Jews hiding out in the town of Xanten, where they had just sat down to their Sabbath meal. The brief chronicle of Rabbi Eliezer bar Nathan reports the occurrence rather straightforwardly:

On that very day the onslaught struck the pious of Xanten, whom they [the crusaders] attacked and killed at the very hour when the Sabbath began. Some of the pious ones [of Cologne] were there, and they celebrated the entry of the Sabbath day as they killed them. For just as one who finds booty rejoices, so did they take delight in worshipping our God and in sanctifying his name; they too sanctified the name of God with their sacrifices [*'akedot*].[1]

Eliezer's record of the massacre leaves little room for doubt that such an attack upon the Jews took place and that Jews died a martyr's death in Xanten. But the more detailed account in the chronicle attributed to Rabbi Solomon bar Samson lends itself to a more thorough—and more interesting—analysis.

On Friday, the fifth of the month [Tammuz], on the eve of the Sabbath at	1
twilight, on the eve of the day of rest, the enemies of the Lord came	2
upon the pious of Xanten. Their enemies fell upon them just as the	3
Sabbath had begun and as they had sat down to eat, sanctified the day	4
with the *Kiddush* prayer, and recited the blessing of *ha-Motzi* over the	5
bread. They heard the voice of the oppressor, and the seething waters	6
beset them; they had eaten but a taste of bread together with their	7
blessing.	8

Their leader exlaimed: "Son of Aaron the priest, you are worthy   9
of grandeur." Woe, woe for those who have perished and are no   10
longer to be found. So my lyre is given over to mourning, my pipe   11
to accompany weepers. For everyone who heard [this priest's] voice   12
as he prayed would say, "His sound is like that of the lyre and the pipe,   13
the drum and the flute"; and his prayer would ascend to heaven before   14
the divine throne, where it would become a crown and diadem for the   15
heavenly God, the king of kings of kings, the holy one, blessed be he.   16
But the persecution had been decreed, and it became a sort of iron   17
griddle separating us from our father in heaven. It stifled our prayer,   18
and we could not find on our behalf even one advocate among a   19
thousand angels. God had come to put this generation to the test, to   20
make known his love for them to his entire heavenly entourage. Thus   21
did King David declare, "Therefore did maidens ['*alemot*] love you"—   22
meaning, they loved you unto death [revocalizing the same Hebrew   23
consonants as '*al mavet*]. So, too, did he say, "It is for your sake that   24
we are slain all day long, that we are regarded as sheep to be   25
slaughtered."   26
And this pious man of faith, the priest ranking above his brethren,   27
spoke to the group gathered to eat with him at the table: "Let us recite   28
the grace after meals to the living God, our father in heaven, since the   29
table is now set before us in place of the altar. Now that the enemy has   30
attacked us today, let us arise and ascend to the house of the Lord and   31
quickly do the will of our creator: that even on the Sabbath each man   32
slaughter his son, daughter, and brother in order to bestow a blessing   33
upon ourselves today. Let no man have mercy on himself or on his   34
fellow, and let the last one remaining slaughter himself with a knife to   35
his throat or plunge his sword into his stomach. Let not the wicked   36
hands of the impure defile us with their abominable rites, but let us   37
offer ourselves as a sacrifice to God brought on the altar of God, total   38
burnt offerings to the most high. And we shall live on in that world of   39
eternal daylight, in the Garden of Eden, in the illuminating radiance of   40
God, where we shall behold him face to face in his glory and grandeur.   41
There shall everyone be given a golden diadem on his head, with   42
precious stones and pearls inlaid in it. There shall we dwell among the   43
pillars of the world, dining in the Garden of Eden in the fellowship of   44
the righteous, numbering among the company of Rabbi Akiba and his   45
colleagues, sitting on a throne of gold. Each and every one of us shall   46
point him out with his finger and proclaim, 'This is our God; we   47
trusted in him, and he delivered us. This is the Lord in whom we   48
trusted; let us rejoice and exult in his deliverance.' There we shall   49
observe the Sabbaths; for here in this world of darkness we cannot   50
keep the Sabbath, observing it as required."   51
All of them responded aloud, of one voice and mind, "Amen, let it be   52
so, and may this be the will of God." The pious Rabbi Moses began to   53
lead the grace after meals, since he was a priest of the supernal God,   54

and he recited, "Let us bless our God whose food we have eaten."   55
They responded, "Blessed is he, our God, etc." And he recited, "May   56
the merciful one avenge the spilled blood of 'your' servants [instead   57
of *his*]—and the blood yet to be spilled—during the lifetime of   58
those who survive us, before their very eyes. May the merciful one   59
save us from evil men, from persecution, from idolatry, from the   60
impurity of the Gentiles, and from their abominable rites." And he   61
recited many other blessings concerning those events, on account of   62
the decree imposed upon them. So have I heard from my ancestors and   63
the other elders, engaged in their work, who saw this great occurrence.   64
Then when they got up from the table, the pious one said to them: 65
"You are children of the living God; proclaim aloud and in unison,   66
'Hear O Israel, the Lord is our God, the Lord alone,'" and so they did.   67
"And now, delay no more; the time has come to act, to offer to him the   68
sacrifice of our lives."   69
On the eve of the Sabbath at twilight they offered themselves as a   70
sacrifice to God in place of the daily twilight offering, and they   71
themselves came to be like the daily morning offering. Just as one   72
rejoices when he finds booty and at reaping time, so they delighted   73
and rejoiced in worshipping God and in sanctifying his great and holy   74
name. Delighted and joyful, they all came before the most powerful   75
God, and of their likes it says in Scripture, "like a groom coming forth   76
from the chamber, like a hero, eager to run his course." Thus did they   77
rejoice in running and entering into the innermost recesses of the   78
Garden of Eden. Of them the prophet foretold, "No eye has seen [such   79
things], O God, but you, who act for those that trust in you."[2]   80

On its most obvious level, this story serves to glorify the Jewish martyrs of Xanten. Nowhere does the chronicle intimate that death comes to
punish them for their sins. Rather, God has put them to the test, "to make
known his love for them," precisely as they busy themselves with sanctifying his holy day, reciting the *Kiddush* over the wine, the blessing of *ha-
Motzi* over the bread, and *Birkat ha-Mazon* at the end of their abbreviated
meal. Led by the pious priest Rabbi Moses, they rise to the occasion and
pass the test with flying colors. Not only do they submit to death to avoid
contamination by the "seething waters" of baptism, but they remove all
initiative from the hands of their enemies and into their own. Inflicting
their own deaths upon themselves, they transform their ruin into spiritual
victory, their brutal slaughter into a ritual of self-sacrifice. Thus do they
prove the extent of their love for God. Blessing and prayer precede the
sacrifices, and the most cherished reward follows them immediately. The
martyrs enter directly into the uppermost levels of paradise. The company
of Rabbi Akiba and other exemplary martyrs of old in paradise confirms

their worthiness. Here in the Garden of Eden they live anew, dining, rejoicing, observing the Sabbath properly without impediment, beholding the divine countenance, and reaffirming their faith in utter glee. One can hardly overlook the nearly ecstatic sense of religious fulfillment, attributed by the story to its heroes, to be sure, but intended no less to inspire its Jewish readers who continued to live in danger of crusading violence. No doubt with scenes like this in mind did Israeli historian Yitzhak Baer, as noted in Chapter 2, declare that "we taught the world the idea of martyrdom," and that during the First Crusade "this idea was realized in the very body of the people."[3]

This reading of the martyrdom in Xanten has much to commend itself. It explains a great deal concerning the character, purpose, and function of the tales of 1096 preserved in the three Hebrew chronicles. I have given it relatively short shrift here *not* in order to discount its validity or significance but simply because it is the standard reading of the story, which many investigators have already elaborated, well and at length.[4] I hope in this book to demonstrate that this standard interpretation is not airtight or sufficient. It has cracks, as it were; it fails to explain other, generally more subtle aspects of the stories, which lead us to different, conflicting readings of the same passages that I consider simultaneously valid. If these various readings appear contradictory, perhaps this is because the very origin of the stories in the chronicles reeks of contradiction. On the one hand, they glorify the martyrs. On the other hand, they originate, develop, and find their way into writing among the survivors of the 1096 persecutions, who chose the opposite path, not of death but of life, often at the price of conversion to Christianity.

This anomaly points to a crack in the standard, "heroic" interpretation of the Xanten story when we consider the following: The chronicle reports (line 52) that *all* of the Jews assembled assented enthusiastically to Rabbi Moses' charge that they kill one another as martyrs. Within several lines, however, the narrator attests to the veracity of his story by noting (lines 63–64), "So have I heard from my ancestors and the other elders, engaged in their work [of the community], who saw this great occurrence." In other words, not all of the Jews gathered for this Sabbath dinner in Xanten martyred themselves. Some, including the storyteller's own progenitors, chose to remain alive, perhaps mitigating the power of the tale, but certainly complicating its meaning. We thus proceed to a more rigorous analysis of our text, applying the guidelines outlined in Chapter 3, delving

into the difficulties, the symbols, and the intertextual allusions that it contains. Our discussion revolves around three dimensions of the story.

Earthly and Heavenly Time

Our story does not wait until its second half in order to awaken the reader to its complexity. In its very first line, we read that the crusaders came to Xanten "on Friday, the fifth" of the Hebrew month of Tammuz; yet in 1096 the fifth of Tammuz fell on Saturday, not on Friday! Did our text inadvertently make a mistake?[5] Perhaps, but I tend to think not. The likelihood of such error seems minimal. All three of the chronicles make an effort to date the attacks upon the Jews of the Rhineland with precision. In the chronicle of Eliezer bar Nathan and that attributed to Solomon bar Samson, this is especially true with regard to the slaughter of those Jews who had fled from Cologne to other towns in the vicinity; and Eliezer, we should note, correctly dated the first Friday of Tammuz 4856 (1096) as the fourth.[6] The fourth of Tammuz always falls on the same day of the week as the Jewish festival of Shavu'ot (Pentecost, on the sixth of Sivan). Inasmuch as our Solomon bar Samson narrative correctly notes that the main attack on Mainz Jewry occurred on Tuesday, the third of Sivan, which places both Shavu'ot and the fourth of Tammuz on Friday, shouldn't it have known better than to call the fifth of Tammuz a Friday? Curiously, immediately after the episode at Xanten the Solomon bar Samson text alters its method of dating—"and it came to pass on the [first] Sunday of Tammuz"[7]—and thereby avoids extending its incorrect chronology into an additional week. How, then, ought one to explain the confusion? In Chapter 2, we cited historian Karl Morrison's suggestion that twelfth-century historical texts often communicated their meaning in silences or "loose ends" pertaining to time. And here, in the Xanten episode's seeming conflation of Friday, the fourth of Tammuz, and Saturday, the fifth, our story might betray one of its central concerns.

Compounding the inexactitude in dating the scene at Xanten, the chronicle brackets its story with references to the time of day when the martyrdom occurred: "on the eve of the Sabbath at twilight" (lines 1–2, 70). Just as the misleading date makes one unsure as to whether the time is Friday, the fourth of the month, or Saturday, the fifth, so does the specified hour. On the Jewish ritual and liturgical clock, a twenty-four-hour day begins at nightfall, when the preceding day ends. Owing to their greater

sanctity, however, the Sabbath and other holy days begin early, at dusk, some twenty to forty minutes before nightfall. Our narrative's repeated reference to twilight, therefore, makes it doubly difficult to know if it is Friday or the Sabbath; before the nightfall that marks the end of Friday but after the sunset that introduces the Sabbath, the twilight belongs to both days. Along similar lines, the text first specifies that the events occurred on Friday (line 1); it then moves to the ambiguous twilight (line 2); it then proceeds to the beginning of the Sabbath (line 4); it refers to the slaughter as transpiring on the Sabbath itself (line 32); and it returns, as we noted, to twilight (line 70). We know that medieval German Jews often recited their evening prayers early, such that they commonly began their observance of the Sabbath before nightfall. As a result, they may not have found such ambiguity in this story disturbing.[8] Yet for just this reason, the transitional nature of the story's time frame may have resonated with meaning for them.

Just as Rabbi Moses the priest prodded his followers to exchange life in this world for life in "that world of eternal daylight" (lines 39–40), so did classical rabbinic traditions cherished by medieval Jews commonly compare salvation both to a world of unending daylight and to a world of unending Sabbath rest. Rabbinic texts from the talmudic period understood the "psalm for the Sabbath day," Psalm 90, as yearning for "the day that is an unending Sabbath,"[9] in which, as one tradition elaborated, "there is neither eating, nor drinking, nor the transaction of business, but in which the righteous sit, their heads crowned, and are sustained by the radiance of God's presence."[10] Labeling the sabbatical "day of rest" *margo'a* (line 2), a term understood by twelfth-century Hebrew poets to denote a more permanent state of tranquillity as well,[11] our chronicle seems to express this notion of salvation, in which Friday, the weekday, represents the passing experience of life in this world, while the Sabbath denotes the ultimate, eternal fulfillment of the world to come. We find this contrast echoed in a rabbinic midrash, which likewise hints at Rabbi Moses' promise that the martyrs will reside in paradise in "the fellowship of the righteous" (lines 44–45). The parable concerns

two wicked men that consort with each other in this world. One repents before his death while the other does not repent. When the time comes, one numbers among the fellowship of the righteous and the other among the fellowship of the wicked. When the latter sees his friend, he exclaims: "Woe is me; perhaps there is inequity here. He and I stole together; he and I murdered together. Yet he numbers among the fellowship of the righteous and I among the fellowship of the wicked." They reply to him [in the heavenly court]: "Utter fool . . . , when your friend understood

this he repented from his evil way, and you had the capacity to repent but did not!" He says to them: "Give me a chance to go and repent." Yet they reply: "Utter fool, don't you know that this [other] world resembles the Sabbath, and that the world you have come from resembles the day preceding the Sabbath? If a person makes no preparation on Friday, what will he eat on the Sabbath?"[12]

This midrash sheds interesting light on our story. The ambiguity of what happened in Xanten, wavering from Friday to the Sabbath as it does, suggests that time in this tale is not simply earthly and temporal, but heavenly and otherworldly as well. The martyrs stood on the verge of a critical transition, and not merely that between today and tomorrow. Attacked by the crusaders on the brink of the Sabbath, these Jews straddled the proverbial fence between one world and the next: the world of Friday, of physical existence, of a gloomy, tiresome lack of fulfillment on the one hand, and the radiant world of the Sabbath, of eternal light, repose, and salvation on the other hand. Rabbi Moses instructed his fellow Jews (lines 49–51) that there, in that other world, "we shall observe the Sabbaths, for here in this world of darkness we cannot keep the Sabbath, observing it as required." To live here, in this world, as a Christian (with the promise of punishment in the next world) or to die here and enjoy the eternal rewards of paradise after death—did such a choice leave the committed Ashkenazic Jew any room for doubt?

The apparent confidence of the narrative might indicate that no, it did not, but a more subtle reading might suggest otherwise. Alongside the rabbinic homilies likening the salvation of the next world to an unending Sabbath day, one finds the tradition that the unending Sabbath day (*yom shekulo Shabbat*) also refers to a thousand-year-long period of utter destruction that will follow upon six thousand years of life in this world. In that millennial age, nothing whatsoever will exist besides God himself.[13] Perhaps, as with specifying time, our story evokes associations concerning an extraterrestrial Sabbath that are not unambiguous.[14] If an eternal Sabbath possibly heralded ruin, the end of existence rather than eternal life, then the choice between martyrdom and submission to baptism might not prove as uncomplicated as we imagined.

Ambiguities of Heroism

When we recall that the martyrs of Xanten—or any other Jewish community attacked in 1096—did not live to tell their tale, but that the narratives

in the chronicles aired the memories, worldview, and needs of the survivors, it should not surprise us that these stories reflect some measure of doubt. The choice between baptism and death was mind-boggling for the Jews of the Rhineland, and one wonders how he or she would have reacted in their predicament. Indeed, at the same time as our stories glorify the martyrs, boosting morale within Jewish communities that survived the persecutions and responding to the threatening, notably anti-Jewish ideology of crusading from without, they naturally expressed the guilt and the doubts weighing onerously upon the survivors. As the martyr came to represent the exemplary hero for Ashkenazic Jews, how could those who themselves or whose parents had found temporary refuge in Christianity, thereby escaping a martyr's death, justify that decision? How could they look at themselves in the mirror every day when they woke up in the morning? Here were Jewish communities suffering from serious wounds, not the least of which was the guilt-ridden trauma of their survival. The key to any process of psychotherapy lies in having the patient verbalize his or her critical transforming experiences; as we noted at the end of the previous chapter, victims of trauma in particular must offer testimony in order to heal and overcome their guilt. I believe that the martyrs' tales in our chronicles also served to verbalize such testimony, facilitating a process of collective "therapy" for the Jewish communities that told them and disseminated them.

How did these tales function so? As we shall see, the martyrs at the center of the stories, those who heroically sanctify God's name with their death and often inflict such death upon themselves, are often not quite so simple as they might first appear. Careful reading reveals characters less than perfect, characters depicted with ambivalence, characters who at one and the same time embody both the perfection of the deceased martyr-hero and the misgivings of the survivor who had submitted to baptism in order to go on living as a Jew. If the Xanten narrative somehow blurs the distinction between Friday and Saturday, so too does it conflate victim and survivor, with equally important ramifications. Consider an array of intertextual associations that contribute to such a reading of our story.

1. Line 9: "Son of Aaron the priest." This epithet surely serves to elevate the hero of this episode in status and stature. But "son of Aaron the priest" also brings to mind the two sons of the biblical Aaron, Nadav and Avihu, whom God punished for offering "alien fire" upon his altar. Among the many rabbinic interpretations of the details of their sin, one midrash suggested that they offered a sacrifice that was neither the daily twilight

offering nor the daily morning offering—those two very sacrifices with which our narrative proceeds to equate the martyrs (lines 70–72).[15] Did some Jews at Xanten, linked expressly to the hero of the story, resort to the alien fire of a different cult? Was the sacrifice unacceptable to God that of the martyrs or that of the forced converts?

2. Lines 10–11: "Woe, woe for those who have perished and are no longer to be found." As the narrator laments the absence of the martyred Rabbi Moses the priest, he uses a phrase that evokes memories of truly accomplished leaders who succumbed to doubt in reflecting about God, just as some of the Jewish converts in 1096 undoubtedly had their doubts. In one instance, a midrash attributes such a phrase to Elisha ben Abuya, a colleague of the famed scholar-martyr Rabbi Akiba and teacher of Rabbi Meir, who left the fold of the community because his faith could not withstand his doubt.[16] In a better-known classical rabbinic *aggadah*, God uttered this phrase to bemoan the absence of the Hebrew patriarchs to Moses in Egypt. For they, God explained, never questioned his mandates to them, while Moses—whose name the Jewish leader in Xanten shared—doubtfully questioned and resisted, even though God had revealed more of himself to him than to Abraham, Isaac, or Jacob.[17]

3. Lines 19–20: "We could not find on our behalf even one advocate among a thousand angels." The text has adopted the words of Job 33:23 to underscore the helplessness of the martyrs' situation; they lack even a single vote of confidence in heaven. In its biblical context, however, this verse appears in Elihu's rebuke of the saintly Job for his theological arrogance. Might our text be questioning the image of perfection exuded by the martyrs? The Talmud cites the verse in its description of the heavenly tribunal that will judge human souls. Even if 999 angels clamor for a soul's condemnation and but one defends it, that soul will be saved. "And who are the advocates of a human being? Repentance and good deeds."[18] Precisely these are the means whereby the storytellers have sought to justify their survival, which contrasts so blatantly with the martyrs' death. They, we recall, had no advocate.

4. Lines 22–26: "'Therefore did maidens ['*alemot*] love you'— meaning, they loved you unto death [revocalizing the same Hebrew consonants as '*al mavet*]. . . . 'It is for your sake that we are slain all day long, that we are regarded as sheep to be slaughtered.'" The chronicle quotes two biblical verses, Song of Songs 1:3 and Psalm 44:23, which were commonly understood in rabbinic tradition as referring to martyrs, those who, loving

God "unto death," make their way like sheep to the slaughter.[19] Yet again, rabbinic tradition also applied these verses specifically to the imperfect, the sinners, and the doubters of Israel. One homily links "for your sake that we are slain all day long" to the third of three shiploads of Jewish youths taken captive by the Roman Vespasian and destined for sexual slavery, who, unlike the first two groups, presumably had doubts and hesitated before plunging into the sea as martyrs.[20] Perhaps more telling, another midrash suggests that Song of Songs 1:3 can denote *ba'ale teshuvah*, those who repent and return to the faith after having left it.[21] The same source also allows for understanding Song of Songs 1:3 as referring to the third group in Zechariah 13:9: "And that third I will put into the fire. . . ." Numerous rabbinic sources identify this third group as one of three whose fate is sealed on judgment day; the first includes only the perfectly righteous, the second the irreparably wicked, and the third the majority, those of an intermediate status who must be cleansed of their iniquity with punishment before receiving any heavenly reward.[22] These were all apt comparisons for the converts of 1096, now returned to Judaism—penitent *ba'ale teshuvah*, who acknowledged their checkered past as well as their need to prove their worthiness. Such individuals needed to believe that the completion of the same prophetic verse from Zechariah would ultimately be theirs as well: "They will invoke me by name, and I will respond to them. I will declare, 'You are my people,' and they will declare, 'The Lord is our God.'"

5. Lines 32–34: "Each man *slaughter* his son, *daughter*, and brother in order to bestow a blessing upon ourselves today." Except for the two italicized words, this phrase derives from the biblical story of the golden calf, in which Moses ordered the Levites to slaughter those of their kinsmen that had sinned against God and thus to secure divine blessing for themselves (Exodus 32:27–29). In 1096, however, slaughterer and slaughtered were ultimately one and the same. Might the chronicle hint at some sinful dimension to the heroes of this story, even as it extols them for their zeal? Perhaps identifying Rabbi Moses as "son of Aaron the priest" (line 9, see above) also confirms this allusion to the sin of the golden calf, a sin of idolatrous worship that many commentators of the talmudic and medieval periods attributed not to the malice of the Israelites but to misunderstanding, extenuating circumstances, and the pernicious influence of pagans who left Egypt with them.[23] Like the martyrs of Xanten, the Israelites who compelled Aaron to make the idol felt abandoned by God and by Moses, and Aaron himself feared for his life; they concluded that they had no other viable option. So did those Jews in 1096 who chose not to martyr themselves.

6. Lines 46–49: "Each and every one of us shall point him out with his finger and proclaim [Isaiah 25:9], 'This is our God; we trusted in him, and he delivered us. This is the Lord in whom we trusted; let us rejoice and exult in his deliverance.'" This description of what the martyrs should expect in paradise immediately evokes the talmudic description of a future "dance of the righteous," among whom God would sit, so that they would point to him in this fashion.[24] Yet a rabbinic midrash also understands Isaiah's prophecy as referring to the future return of the sinful and wicked, who in times of distress used to say, "Where is your God?" (Psalm 42:4), but at the end of days will acknowledge, "This is our God."[25] Whom did the Jews attacked in 1096 resemble, the utterly righteous or sinners who doubted the providence of God but who eventually reassumed their faith?

7. Line 52: "All of them responded aloud, of one voice and mind." The chronicle surely seeks to praise the martyrs for the unanimity of their resolve, but the phrase "of one voice and mind" (*peh eḥad be-lev eḥad*) invariably reminds the traditional Jewish reader of a standard rabbinic expression for hypocrisy: pronouncing one word with one's mouth and another with one's heart (*eḥad ba-peh ve-eḥad ba-lev*). According to the Talmud, this characteristic among human beings ranks among those that God despises more than any other.[26] At least one midrash attributed such hypocrisy to Esau, the progenitor of Rome and of Christianity in rabbinic tradition, since he begged his father Isaac for his blessing at the same time as he prayed for Isaac's death.[27] Curiously, while the martyrs of Xanten proclaimed their willingness to die with "one voice and mind," *peh eḥad be-lev eḥad*, their fellow Jews who survived to tell the martyrs' story found temporary refuge in the Christian legacy of Esau. What more aptly captures the insincerity of their forced conversion to Christianity than their pronouncing one word with their mouth and another with their heart, *eḥad ba-peh ve-eḥad ba-lev*?

8. Line 54: "He was a priest of the supernal God" (*kohen le-El 'elyon*). The Hebrew Bible uses this phrase (Genesis 14:18) in identifying a single individual, Melchizedek, who celebrated Abraham's victory in the war between the Canaanite kings. Melchizedek appeared bearing bread and wine, and, in Christian tradition, he thus became a prototype of the priest administering the sacrament at the mass, a motif to which we shall return in the next section of this chapter.[28] Yet in Jewish perspective, underscoring Rabbi Moses' priestly lineage certainly suits the sequence of events in our story. When Jews recite the grace after meals, the master of the household or the leader of the community customarily defers to a priest, a *kohen*, at the table

and offers him the honor of leading those present in blessing and thanking God.[29] Exactly this transpired at Xanten; perhaps the Jewish leader's words to Rabbi Moses (lines 9–10), "Son of Aaron the priest, you are worthy of grandeur," actually mean that he should take precedence and preside over the prayers. The narrator's ensuing praise of Rabbi Moses' powers of prayer (lines 12–16) would thus make perfect sense. But, in this instance, not even Rabbi Moses' prayer could offset the heavenly decree, and the grace after meals evolves into a ritual of preparing for martyrdom.

Does the figure of Melchizedek help us to understand Rabbi Moses? Evidently responding to the Christian glorification of Melchizedek and his role in foreshadowing the priest and sacrament at the mass, rabbinic tradition found fault with him. Having produced bread and wine, Melchizedek declared (Genesis 14:19–20), "Blessed be Abram of God most high, creator of heaven and earth, and blessed be God most high, who has delivered your foes into your hands." Yet while the New Testament (Hebrews 7:3) lavished praise upon Melchizedek—"resembling the Son of God he continues a priest for ever"—the Talmud and midrash record that Abraham himself rebuked the priest: "Does one place the blessing of the servant before the blessing of his master?!" This blessing gave precedence to Abraham over God, and God therefore took the priesthood away from Melchizedek's progeny and bestowed it upon the descendants of Abraham.[30] Melchizedek had erred in paying homage to creature as if he were creator, which, in Jewish eyes, was the essential error at the heart of Christianity. Yet our story esteems Rabbi Moses for his priestly pedigree and for his likeness to Melchizedek. Does it thus make room among its heroes for those who, instead of dying as martyrs, worshipped a son as if he were the Father?

9. Line 66: "You are *children of the living God.*" Rabbi Moses' inspiring call to martyrdom employs the words of Hosea 2:1, where the biblical prophet anticipated restoration and redemption. These would come on the heels of a much less desirable state of alienation and rejection, in which God would say to Israel (Hosea 1:9): "you are not my people, and I will not be your [God]." Who, then, were the real children of the living God? Our story tells its Jewish readers that *you,* the Jews, are children of the living God, not the Christians who now prided themselves as having inherited the status of God's elect. But who among the Jews were truly heroic? One midrash suggested that these were the righteous martyrs who sacrifice their lives for the unity of God's name, lovesick for God even unto death, as we have seen that Song of Songs 1:3 intimated to the rabbis.[31] Yet the reversal in God's attitude toward his people as prophesied by Hosea led other rabbinic

voices to understand these children of God as penitent sinners, as those who had spurned God and then returned to him, inasmuch as "from the fall of the righteous follows their exaltation."[32]

10. Line 68: "The time has come to act" (*ba ha-'et la'asot*) emphasizes how the moment is critical, how reasoning and words no longer suffice; the moment requires an immediate decision and action, costs notwithstanding. Here in Xanten, the Jews must choose between baptism and death, and, curiously, the narrative's obvious allusion to Psalm 119:126—"It is a time to act for the Lord, for they have violated your teaching"—might point in more than one direction. On the one hand, as the Talmud explained, a straightforward reading of the verse called for action *because people have violated the laws of God's Torah*; perhaps one might consider this a vote for martyrdom over conversion to Christianity.[33] On the other hand, rabbinic tradition more often understood this verse as licensing violation of God's law in extenuating circumstances, presumably in order to fulfill God's will more effectively: *Because the time has come to act on God's behalf*, they have violated his law.[34] What violation might the Xanten story have in mind? The temporary conversion of the survivors, perhaps; or perhaps the martyrs' suicidal infliction of death upon themselves, which Jewish legal tradition generally did not license before the persecutions of 1096.[35] This biblical allusion hints at ambivalence concerning both courses of action open to the Jews in Xanten on that fateful Friday night.

11. Lines 72–74: "Just as one rejoices when he finds booty and at reaping time, so they delighted and rejoiced." The chronicle alludes to Psalm 119:162, in which the poet declares that he delights in God's teaching "as one who finds much booty." Commenting on this Psalm, the great rabbinic authority Rashi (Solomon ben Isaac of Troyes), who lived and wrote in northern France at the time of the First Crusade after having studied at rabbinic academies in the Rhineland, quoted a midrash that circulated among his students during the twelfth century.

Our sages preached [that the divine teaching in question in this verse] concerns circumcision. For David [the presumed author of the Psalm] was in the bathhouse where he saw himself without his ritual garment [*tzitzit*] and without phylacteries [*tefillin*] and without the Torah. "Woe unto me," he said, "for I am stripped of all the commandments." But when he beheld his circumcision he rejoiced.[36]

Again, the chronicle uses this verse from Psalms to attribute the joy of obeying God's Torah to the martyrs of Xanten. But it does so with a biblical

text that the rabbinic preacher linked most colorfully to the situation of the Jew who submitted to baptism in 1096. What could better express the emotions of the forced convert at the moment of his immersion in the baptismal font, symbolized here by David's bathhouse? Bereft of all other tangible means to comply with the will of God, he confronts the seal of God's covenant on his flesh, and he rejoices in his resolve to remain a Jew. Albeit imbedded in and between the lines of our narrative, the survivors' post-traumatic need for self-esteem rings loud and clear.

I have taken the reader through so many echoes of ambivalence in the Xanten narrative because the weight of the evidence in this kind of analysis depends on quantity as well as quality. We have proceeded from the premise that texts like this allow for and, in fact, demand simultaneously valid alternative readings that derive from symbolic association and intertextual allusion. Since a particular reader might understand any specific association or allusion differently, isolated references to earlier traditions scattered throughout a text might appear coincidental, far less convincing than an array of evidence pointing in a similar direction. Running like a constant thread through this story, however, nearly a dozen indicators reveal a basic tension between perfection and imperfection, immaculate piety and mediocrity, zeal and doubt in the characterization of its heroes, such that these characters seem to make room for martyrs and survivors alike. The Xanten narrative closes on a similar note (lines 79–80), quoting Isaiah 64:3, "No eye has seen [such things], O God, but you." Various rabbinic sources interpret the prophet as referring to the unknowable, ultimate nature of the reward that God has prepared for the righteous in the next world. But the Talmud offers another reading alongside this one: that biblical prophecies of the future restoration apply strictly to *ba'ale teshuvah*, those who repent of their sinful errors, while the reward of the perfectly righteous remains known to God alone.[37] Just as this story in the chronicle opened on a note of ambiguity, so it concludes, extolling the martyrs but marginalizing them too, hinting that the forcibly converted who have returned to the Jewish community number among the mainstream included in the prophetic vision of redemption.

As we have noted, the narrative describes these *ba'ale teshuvah* as "engaged in their work" (line 64) of rebuilding the community. In view of the symbolic importance of the Sabbath in our text, this phrase may well evoke the talmudic homily in which the angels complain to God that he has given his Torah to mere mortals rather than to them. God responds to the angels somewhat sarcastically: "What is written in it? 'Remember the Sabbath day

and keep it holy.' Are you at all engaged in work that you need rest?! What is written in it . . . ? 'You shall not commit murder; you shall not commit adultery; you shall not steal.' Is there any jealousy among you? Do you at all have an evil inclination?!"[38] The martyrs might have merited an eternal Sabbath, but God intended his commandments for the imperfect. The Sabbath prescribed in the Torah requires work on the first six days of the week, not just rest on the seventh; and the survivors of 1096 and their progeny busy themselves in that work. The chronicle thus declares implicitly that God's covenant and Torah are for them; *ba'ale teshuvah* as they are, the redemption envisioned by the prophets will be theirs.

Confronting the Enemy

Beyond giving expression to problems inside the Jewish communities of the early twelfth century, the narratives of the Hebrew Crusade chronicles offered a response to the hostility directed at Ashkenazic Jewry from the Christian world outside. For those who told, transmitted, and recorded the martyrs' stories between the First and Second Crusades, the primary source of the hostility that threatened them was not the crusader so much as the ideology of crusading, which matured during the same period and, as we have seen, had ominous anti-Jewish overtones. Not surprisingly, then, we find that intertextual allusion and symbolic association in texts such as our Xanten narrative point in another direction, too, using memories of the martyrs to undermine the Crusade, its ideological foundations, and its ideals.

Most obviously, our story lashes out at Christianity. It reports the onslaught of "the seething waters" of baptism (line 6). It fears the designs of "the wicked hands of the impure" that seek to "defile us with their abominable rites" (lines 36–37). And its hero prays for salvation "from evil men, from persecution, from idolatry, from the impurity of the Gentiles, and from their abominable rites" (lines 60–61).[39]

With greater ingenuity, however, the Xanten narrative clearly attempts to beat the crusaders and their ideology at their own game, appropriating from Christianity and its idea of holy war themes and symbols that served the purposes of the Jewish storyteller in twelfth-century Ashkenaz. The crusaders had set out to avenge the martyrdom of Jesus, prepared to emulate the willingness of his self-sacrifice should the need arise. Not only do the Jewish martyrs of Xanten in our story express a willingness to sacrifice them-

selves, but they act upon it, in a manner that unmistakably recalls the events leading to Jesus' demise. Like Jesus, they partake of a last supper of bread and wine; they, too, meet their deaths on a Friday when the skies have darkened, although it is not really night just yet.[40] Building on the motif of the last supper, our story presents Rabbi Moses as ritualizing the sanctification of God's name (*kiddush ha-Shem*) precisely in the fashion that Christianity has actualized the experience of Jesus' death in the daily lives of its believers—in the mass. For as we have noted, the text likens Rabbi Moses to Melchizedek, the "priest of the supernal God" (line 54) whom Christianity considered a prototype of the priest that transmutes (transubstantiates) the bread and wine of the sacrament into the saving body and blood of Christ.[41] Rabbi Moses, too, like the Catholic priest at the mass, presides over a communal meal, in which blessings are recited over the wine and the bread, in which he transforms the table before him into an altar (line 30) for sacrifice that brings salvation to its participants. Only the Jews of Xanten go further than the priest and participants in the mass: Consuming the bread and wine does not suffice. Once these have been consecrated on the "altar" and consumed, the Jews at the table themselves become the sacrificial martyrs, assuming the role of the crucified Jesus in the symbolism of the Christian ritual. Just as Christianity considered Jesus the ultimate sacrifice that replaced the sacrifices of the Jewish temple in Jerusalem with his own, so do the Jews of our story become the sacrificial victims of the ancient temple cult. "On the eve of the Sabbath at twilight they offered themselves as a sacrifice to God *in place of* the daily twilight offering, and they themselves came to be like the daily morning offering" (lines 70–72).

"Let us arise and ascend to the house of the Lord" (line 31). Rabbi Moses' charge to the Jews of Xanten echoes Isaiah 2:3, "The many peoples shall say, 'Come let us go up to the mount of the Lord,'" and Jeremiah 31:5, "The day is coming when watchmen [*notzerim*] shall proclaim on the heights of Efraim, 'Come let us go up to Zion, to the Lord our God.'" The twelfth-century Jew would surely have linked such biblical prophecies to calls for crusading in Christian Europe; Isaiah hears such a cry of ascent arising among the Gentile nations, Jeremiah among the *notzerim*, literally watchmen, but in medieval Hebrew the word for Christians. The Hebrew chronicle of the persecutions responds to the ideological challenge of the Crusade in kind: The Jewish martyrs, hints our story, have themselves undertaken the genuine holy war.

But the reader might react, and correctly, that unlike the crusaders, the Jewish martyrs of 1096 hardly obeyed the call of ascent to the house of

the Lord by setting out for Jerusalem. Rather, as we saw in Chapter 3, they saw their communities in the Rhineland as substitutes for Zion and the temple, filled with images of temple, altar, and sacrificial cult. We can better understand this dimension of the chronicle's response if we recall, as explained in Chapter 1, that the Christian ideology of crusading matured only in the aftermath of the First Crusade and in chronicles that derived from the monastery, expressing a monastic perspective on the Crusade and exuding monastic values. These chronicles, as British historian Jonathan Riley-Smith noted, perceived the crusaders as "temporary religious, professed into what looked to them like a military monastery on the move." Moreover, as Riley-Smith explained,

nowhere is the picture of a secular but semi-monastic way of the cross clearer than in these writers' treatment of martyrdom. I have already described how the conviction that their dead were martyrs grew among the crusaders as their triumph became apparent. . . . Martyrdom was for them [the monastic chroniclers of the First Crusade] an expression of the crusaders' love for God and their brothers. It was a voluntary act by which they exchanged temporal for eternal life. They died for Christ, who had died for them, and for the faith, of which they were witnesses.[42]

It is this monastic perspective on crusading which the Xanten tale appropriates and to which it responds.

As we saw in the preceding chapter,[43] monastic writers of the twelfth century like Bernard of Clairvaux deemed the sanctity of their own monasteries as equivalent to or even surpassing that of Jerusalem. So, evidently, did the Jews of Xanten, who ascended to the house of the Lord at their Sabbath table turned altar on the banks of the Rhine. Important monastic theologians of this period described the spiritual reward of the self-sacrificing monk in terms of perfect Sabbath rest,[44] just as the Sabbath figures so centrally in our Xanten narrative. Finally, our story's citation of Psalm 44:23 (lines 24–26), "It is for your sake that we are slain all day long, that we are regarded as sheep to be slaughtered," allows for a still more revealing comparison between the Jewish zeal for sanctifying God's name and contemporary Christian monasticism.

As early as the middle of the first century, the apostle Paul—once a Jew named Saul—expressed the steadfastness of his faith in the following terms: "Who shall separate us from the love of Christ? Shall tribulation or distress or persecution or famine or nakedness or peril or sword? As it is written, 'It is for your sake that we are slain all day long, that we are regarded as sheep to be slaughtered.'"[45] Understandably, Paul's teaching

struck a resonant note in the worldview of medieval monks and nuns. Some eleven hundred years after Paul, a mid-twelfth-century German abbot named Hermann who, like Paul, had converted from Judaism to Christianity, recounted in his autobiography how the selfless self-sacrifice of monks first induced him to question his ancestral faith and gravitate toward the church.

While, groaning within myself, I considered these things and (if it is pious to express it this way) after a certain fashion wrestled with God for judgment in favor of these monks. Straightway a heavy scruple of doubtfulness arose in my heart concerning the mutually contrary and diverse laws established by Jews and Christians. For since God's nature is good and his judgment mercy, I saw that it would be most appropriate for him to show the way of truth to his servants who truly "slay themselves all day long" for him, according to the word of the Psalm.[46]

Much as this previously Jewish abbot recalled these monks in his memory, so did the Jewish survivors of 1096 recall and present the heroes of 1096 in their communities; true self-sacrifice proved one's status as God's chosen. Curiously, one notes that a willingness to sacrifice oneself alone did not convert "Hermann the sometime Jew," as he is remembered, to Christianity. It was a willingness of monks and nuns to give of themselves on behalf of others—of fundamental importance in the theology of medieval monasticism—that truly captured his heart and soul. And when our narrative thus presents the Jews slain in Xanten as martyrs in a monastic mode, it may well have had such altruism in mind. One midrash declared summarily: "No nation in the world is killed in sanctification of God's name and offers itself up to be slain besides Israel, as it is written, 'It is for your sake that we are slain all day long.'"[47] And another rabbinic source preached with reference to the doves in Song of Songs 1:15: "Just as the dove extends its neck to the slaughter, so does Israel as it is written, 'It is for your sake that we are slain all day long.' Just as the dove atones for sins, so do Israelites atone for the nations."[48]

Simply put, the Hebrew chronicle claimed for the Jewish martyrs of 1096 the zeal of the crusader, the selfless altruism of the monk, and the salvific effectiveness of Jesus' self-sacrifice on the cross. At the same time as our story allowed early twelfth-century Jews to wrestle with the guilt that accompanied their survival of the persecutions, so too did it facilitate Jewish victory over the crusader—not a victory of physical combat, to be sure, but a narrative victory, a victory of memory and ideology. The last supper of the Jews killed in Xanten transposed the battlefield of the Crusade from the physical realm of flesh and blood to the discursive realm of symbol and spirit.

Chapter 5
Master Isaac the Parnas

From Xanten and the suburbs of Cologne we retrace our steps back up the Rhine to Mainz, and one month back in time. Reports of martyrdom in the Mainz Jewish community dominate each of the three surviving Hebrew chronicles of 1096, and we shall accordingly devote this chapter and the following two to several exemplary Jewish martyrs who perished in Mainz and to the nameless survivors who told their stories.

The chronicles relate that the crusaders massacred the Jews of Mainz on the third of Sivan, 4856, that is, May 27, 1096, when hundreds of Jews, perhaps over a thousand, met their deaths. Yet we also read of several Jews who then escaped destruction only to die within the next few days, and these characters in our sources, who thereby blend attributes of survivors and martyrs, will concern us in this chapter and again in Chapter 7. We begin here with Isaac the *parnas,* or community warden, whom historians typically remember as a hallmark example of the new ideal type of Jewish martyr who boldly inflicted death upon himself.[1] On that same fateful day of the third of Sivan/May 27, when the crusaders killed his wife, Isaac submitted to forced baptism, hoping thus to prevent them from kidnapping his two children and raising them as Christians, which other contemporary sources confirm as a well-grounded fear.[2] Three days later, however, Isaac regretted his conversion and proceeded to kill himself, his mother, and his children, even after the most imminent danger had passed. The brief chronicle of Eliezer bar Nathan relates his story thus:

Two pious men were saved on that very day, because they defiled	*i*
them against their will; one was named Master Uri and the other	*ii*
Master Isaac, whose two daughters were with him. Yet they too	*iii*
greatly sanctified the name of God, and they submitted to a death so	*iv*
unusual that it is not listed in any of the biblical admonitions. For on	*v*
the day before Pentecost Master Isaac ben David the community	*vi*
warden slaughtered his two daughters who were with him, and he	*vii*
set his house on fire. He and Master Uri then went to the synagogue in	*viii*

front of the holy ark, and there they died before the Lord. For there   *ix*
they submitted to the flames without hesitation. Regarding them and   *x*
others like them it is written, "He who sacrifices an offering of   *xi*
thanksgiving honors me."³   *xii*

Even this brief report of what befell Masters Isaac and Uri does not lack symbolic overtones that suggest ambivalence. Isaac and his two daughters' forsaking a Christian life in order to sanctify greatly the name of God (line *iv*) evokes the biblical scene of Lot with his two daughters leaving Sodom and Gomorrah, where the midrash reports there was great desecration of God's name.⁴ In further contrast to the biblical narrative of Lot in Sodom, the chronicle relates that Isaac enters the fire in order to die rather than flee from it in order to live. Nevertheless, as suggestive as this might be, one must turn to the chronicle of Solomon bar Samson to appreciate the full impact and depth of Isaac's story.

For these things do I weep, my eyes flow with tears—over the burning   1
of the temple of our God and the burning of Master Isaac ben David   2
the community warden who was burned to death in his house. Now I   3
shall relate and inform everyone how this came to pass. On the fifth of   4
Sivan, on the day before Pentecost, these two pious men, Master Isaac   5
ben David the warden and Master Uri ben Joseph, proceeded to meet   6
their maker, greatly sanctifying the name of their creator. For on the   7
third [of the month], on the very day when the community was slain,   8
these two pious men were saved for hell, when the enemy defiled them   9
against their will; they therefore submitted to a death that is not listed 10
in any of the biblical admonitions.   11
Master Isaac the pious came to his father's house to see the treasures   12
hidden there since his father's lifetime; he came to the cellar and saw   13
that the enemy had not touched it. He said to himself: "What is all   14
this wealth worth to me now, now that the enemies have fulfilled their   15
purposes in me to distance me from the Lord and to make me rebel   16
against the Torah of our holy God? Furthermore, a certain priest   17
sought to revive me by having me dine with him. Do I still have any   18
rightful use for this money? Gold and silver do not accompany a   19
person to his eternal resting place, only repentance and good deeds."   20
He reflected to himself: "I shall repent and be fully wholehearted with   21
the Lord God of Israel until I repay him with my life and fall by   22
his hand; perhaps he will be gracious so that I can still reach my   23
companions and in their company approach the great light. He who   24
scrutinizes human hearts well knows that I did not obey the enemy   25
except to save my children from the children of wickedness, so that   26
they should not be raised in the error of their faith. For they [my   27
children] are young; they cannot distinguish between right and wrong."   28

He went to his father's house and hired workers, and they repaired the   *29*
doors of the house that the enemy broke. When they finished repairing   *30*
the doors on the fifth of the month, the eve of Pentecost, he came to his   *31*
mother and told her what he intended to do. He said to her: "O, my   *32*
mother, my lady, I have decided to sacrifice a sin-offering to the God   *33*
of heaven, so that I can find atonement in it." When his mother heard   *34*
her son's words, she made him swear—inasmuch as he was   *35*
God-fearing—not to do such a thing. For she was overcome with   *36*
compassion for him; he alone remained of all her loved ones. His   *37*
saintly wife had been slain—Mistress Skolaster, who was the daughter   *38*
of Rabbi Samuel the Great—and his mother herself was confined to   *39*
bed, because the enemy had inflicted several wounds upon her; her son   *40*
Master Isaac had saved her from death without defilement after they   *41*
had polluted him. Her son Master Isaac the pious did not comply with   *42*
her words.   *43*
He came and shut the doors of the house, enclosing himself, his   *44*
children, and his mother on all sides. And the pious one asked his   *45*
children, "Do you want me to sacrifice you to our God?" They said to   *46*
him, "Do with us what you wish." The righteous one responded, "My   *47*
children, my children, our God is true; there is no other." Master Isaac   *48*
the righteous took his two children, his son and his daughter, through   *49*
the courtyard in the middle of the night and brought them into the   *50*
synagogue in front of the holy ark. There he slaughtered them in   *51*
sanctification of the great name of God, powerful and exalted, who   *52*
commanded us never to compromise our untainted fear of him, but to   *53*
hold fast to his holy Torah with all our heart and with all our soul. He   *54*
sprinkled from their blood on the pillars of the holy ark, so that they   *55*
should be remembered before the one God who sustains the world and   *56*
before the throne of his glory. [He said,] "May this blood cleanse me of   *57*
all my sins."   *58*
The pious one returned through the courtyard to his father's house and   *59*
ignited the building at its four corners. His mother remained in the   *60*
house and was burned in sanctification of God's name. The pious   *61*
Master Isaac then went back once again to burn the synagogue and   *62*
ignited the fire at all the entrances. And the pious one went repeatedly   *63*
from one corner to another, his hands spread forth toward the sky to his   *64*
heavenly father, and he prayed to the Lord out of the fire in a loud,   *65*
pleasant voice. The enemy shouted to him through the windows: *66*
"Wicked man, get out of the fire; you still can be saved." They   *67*
extended him a beam to pull him from the fire, but the righteous one   *68*
did not want it. There was burned a blameless, upright, God-fearing   *69*
man; his soul is interred in the lot of the righteous in the Garden of   *70*
Eden.   *71*
Now Master Uri was party to the same plan to burn the synagogue,   *72*
since they had heard that their attackers and the local residents were   *73*
talking about converting it into a house of idolatry or a building for   *74*

minting coins. When Master Isaac set his father's house and the   75
synagogue afire, Master Uri was in a different house, but he wanted to   76
help Master Isaac burn the synagogue and there to sanctify God's   77
name with his friend. Yet he could not get to him, because the   78
attackers had arisen from their beds in the middle of the night,   79
having sensed the fire; and before he reached him, they killed him on   80
his way before he arrived at the fire where Master Isaac burned to   81
death. There both of them, wholehearted and of one mind, fell   82
together before the Lord for the sake of his name, "[Lord] of hosts."   83
Regarding them and others like them it is written, "He who sacrifices   84
an offering of thanksgiving honors me."   85
Some say that the forced converts heard that they wanted to convert   86
the synagogue into a mint, and therefore the pious one burned it, such   87
that he himself burned to death inside the synagogue. Others say that   88
the enemy wanted to convert the synagogue into a house of idolatry,   89
and for that reason did they burn it.   90
A year before the coming of the day of the Lord—before the onset of   91
persecution—most of the rabbis in all the communities died. So too   92
did the dignitaries in Israel, fulfilling what was written, "Because of   93
evil was the righteous taken away."⁵   94

Hebrew literature scholar Ezra Fleischer has argued vehemently that Isaac's emotions and actions transpired exactly as the chronicle describes them. Commenting on the significance of this "most vivid" portrait, the longest description of any one individual martyr in all three of the Hebrew Crusade chronicles, medievalist Robert Chazan has similarly affirmed its credibility. "It is the portrait of a man maddened by suffering, pain, and guilt and consumed by a powerful drive for repentance and atonement. The act of conversion shattered Isaac, leaving him possessed by the desire to undo the sin which he felt he had committed." And historian Yisrael Yuval concludes that the narrator identifies completely with Isaac's slaughter of his children, his mother, and himself, an act fully justified in the reflection (lines 69–70), "There was burned a blameless, upright, God-fearing man."⁶ One surely should not doubt that Isaac's story would have elicited similar reactions from many of its contemporary readers, but such a straightforward reading of this tale barely probes the surface of its rich, highly charged, at times even confounding narrative.

What Is Wrong with This Picture?

Much as we found in the chronicle's account of martyrdom in Xanten, so do inaccuracy and contradiction, too blatant to be entirely unintentional,

bracket the story of Isaac the *parnas*, suggesting to the reader that it contains more than meets the eye. The tale begins by proclaiming its grief over
"the burning of Master Isaac ben David . . . who was burned to death in
his house" (lines 2–3), while the end of account makes clear (lines 62ff.)
that Isaac did not die in his house at all but in the synagogue. Moreover,
virtually in the same breath the story's concluding paragraph belabors the
failure of Master Uri to join Isaac in the burning synagogue but then reca-
pitulates that the two men (lines 82–83), "wholehearted and of one mind,
fell *together* before the Lord."

Isaac's story actually outdoes that of the martyrs of Xanten in its difficulty, and the list of details that appear inaccurate, contradictory, or clearly
unreasonable only continues. How, for example, can anyone know what
Isaac said to himself by way of rationalizing his actions—both those of the
third of Sivan, when he accepted baptism, and those about to occur on the
fifth and sixth, when he martyred himself and his family? In the Xanten
narrative, the storyteller explains how he learned what had happened; in
Isaac's case, not only have we no "footnote" for the reconstruction of the
events, but the text cites no authoritative basis whatsoever for determining
his thoughts. Still, the power of this story derives in large measure from
Isaac's ruminations (lines 14–28), which the narrative does not pass over
too hastily; any message that this story might have conveyed in its original
context depends directly on Isaac's rationale for his behavior. What can we
conclude, other than that he or she who has survived to tell the martyr's
story has seen fit to speak for the martyr as well?

Where did Isaac find workers to repair his house (line 29)? Certainly
not among the crusaders or the local population of Mainz that joined in
the attack on the Jews, and the story reports that the Jewish community
had already been destroyed (line 8). Perhaps Isaac hired other Jews, who,
like himself, had survived by submitting to baptism, to restore his father's
house filled with its ancestral treasures. What could better symbolize the
restoration of the Jewish community by the survivors after the violence had
subsided? But Isaac, who did not number among the Jews who martyred
themselves during the attack, also failed to reconcile himself to survival, to
invest himself in the reestablishment of a viable Jewish settlement in Mainz.
Neither role, that of martyr or survivor, seemed to suit him.

Isaac rationalized that he submitted to baptism in order to provide for
his children, whom the Christians would otherwise have taken away and
raised in the church, "for they are young; they cannot distinguish between
right and wrong" (lines 27–28). If Isaac's children could not yet distinguish

between right and wrong, why did he ask them only several hours—less than twenty lines—later (line 46), "Do you want me to sacrifice you to our God?" Surely they had not yet matured sufficiently so as to make such a decision wisely!

Our story ostensibly casts Isaac's slaughter of his children as the most noble and selfless of actions. "There he slaughtered them in sanctification of the great name of God, powerful and exalted, who commanded us never to compromise [*le-hamir*] our untainted fear of him, but to hold fast to his holy Torah with all our heart and with all our soul" (lines 51–54). But how noble and selfless does Isaac emerge from this picture, when he himself compromised his untainted fear of God—the Hebrew verb *le-hamir* also denotes conversion to another religion—and now holds up his naive, ignorant children to a higher standard of piety? Indeed, one wonders how the sacrifice of the children could mark a repentant return from Christianity to Judaism, when Isaac declared over their freshly killed bodies (lines 57–58), "May this blood cleanse me of all my sins." Which one of the medieval religions at war in Mainz more highly prized the sacrifice of the child by the father as facilitating atonement for sin, Judaism or Christianity?[7] Does the character of Isaac hereby give expression to the doctrine of the church, in which the Jewish survivors of 1096 found temporary refuge, at the same time as it rejects it so zealously? Ironically, Isaac sets out to "repent and be fully wholehearted [*tamim*] with the Lord God of Israel" (lines 21–22), when the biblical commandment to "be wholehearted [*tamim*] with the Lord your God" follows immediately on the ban against child sacrifice (Deuteronomy 18:10–13). Scripture also mandated that the paschal lamb, in whose sacrifice Christianity beheld a model of the crucifixion, be "without blemish," or *tamim* (Exodus 12:5).

As doubts begin to enter the reader's mind concerning the hero of our story, the narrative only fortifies them. At the beginning of the scene (line 1), the chronicle sees fit to bemoan the loss of Isaac and his friend Uri with the very biblical words that mourn the destruction of Jerusalem (Lamentations 1:16), "for these things do I weep, my eyes flow with tears." By implication, the loss of the community of Mainz, its synagogue, and its *parnas* are tantamount to that of Jerusalem, the temple, and its priests. But, if Isaac was so important, why does the chronicle note at the end of our story (lines 91–94) that most of the Ashkenazic communities' notables, rabbis and other dignitaries, had already died one year ago? If, as the prophetic verse (Isaiah 57:1) quoted there by the chronicle suggested, "because of evil was the righteous taken away"—according to various rabbinic commentaries, this

meant that the righteous die before their time to avoid the tribulations of an evil age[8]—what should we think of Isaac the *parnas*? The narrative labels Isaac righteous (*tzadik*) three times and pious (or saintly—*hasid*) nine times. Does it protest too much?

Reading our narrative properly demands that we engage in careful detective work, not unlike the games we played as children trying to identify the parts of a picture that did not make sense. Irony abounds in Isaac's story. While the details that we have already highlighted are themselves rather suggestive, we must probe further in order to appreciate the depth and complexity of this tale.

Time, Women, Salvation

Toward the end of Chapter 2, we encountered the analytical framework proposed by medievalist Karl Morrison for reading twelfth-century historical writing. Morrison suggested that, as much as such texts include information for the enlightenment of their readers, they also transmit meaning through silence, incompleteness, and an impression of being disjointed in their reporting of events. Such texts invite their readers to engage in an imaginative process of interpretation that decodes multisensory images and the symbols within them and thus to participate actively in the process whereby historical writing leads them to spiritual fulfillment and renewal. In Morrison's words, "the power of history to amuse, enlighten, and convert depended on the ability of readers to see themselves playing roles in the spaces between the lines of the texts, to relive with ardor, pity, and dread the events recounted."[9] Morrison argued that narratives of martyrdom exemplified this partnership of interpretation between text and reader, and that silence or loose ends concerning three subjects in particular helped to guide readers toward a historical text's underlying message: time, women, and salvation.

Curiously, loose ends or unanswered questions regarding each of these three themes assume significance in the story of Isaac the *parnas*. We have already noted that something is not quite right in the temporal orientation of this narrative: Only after concluding its account of Isaac and Uri does the chronicle "recall" the death of the community rabbis and dignitaries one year prior to present events; and only following the story of Isaac's demise on the night between the fifth and sixth of Sivan does the chronicle report the death of Isaac's wife on the third of the month.[10]

More important, as in the Xanten narrative, time in Isaac's story clearly has symbolic importance too. The fifth of Sivan marks the third of the three days of preparation or abstinence that God commanded the biblical Israelites prior to striking a covenant with them and revealing the Torah at Mount Sinai. It is also the eve of *Shavu'ot,* or Pentecost, the festival commemorating the covenant and revelation at Sinai, which, like the Sabbath, begins at sundown on the previous day. Isaac therefore died on Shavu'ot "in the middle of the night" (line 79), a night when traditional Jews remain awake studying the Torah in order to prepare themselves for renewing their covenant with God.[11] "The middle of the night" is also the time specified in the Bible for the slaying of the firstborn in Egypt (Exodus 12:29) and for the initial nocturnal encounter of Boaz and Ruth (Ruth 3:8), ancestors of the Davidic messiah—both of which events figure prominently in traditional Jewish messianism. In a word, the timing of Isaac's martyrdom is laden with symbolic baggage. It comes at a critical moment, when, as with the exodus from Egypt, the revelation at Sinai, and the birth of the savior—fateful moments of salvation, election, and redemption—the destiny of the Jews hangs in the balance.

The treatment of women in our story similarly awakens the reader to its problematic nature. Although one would expect the typically male authors of medieval historical text to characterize men as superior—stronger, more resolute, and more intelligent—to women, this narrative appears to reverse their traditional roles.[12] Isaac's wife Skolaster dies a martyr's death with the rest of Mainz Jewry on the third of Sivan, while Isaac submits to baptism so that he can look after the children. (Skolaster's very name resounds with irony: Unattested in any source known to me as the name of another Jewish woman, "Skolaster" actually means a clerical schoolman—that is, a Christian and a male!—in medieval German.)[13] Isaac's mother has also survived the massacre, but, unlike her son, she escaped both death and conversion to Christianity. Curiously, when Isaac informs her (lines 32–34) that he has decided to sacrifice his two children as a sin-offering to God so that *he* "can find atonement in it," the chronicle notes (lines 36–37) that "she was overcome with compassion for *him.*" Why compassion for Isaac? Her grandchildren, not her son, were the intended victims. Yet, unlike her son, *she* understands how misguided his intentions actually are. For how could a Jewish father be cleansed of his sins by putting his children to death?

Finally, ambiguity clouds the theme of salvation in Isaac's story as well. Forms of the Hebrew verb "to save" (*n-tz-l*) appear several times in

this scene, but in each instance with unmistakable ironic overtones. When the chronicle relates that Isaac and his companion Uri at first escaped death by submitting to baptism, it states (line 9) that "these two pious men *were saved* [*nutzelu*] for hell." Isaac rationalizes that he thus succumbed in order "*to save* [*le-hantzil*] my children from the children of wickedness" (line 26), and he thereupon undertakes to slay them. Soon thereafter we read of Isaac's mother (line 41) that he "*had saved* [*hitzil*] *her* from death" too, but within several sentences in the text he sets fire to their house with her inside, in open defiance of her will.

Such irony extends to the chronicle's use of biblical phrases that originally expressed a person's wish to save his or her loved ones, but in our story accompany Isaac's killing of his children and mother. Isaac's call to his son and daughter (lines 47–48), "My children, my children," reads exactly like David's lament over his slain son Absalom (2 Samuel 19:1), which the Talmud understood as expressing the hope that his soul might be spared the suffering of hell.[14] When Isaac's mother is "overcome with compassion" (lines 36–37), the chronicle's language alludes directly to the story of Joseph, overwhelmed with compassion for his long-lost brothers (Genesis 43:30), and the famous judgment of Solomon (1 Kings 3:26), in which the real mother compassionately offers to give up her child in order to save his life.[15] Isaac related to his loved ones far differently.

Perhaps more telling still, the narrative's words (lines 44–45) that Isaac "shut the doors of the house, enclosing himself, his children, and his mother on all sides" recall God's shutting the ark with Noah and family inside (Genesis 7:16). Such a phrase of closure also appears four times in one chapter (2 Kings 4), describing the miracles performed by the prophet Elisha for the poor widow and her children and for the Shunamite woman and her son. Yet again, in Isaac's story, shutting the family in precipitates their destruction, not their salvation.

Most interesting of all, the same phraseology appears in the prophecy of Isaiah (26:20): "Go, my people, enter your chambers, and shut your doors behind you; hide but a little moment, until the indignation passes." Rabbinic interpreters of this verse understood its mandate in a variety of ways. One interpretation understood that the prophet called for flight from oppression until the imminent danger passes.[16] A different reading called for seeking spiritual refuge, in synagogues and houses of study, as Rashi suggested in his commentary on Isaiah. On a more symbolic level, other midrashim counseled, "If affliction besets you, go and look in the inner recesses of your heart, and know that afflictions beset you as a result of

your sins."[17] Curiously, Isaac experiments with each one of these three responses to catastrophe, and each one proves disappointing. Isaac first seeks to flee his attackers until the threat of their violence subsided, but he does so only at the cost of his religious identity. In scrutinizing the inner recesses of his heart, he regrets his actions and sets out to change his ways. In this process he loses a balanced perspective, and he sacrifices his children to atone for his sins. At last he shuts himself up within the synagogue; yet here, too, only destruction awaits him. Isaac has no way to act upon Isaiah's instructions; no solution to his problem—to that of the heroes of the Hebrew Crusade chronicles, be they martyrs, survivors, or both—proves entirely viable.

"Get Out of the Fire/Light [*ur/or*], You Still Can Be Saved [*le-hinnatzel*]"

This final occurrence of the verb "to save" in Isaac's story (line 67) warrants a section of this chapter unto itself, and we must here take note of an additional wordplay. The Hebrew words *or* and *ur*, meaning light and fire, respectively, are written exactly the same—*aleph-vav-resh*—and differ only in their pointing or vocalization. The unvocalized text of the chronicles thus allows for potential—and meaningful—confusion between the two words, which appear in various permutations throughout our story.

As is well known, the symbolic language of religions typically uses light to denote the divine, enlightenment, and salvation, while using fire to suggest destruction, punishment, and hell. No wonder that Isaac yearns (line 24) to reside in the company of other martyrs in heaven and thereby to reach "the great light" (in Hebrew *ha-ma'or ha-gadol*, a form of *or* which allows for no confusion with *ur*).[18] On the other hand, Isaac's compatriot in our story is named Uri, meaning *my fire*, and one cannot but wonder if somehow the narrative balances our hero's heavenly, otherworldly aspirations with a hint of an orientation toward the underworldly. The contrast between *or*/light and *ur*/fire reaches a climax near the end of the scene, in a passage worth quoting once again.

The pious	61
Master Isaac then went back once again to burn the synagogue and	62
ignited the *fire* at all the entrances. And the pious one went repeatedly	63
from one corner to another, his hands spread forth toward the sky to his	64
heavenly father, and he prayed to the Lord out of the **fire** in a loud,	65

pleasant voice. The enemy shouted to him through the windows: 66
"Wicked man, get out of the *fire*; you still can be saved." They   67
extended a beam to him to pull him from the *fire*, but the righteous one   68
did not want it. There was burned a blameless, upright, God-fearing   69
man; his soul is interred in the lot of the righteous in the Garden of   70
Eden. . . .   71
When Master Isaac set his father's house and the   75
synagogue afire, Master Uri was in a different house, but he wanted to   76
help Master Isaac burn the synagogue and there to sanctify God's   77
name with his friend. Yet he could not get to him, because the   78
attackers had arisen from their beds in the middle of the night,   79
having sensed the *fire*; and before he reached him, they killed him on   80
his way before he arrived at the *fire* where Master Isaac burned to   81
death. There both of them, wholehearted and of one mind, fell   82
together before the Lord for the sake of his name, "[Lord] of hosts."   83
Regarding them and others like them it is written, "He who sacrifices   84
an offering of thanksgiving honors me."   85

Five times in this passage (lines 63, 67, 68, 80, 81) the chronicle uses the ambiguous word *ur* for fire, allowing for confusion with *or*/light; the fact that an alternative nonambiguous term for fire—*esh* (as in line 65)— also appears suggests that the storyteller was sensitive to the conflicting implications of his vocabulary. And perhaps the key to unlocking the meaning of this scene lies precisely in this ambiguity. Isaac prepares to meet his maker on the night of Shavu'ot, the commemoration of the revelation at Mount Sinai, when God revealed the Torah to Israel from "out of the fire" (a phrase repeated ten times in Deuteronomy chapters 4–10), recalling Isaac's final prayer before his death (line 65). Yet this night is also the Christian Pentecost, when, fifty days after the crucifixion, Jesus revealed himself once again to seal his covenant with his disciples, and "there appeared to them tongues as of fire" (Acts 2:3). On this night, as we have noted,[19] traditional Jews remain awake to study Torah in a vigil called a *tikkun*, in which they prepare to reaffirm the covenant on the next day. For their part, medieval Christians also conducted nocturnal vigils on this night of Pentecost (much like the vigils of Easter) rituals in which light and candles figured prominently, when the first of four biblical readings was *the sacrifice of Isaac*, and when the sacrament of baptism, that of entering into the covenant, was commonly performed.[20]

What message, then, does the ambiguity of *or/ur* contain? On a grand cosmic level, before us lies a portrait of the conflict between two covenants on a night most appropriate for their encounter; no wonder that (lines

79–80) "the attackers had arisen from their beds in the middle of the night, having sensed the *fire*" or *light* from the synagogue and from their churches alike. On an individual level, Isaac's story exemplifies the conflict between the Ashkenazic Jew and the Crusade and the dilemma that this Jew confronted: to refuse to submit to the enemy, probably at the cost of one's life, or to accept baptism. As our narrative reaches its climax (lines 67–68), Isaac's enemies extend a beam to him in order to extricate him from the burning synagogue. The Hebrew word for beam is *toren*, also the word for the mast of a ship, which in the midrash serves as a symbol of idolatrous worship and which bears the shape of a cross.[21] Yet, as one recent investigator has proposed, the sound of the word *toren* also suggests *Torah*,[22] the law of the covenant being reaffirmed on Shavu'ot. When, offering Isaac the *toren*, the Christians outside the blazing house of worship cry out (line 67), "Wicked man, get out of the *ur/or*, you still can be saved," their words suggest diametrically opposed possibilities to the Jew in crusader Ashkenaz. For Isaac the martyr, they clamor for him to leave the *or*, the light of Judaism, and the synagogue and to save his body, but on a spiritual plane to be "saved for hell" (line 9), as the chronicle would have it. For their part, Isaac's attackers offered him the option to leave the *ur*, the spiritually lethal fire of Jewish error as well as the fire of the burning building. For the Jewish survivors who found temporary refuge in the church, however, the word spelled *aleph-vav-resh* denotes both *or*/light and *ur*/fire. Just as Isaac had done on the third of Sivan, they left the synagogue in order to escape the fire, to live, and, eventually, to return to what they deemed the light.

Torn between *ur* and *or*, between fire and light, between the vigils of Pentecost and the *tikkun* of Shavu'ot night, and between survival as a temporary Christian and martyrdom as a Jew, what course does our hero steer? In fact, he chooses both, first one and then the other. Granted, Isaac yearns to repay God for his transgression (line 22) by dying a martyr's death, and, by the end of the tale, he does. At first glance, one might sense that the narrative accords him nothing but praise (lines 69–70): "There was burned a blameless, upright, God-fearing man; his soul is interred in the lot of the righteous in the Garden of Eden." And yet one must note how this "blameless, upright, God-fearing man" recalls the Bible's description of Job (Job 1:1), who suffered without renouncing God, to be sure, but who struck a contemporary Ashkenazic commentator like Rashi as not perfectly righteous: "In dealings between him and his creator he was not righteous."[23] In a similar vein, our narrative emits conflicting signals concerning Masters Isaac and Uri when it concludes (lines 84–85), "Regarding them and others

like them it is written, 'He who sacrifices an offering of thanksgiving honors me.'" On the one hand, various classical rabbinic sources identified the subject of this verse (Psalm 50:23) as the self-effacing devotee of God or as the penitent sinner;[24] on the other hand, the Talmud linked the verse to the original disciples of Jesus, worthy of death and destruction.[25] To which group did Isaac belong? As we shall see, the way in which Isaac martyred himself—just like the manner in which he killed his children and mother—raises more questions than it puts to rest.

Sacred Parody

Ironic does not suffice to describe the taunt leveled at Isaac by his attackers (line 67): "Wicked man, get out of the fire." These words express bitterness, frustration, perhaps even anger on the part of the survivors telling Isaac's story, especially if we recall that to get out of the fire is exactly what Isaac did two days earlier. Did that make him a wicked man? Or did killing himself, his mother, and his children make him wicked? How did a story like this function in communities of Jews that lived on after 1096 in order to tell it?

Isaac's end hardly exemplifies what recent studies of suicide and martyrdom in ancient times have termed "a noble death."[26] To the contrary, the description of Isaac's last hours—his slaughter of his children to cleanse himself of sin, his defiance of his crippled mother's last request, his indecisiveness and frenzy moving from his house to the synagogue and back and forth again, leaving death in his trail at every turn, and then running wildly from one corner of the burning synagogue to another—all these blend the ridiculous with the pitiful. As in the story of the martyrs of Xanten, the chronicle clouds the transparent grandeur of its heroes. Isaac runs aimlessly in the synagogue with "his hands spread forth toward the sky" (line 64), and the text asserts that they extend upward "to his heavenly father." But the Hebrew here may well allude to the words of the psalmist (Psalm 44:21–22), "If we forgot the name of our God and *spread forth our hands to a foreign god*, God would surely search it out, for he knows the secrets of the heart." Considering that in the very next sentence (Psalm 44:23), the biblical poet mentions the devoted self-sacrifice of the martyr—"It is for your sake that we are slain all day long"—one wonders whether or not the chronicle thus casts Isaac in a favorable light. Surely, in his resolve to die a martyr's death, he extends his hands "to his heavenly father," not "to a

foreign god." In the very same breath, however, the chronicle raises doubts, reporting (lines 63–64) that "the pious one went repeatedly from one corner to another." This image recalls the rabbinic legend that at the time for the temple in Jerusalem to be destroyed, torch-bearing angels descended from heaven, ignited the sanctuary and its four corners, and razed it to the ground. Then, "when the high priest saw that the temple was burning, he took the keys and threw them toward the sky. 'Here are the keys to your house,' he stated; 'within it I have been a deceitful caretaker.'"[27]

As the *parnas* of his community, Isaac in the synagogue of Mainz fills the role of the high priest in the temple of old. As the flames consume his sanctuary, his mother, and himself, why does Isaac evoke both pity and ridicule? Does he, too, whether in converting to Christianity or in igniting the fire, emerge a deceitful caretaker? Does he truly deserve the tribute of our story's opening lament (line 1), "for *these* . . . do I weep"? Or should we read this, too, as ironic?

My Israeli friend and colleague Israel Yuval has also read Isaac's story against the background of rabbinic legends of the destruction of Jerusalem, the imagery of the sacrificial cult that abounds in our chronicles' tales of martyrdom, and the importance of sacrifice in bringing about the final redemption. Within the *ur*, he maintains, within the fire that consumes the structure of the sanctuary and the flesh of the sacrifice, lies the entryway to the *or*, the light of the messiah, and, ultimately, the "great light" (line 24) of eternal glory. Yuval concludes his reading with passion: "Again and again have I read the story of Rabbi Isaac and have discerned in it neither sarcasm nor irony nor parody—only history."[28]

I disagree. Not that I reject Yuval's "messianic" reading of the story that highlights motifs of destruction, sacrifice, and redemption. I accept it, as one dimension of what this rich and intricately woven narrative serves to communicate; the chronicles surely present the glorious acts of martyrdom in 1096 as worthy of moving God's plan for the history of the world along toward the salvation of Israel. Nevertheless, beside this "high road" of interpreting Isaac's story, I cannot ignore the ridicule, the sarcasm, the sense of utter helplessness, and the irony with which it depicts him and his situation. Indeed, virtually every Ashkenazic Jew during the crusading era shared Isaac's quandary, whether personally or vicariously, whether in actual fact or in theory. The parody of sacrifice, sanctuary, and priest/*parnas* at work in the case of *Isaac the forced convert* versus *Isaac the martyr* places the survivor of the 1096 persecutions at center stage in the chronicles' narrative, right alongside the Jew who was killed—or who killed himself. No less

important, just as Isaac aired his prayer of agony to God, hands out-stretched toward heaven, so too does his story allow the survivors, many of whom had submitted to baptism, to vent their guilt, frustration, and resentment over what had befallen them. From the perspective of early twelfth-century German Jewry, distinguished by its self-confidence, firmly convinced of the perfection of its collective piety, God and history had shortchanged them in 1096; their massacre at the hands of the crusaders constituted nothing less than desecration of the first order.

In this mode, not only did the survivors of the persecutions cast fig-ures like Isaac in order to wrestle with themselves and their trauma, but they also told such stories so as to wrestle with God. As Jewish literature scholar David Roskies has proposed, "the most effective means of pro-voking God . . . were still the most indirect: through sacred parody, by imitating on the human, literary level the sacrilege that God had allowed to be perpetrated in history." In order to serve this purpose, the martyrs' tales in our chronicles spoke in symbolic ambiguities, pregnant with multiple meanings. In Roskies's terms, theirs was a "poetics of sacrilege . . . , consol-ing even as it bordered on blasphemy." The stories told by the survivors of 1096 demonstrate how the sacred—or even semisacred—text "became an ever more pliant medium of expression each time new possibilities of vio-lence were forced upon it."[29]

Some readers might think that Isaac's slaughter of his mother, his children, and himself—not to mention his destruction of the synagogue of Mainz—pushed the limits of such violence to the extreme. But the chroni-cles could push these limits even further, and they did.

Chapter 6
Mistress Rachel of Mainz

My critics have accused me of transforming acts of Jewish martyrdom into tales of events that never occurred; instead of treating the Hebrew Crusade chronicles as works of history, so they claim, I have mistreated them as literature, mining them for symbols and codes while overlooking the facts. While I have no doubt that the acts of the martyrs directly inspired those who told their stories and those who collected these stories in the chronicles, this hardly proves that in their specific episodes the chronicles preserve an accurate, play-by-play account of what *in fact happened in the Rhineland in 1096*. Without corroboration in other sources—which, in almost every case, does not exist—we have no way of knowing whether they do or do not. Rather, the richness of their symbolism, the narrative games at play in their reporting, and their origin among those who survived the massacres are all part of the historical truth that the stories do embody and express. Particularly in our post-Holocaust age, we must wrestle with collective memory as evidence of "fact," or as historical data unto itself. Furthermore, if elements in the martyrs' tales of 1096 seem more characteristic of works of literature than historical writing—such that one might more appropriately classify our sources as fiction, not chronicles, as Ivan Marcus suggested some twenty years ago[1]—this should hardly devalue them for students of the past. From ancient times until the nineteenth century, most Western intellectuals would have followed the lead of Aristotle in maintaining the opposite: Poetry, drama, and literature in general have a universal relevance; history bears only on particular times, places, and individuals.[2] One should hardly wonder if those who told and edited the stories making their way into the Crusade chronicles had priorities in mind other than those of the modern "scientific" historian.

With such reflections in mind, we return to the narratives of the chronicles, to the tale of medieval Jewish martyrdom that many remember as the most grizzly and horrendous of all, that of Mistress Rachel of Mainz.

The Sources

Like the account of the martyrs of Xanten and that of Isaac the *parnas*, Rachel's story appears in two of the three Hebrew Crusade chronicles; moreover, several prominent motifs in these versions of her tale are echoed in a piyyut, a liturgical poem, by an Ashkenazic Jew who survived the persecutions. Despite their length, we must have these sources before us in order to proceed systematically.

"Mainz Anonymous" Chronicle

The "Account of the Persecutions of Old" (the "Mainz Anonymous" chronicle) includes the following scene in its report of the carnage in Mainz:[3]

There there was a distinguished woman, the young Mistress Rachel,	*i*
daughter of R. Isaac b. R. Asher. She said to her companion, "I have	*ii*
four children. Even on them have no mercy, lest these uncircumcised	*iii*
ones come and take them alive and they be maintained in their error.	*iv*
Sanctify [God's] holy name in them, too." One of her companions	*v*
came and took the knife, and when [Rachel] saw the knife she burst	*vi*
into wild and bitter sobbing [Genesis 27:34], and she struck her face,	*vii*
shouting out, "O Lord, where is your steadfast love." She took her	*viii*
younger son Isaac—he was most pleasant—and slaughtered him, and	*ix*
she stretched out her arms [or sleeves] between the two brothers and said	*x*
to her companion: "By your life, do not slay Isaac in front of Aaron."[4]	*xi*
As for the lad Aaron, upon seeing that his brother had been slain he	*xii*
shouted, "My mother, my mother, do not slay me"; and he went and	*xiii*
hid under a box. [Rachel] then took her two daughters Bella and	*xiv*
Madrona and sacrificed them to the Lord, God of hosts, who	*xv*
commanded us not to compromise our untainted fear of him and to be	*xvi*
totally wholehearted with him. When the righteous woman finished	*xvii*
sacrificing her three children to our creator, she raised her voice and	*xviii*
called out to her son, "Aaron, Aaron, where are you? I shall not have	*xix*
mercy nor spare you either." She pulled him by his leg out from under	*xx*
the box where he had hidden and sacrificed him to God the powerful	*xxi*
and the exalted. She then placed them on her lap in her two arms, two	*xxii*
on one side and two on the other, and they were writhing on her	*xxiii*
until the crusaders took the room, and they found her sitting and	*xxiv*
lamenting over them. They said to her, "Show us the treasure that you	*xxv*
have in your arms." When they saw that the children were slaughtered	*xxvi*
they beat her and killed her. Of them and of her it is written in	*xxvii*
Scripture [Hosea 10:14], "Mothers and babes were dashed to death	*xxviii*

together." For she died along with them just as that other righteous   *xxix*
woman died with her seven sons; of her it is written in Scripture   *xxx*
[Psalm 113:9], "a happy mother of children."   *xxxi*

Here we have a heartrending account of a Jewish woman mustering the courage to sacrifice the fruit of her womb so that they would not fall captive to the crusaders and be raised as Christians in Christian homes. In the version of the Mainz Anonymous, the story of Rachel has recently figured prominently in scholarly debates as to the chronological order of the various chronicles,[5] and a good number of investigators have argued that this is the earliest recollection of Mistress Rachel that we have. Yet two other sources deserve mention.

Solomon bar Samson Chronicle

As in previous chapters, the longer narrative in the chronicle attributed to Solomon bar Samson proves to be much more fertile ground for our method of analysis, and we need to quote its story of Rachel in full.

Who ever witnessed the like of this? Who ever heard of something   *1*
like the deed of this righteous, pious woman, the young Mistress   *2*
Rachel, daughter of R. Isaac b. R. Asher, wife of R. Judah. She said to her *3*
companions, "I have four children. Even on them have no mercy, lest   *4*
these uncircumcised ones come and take them alive and they be   *5*
maintained in their error. Sanctify the name of the holy God in them, too." *6*
One of her companions came and took the knife to slay her son, and when   *7*
the children's mother saw the knife she burst into wild and bitter sobbing, *8*
and she struck her face and her breast, saying, "O Lord, where is your   *9*
steadfast love." The woman [Rachel] said to her companions in her   *10*
misery: "Do not slay Isaac in front of his brother Aaron, so that he   *11*
[Aaron] should not witness his brother's death and run away from us."   *12*
The [other] woman took the lad, small and very pleasant as he was,   *13*
and slaughtered him, and the mother stretched out her arms to receive   *14*
their blood, and she received the blood in her sleeves instead of in the   *15*
cultic chalice of blood. Upon seeing that his brother had been slain,   *16*
the lad Aaron shouted, "My mother, do not slay me"; and he went and   *17*
hid under a box. She still had two daughters, Bella and Madrona,   *18*
stately and beautiful virgins, daughters of her husband R. Judah, and   *19*
the girls took the knife and sharpened it so it would have no blemish.   *20*
[Rachel] then extended their necks and sacrificed them to the Lord,   *21*
God of hosts, who commanded us not to compromise our untainted   *22*
fear of him and to be totally forthcoming with him, as it is written in   *23*
Scripture, "You must be wholehearted with the Lord your God."   *24*

When the righteous woman finished sacrificing her three children to 25
their creator, she raised her voice and called out to her son, "Aaron, 26
Aaron, where are you? I shall not have mercy nor spare you either." 27
She pulled him by his leg out from under the box where he had hidden 28
and sacrificed him to God the powerful and the exalted. She then 29
placed them on her lap in her two arms, two on one side and two on the 30
other, and they were writhing on her until the enemy took the room, 31
and they found her sitting and lamenting over them. They said to her, 32
"Show us the treasure that you have in your arms." When they saw the 33
children and that they were slaughtered, they beat her and killed her 34
along with them; her soul expired, and she died. Of her it is written in 35
Scripture, "Mothers and babes were dashed to death together," as was 36
she along with her four children, just as the righteous woman died with 37
her seven sons; and of them it is written in Scripture, "a happy mother 38
of children." The father, well-built and handsome, screamed, crying 39
and wailing, when he beheld the death of his four children. He went 40
and threw himself on the sword in his own hand; his entrails came out, 41
and he lay in the middle of the road, drenched in blood.[6] 42

"I said, 'Look away from me'"

Finally, we must quote from "I said, 'Look away from me,'" a *piyyut* written by Kalonymos bar Judah, who belonged to one of the most distinguished rabbinic families of the Rhineland, who witnessed the events of 1096, and whose memories inspired several noteworthy liturgical laments. Describing the heroism of the Jewish martyrs in his poem, he wrote more generally of the horrors of parents slaughtering their children to prevent their capture and baptism.

The father subdued his compassion, brought his children to sacrifice *a*
like lambs to the slaughter; indeed, he prepared the slaughterhouse for *b*
his own children. When the women set aside the children of their own *c*
tender care for the slaughter, and dragged them to the shambles, they *d*
said to their mothers: "Behold, we are being slaughtered and *e*
massacred." Who can hear the father proclaim his faith in the words of *f*
the *Shema* while his son is being slaughtered and refrain from shedding *g*
tears? Who has seen or heard the like? The stately, beautiful virgin, *h*
daughter of Judah, did whet and sharpen the knife and stretched out her *i*
neck; the all-observing eye saw it and did bear witness. The mother *j*
was afflicted and breathed forth her soul, when she reconciled herself *k*
to the sacrifice, as a happy mother prepares a meal for her *l*
children. Betrothed maidens and wedded daughters did exult as they *m*
danced joyfully to meet the scourging sword, that their blood be shed *n*
upon the bare rock, never to be covered. The father turned away *o*

weeping and wailing, plunging himself down to be pierced through by   *p*
his own sword, wallowing in his own blood upon the highway. The   *q*
fruitful tree (or woman) acknowledged the justice of her sentence when   *r*
she offered her branches, and she received it in her sleeves instead of   *s*
in the cultic chalice of blood, as she sobbed and stretched out her arms.[7] *t*

In view of a poetic lament such as this, the detective work required of the
modern reader takes on an additional dimension. While the passages from
the chronicles that we quoted above describe a particular scene from the
violence that transpired in Mainz, the poem generalizes concerning the heroic willingness of the Jews to sacrifice themselves and their loved ones.
What does this passage have to do with the story of Rachel of Mainz? The
father (lines *a*, *o*) and the mother (line *j*) sacrificing their children represent
the typical Ashkenazic Jewish parents of 1096; the "daughter of Judah" (line
i) surely does not refer to one specific individual, child of a man named
Judah, but to the representative Jewess, daughter of the nation of Judah.
Indeed, the English translation of the poem that we have used here quite
reasonably reads "daughters of Judah" (line *i*), "mothers" (line *j*), and
"fathers" (line *o*), and we have reverted to the singular only to preserve the
potential ambiguity of the Hebrew original. Yet there clearly must be some
connection between prose and poetry, given their mutual concern with the
slaughter of children by their mother and the specific motifs which they
share: the "happy mother" (lines *xxxi*, 38–39, *l*) with outstretched arms
(lines *x*, 14, *t*) catching the blood in her sleeves instead of the cultic chalice
(lines 15–16, *s–t*), the stately, beautiful virgins, daughters of Judah, who
sharpen the sacrificial knife and then offer their necks to be slaughtered
(lines 19–21, *h–j*), and the father who impales himself on his sword (lines
41, *p–q*).

Comparing the two versions of Rachel's story in the chronicles with
each other and with Kalonymos's piyyut, some investigators have tried to
figure out which composition came first and which somehow borrowed
from and therefore depends upon the others. Conclusions have varied
widely, and the current wisdom tends to assume the existence of still other
sources, presumably earlier, that the writers of our surviving sources con-
sulted.[8] Such questions of dependence figure relatively little in our present
inquiry; both the narrative prose of the chronicles and the poetry of the
piyyut testify to the collective memories of the trauma-stricken Jewish communities in the wake of 1096. In the pages that follow, we proceed to analyze the character of Rachel of Mainz, the heroine of our story, primarily

with reference to the narrative of the Solomon bar Samson chronicle, drawing from the other two sources where appropriate.

Rachel in Jewish Tradition

The power and significance of Rachel of Mainz flow directly from those of other women, primarily Rachel the matriarch in the Bible and in rabbinic tradition. Who was our young Mistress Rachel? Let us proceed with some care through four different dimensions of the traditions that nurtured her identity, as Jews of the crusading era might have construed it.

Rachel in the Bible

As any reader of the Bible knows well, Rachel was a complicated individual, and her complexity will prove critical to an understanding of Rachel of Mainz. On the one hand, Rachel was the younger, more beautiful, more beloved wife of the patriarch Jacob, who tended the sheep of his father-in-law Laban for fourteen years in order to wed her. On the other hand, Rachel, unlike her older sister Leah, was a barren and bitter woman. Betrayed by her father-in-law who placed Leah in her bridal bed on her wedding night, Rachel failed to bear children for years after she did marry. Despondently, maybe even irrationally, on one occasion she traded Leah her conjugal rights for mandrakes that Leah's son Reuben had collected for her. With tragic irony, the Bible reports that Rachel cried out to her husband (Genesis 30:1), "Give me children, or I shall die." When the birth of her first son then failed to satisfy her, so that she obsessively named him Joseph, "which is to say, 'May the Lord add another son for me'" (Genesis 30:24), Rachel proceeded to bear Benjamin and found death, not life, in childbirth.

Perhaps this tragic duality in the character of the biblical Rachel finds its clearest expression in yet another instance of dramatic irony. When Jacob and his wives finally fled from the clutches of Laban, Rachel stole the *terafim*, the household idols, and took them with her, unbeknown to Jacob. Laban and his sons caught up with Jacob's caravan and accused him of stealing his gods, to which Jacob responded (Genesis 31:32), "Anyone with whom you find your gods shall not remain alive." Laban then searched his daughters' tents, but Rachel sat on the *terafim* and claimed her menstrual period had indisposed her, so that she could not get up. Rebelling against Laban's tyranny, Rachel thus employed her wiles and her femininity to

outwit her father, save her husband from disgrace (and harm), and score a victory against idolatry. Yet Jacob's curse tragically came true.[9] Soon thereafter Rachel died. Jacob buried her in Bethlehem, and not in the family burial plot in Hebron's Cave of the Machpelah, so that even in death, just as in life, Rachel forfeited the spot that was presumably hers to Leah. As an insightful friend once suggested to me, Rachel is a consummate tragic heroine, the Bible's equivalent of Antigone. Betrayed by her father, cursed by her husband, unfulfilled by her firstborn son, she lost her three beds, her marriage bed, her birthing bed, and her grave, to her sister and rival.

The few occurrences of Rachel's name in later books of the Bible preserve the tension in her character. In the closing chapter of the Scroll of Ruth, the people of Bethlehem applauded Boaz's marriage to Ruth, his relative Naomi's Moabite daughter-in-law: "May the Lord make the woman who is coming into your house like Rachel and Leah, both of whom built up the house of Israel" (Ruth 4:11). Jacob's two wives exemplify the fertility that underlay the glory of Israel, and, although her sister's progeny were more numerous, the people saw fit to mention Rachel first. The prophet Jeremiah likewise singled out Rachel as the preeminent mother of Israel, without any mention of Leah. Here, however, the Bible highlights Rachel's tragic dimension together with her importance and stature.

Thus said the Lord: A cry is heard in Ramah—wailing, bitter weeping—Rachel weeping for her children. She refuses to be comforted for her children, who are gone. Thus said the Lord: Restrain your voice from weeping, your eyes from shedding tears. For there is a reward for your labor, declares the Lord; they shall return from the enemy's land. And there is hope for your future, declares the Lord; your children shall return to their country. (Jeremiah 31:14–16)

We encountered Jeremiah 31 in Chapter 4, in the narrative report of the martyrs of Xanten. In medieval Jewish ears, as we saw, this prophecy could easily have alluded to the Crusades even as it foretold the redemption of the house of Israel. "The day is coming when watchmen [*notzerim*] shall proclaim on the heights of Efraim, 'Come let us go up to Zion, to the Lord our God'" (Jeremiah 31:5); and, as we noted, the biblical term for watchmen, *notzerim*, already denoted Christians in rabbinic parlance. Christians in general and crusaders in particular unquestionably identified with the prophet's vision of a new covenant or testament: "The time is coming, declares the Lord, when I will make a new covenant with the house of Israel and the house of Judah . . . ; it will not be like the covenant I made with their fathers" (31:30–31).[10] And certainly the prophet's repeated call to the

maiden or virgin of Israel (31:3, 20) rang with overtones of the Virgin Mary, who assumed a prominent role in the ideology of crusading and whose cult enjoyed a widespread revival in Christian Europe beginning in the twelfth century.[11]

But even beyond linking her to the "virgin of Israel," to the call of the *notzerim* to ascend to Zion, and to the new divine covenant of the end of days, Jeremiah 31 casts Rachel as the archetype of the Jewish mother, wailing over her children as they suffer in their exile at the hands of Gentile oppressors. As anthropologist Susan Starr Sered has written, "Rachel is the personification of the vulnerability of Jewish women; she is the quintessential sufferer, even rising from her grave to cry for her children." In a word, she is the "weeping mother par excellence."[12]

Rachel's role as the mother figure who intercedes with God on behalf of her children, who willingly suffers in pursuing this role, and who ultimately succeeds in securing a divine promise of their return and salvation found numerous echoes in rabbinic midrash and in the traditional Jewish liturgy. This image has endured through the centuries; as a twentieth-century pilgrim to Rachel's Tomb in Bethlehem wrote unhesitatingly upon her visit to the shrine, "In the merit of our mother Rachel we will all be healthy and whole."[13] While Rachel of Mainz expedited the physical destruction of her children—and did not intercede for them in the manner of Rachel in Jeremiah 31—one can only understand her function in our story against the background of these traditions.

Rachel and the Liturgy of the Jewish High Holy Days

The prophetic verses of Jeremiah 31 contribute roundly to the liturgy for Rosh Hashanah and Yom Kippur, the Jewish New Year and Day of Atonement, those holiest days of the Jewish calendar when synagogue attendance is at its highest. Even relatively uneducated worshippers remember and anticipate the moving melodies in which cantors typically chant the last of the verses of remembrance (*Zikhronot*) in the prayers for Rosh Hashanah: "Truly, Efraim [son of Joseph, son of Rachel] is a dear son to me, a child that is dandled. Whenever I have turned against him, my thoughts would dwell on him still. That is why my heart yearns for him; I will receive him back in love" (Jeremiah 31:19).

Much more profoundly, the liturgy of these High Holy Days classifies Rachel and the biblical figures of Sarah and Hannah as barren righteous women, all of whom suffered their childlessness with great anguish until

God answered their prayers. The prayers of the New Year and Day of Atonement refer or allude to these heroines repeatedly as they beseech God for mercy and salvation. The readings from the Torah, the Five Books of Moses, designated for the two days of Rosh Hashanah concern Sarah and her son Isaac; on the first day of the new year the *Haftarah*, the reading from the prophetic books of the Bible, tells of Hannah and the birth of her son Samuel; on the second day it consists of Jeremiah 31, highlighting the pathos of Rachel.[14]

The classical rabbis likened each of these three heroines to the "happy mother of children" of Psalm 113:9,[15] and the Talmud offered an explanation for their singular tie to the High Holy Days: "Rabbi Eliezer stated: In [the Hebrew month of] Tishre the world was created. . . . On Passover Isaac was born. On Rosh Hashanah [the first of Tishre] Sarah, Rachel, and Hannah were remembered."[16] This passage also suggests a connection between Rachel and Isaac, and not by happenstance does Jeremiah 31 comprise the *Haftarah* for the Torah's story of the Akedah, the binding of Isaac. Complementing the figure of Isaac bound on the altar, the Isaac who epitomized martyrdom and self-sacrifice, Rachel—the barren (*'akeret bayit*) younger sister who, as the rabbis punned, became "the foundation (*'ikar ha-bayit*) of the house of Israel . . . such that all of Israel bore her name"[17]—evokes the divine assurance that such suffering has proven its worth. "Restrain your voice from weeping," God consoles her, "your eyes from shedding tears. For there is a reward for your labor."

As opposed to the biblical matriarch, our Rachel of Mainz had four children, and as such she recalls symbols, images, and ideas of the Passover holiday—many of them grouped in bundles of four[18]—whose Haggadah liturgy includes a well-known midrash on four children (albeit in this case sons).[19] How does our Rachel relate to the Passover? Perhaps the error of a medieval scribe can help us understand. The Solomon bar Samson chronicle reports (lines 4–5) that Rachel cried to her companions: "I have four children. Even on them have no mercy, lest these uncircumcised ones come and take them alive and they be maintained in their error." The Hebrew for "have no mercy" should be *al taḥusu*; yet the sole surviving manuscript reads *al takhosu*.[20] What happened? It seems that the copyist wrote the Hebrew letter *khaf* instead of *ḥet*, hardly an inconceivable error for an Ashkenazic Jew, who could not give the letter *ḥet* its Sefardic and Middle Eastern guttural pronunciation. But one must note that the word *takhosu* makes no evident sense in this context. It appears only once in the entire Bible, in the list of divine instructions to Moses for preparing the Passover

sacrifice, the paschal lamb whose blood insured the liberation of the Israelites from Egypt. There we read (Exodus 12:4) that if individual families
cannot consume an entire lamb on their own, they can join together; and
"you shall contribute [*takhosu*] for the lamb according to what each household will eat." While the narrative in our Crusade chronicle clearly should
read *al taḥusu* (have no mercy), it nonsensically reads *al takhosu*. In making
this error, the scribe may well have beheld the image of the saving blood-
sacrifice of Passover between the lines of his text; somehow he equated
Rachel's four little children with the paschal lamb. We shall consider below
why this is so telling.

Rachel as Martyr

Jeremiah's image of the long-deceased Rachel weeping over her exiled children led some rabbis to conclude that in order to fulfill this prophecy Jacob
buried her close to Jerusalem, in Bethlehem, and not in the family burial
ground in Hebron. That way Rachel might cry over the children of Israel
as they left Jerusalem and, ultimately, find consolation in them upon their
return. Some asserted that, foreseeing this role, Rachel gave up her designated burial spot in the Cave of Machpelah of her own accord. Indeed,
Rachel loomed large in rabbinic tradition as one who willingly sacrificed
what was rightfully hers for the good of her loved ones and her nation.[21]

In the rabbinic imagination, Rachel's selflessness found its best example on the night when she should have consummated her marriage with
Jacob, but when Leah did instead. In his commentary on Jeremiah's vision
of Rachel bemoaning her suffering children (31:14), Rashi quoted a rabbinic
midrash that focused on God's decree that the First Temple be destroyed.

The patriarchs and matriarchs went to appease the holy one, blessed be he, after
[King] Menasseh placed an idol in the temple, but he was not pacified. Rachel
entered and said to him: "Master of the world, whose mercy is greater, your mercy
or the mercy of a mere mortal? One would think that your mercy is greater. And
yet, did I not take my rival wife into my house—inasmuch as all the labor that
Jacob performed for my father he did entirely for me? As I prepared to enter the
marriage tent they brought in my sister; not only did I keep silent, but I even gave
her my signs! So, too, if your children have brought your rival into your house,
restrain yourself and keep silent!" Said he to her: "You have pleaded their case well.
There is a reward for your labor and your righteousness in giving your sign to your
sister."

Rashi's midrash—which alludes to the tradition that Rachel revealed
to Leah the signs whereby she and Jacob, expecting foul play from Laban,

had agreed to identify one another in the darkness of the bridal tent—recalls another midrashic passage found in *Lamentations Rabbah*. Here Jeremiah rallied Moses and the patriarchs to plead with God at the time of the destruction of the First Temple, but no one succeeded in assuaging his anger. Evidently the only matriarch to take part in this meeting, Rachel brazenly interrupted Moses and presented her arguments to God; ultimately, "the mercy of the holy one, blessed be he, was awakened, and he said, 'For your sake, Rachel, I shall restore the people of Israel to their rightful place.'" What had Rachel said to make God acquiesce? "If I—mortal flesh and blood, dust and ashes, as I am—did not begrudge my rival wife so as to bring shame and disgrace upon her, how could you—living, eternal, merciful king that you are—be so envious of idolatry, that is void of any substance, as to exile my children, who were killed and grossly maltreated by their enemies?!" Rachel recounted her act of kindness to Leah in some detail: "I revealed to my sister all of the signs that I had arranged with my husband, so that he would think she was Rachel. Moreover, I went in under the bed in which he was lying with my sister. He would speak with her, and she would keep silent, while I would respond to everything he said, so that he would not recognize my sister's voice."[22]

In this captivating picture of Rachel's intended wedding night, *the voice* speaking to Jacob while he makes love to his bride *is that of Rachel*, while *the body is that of Leah*! In its unmistakable allusion to the biblical story of Jacob and Esau, this midrash suggests, perhaps, that Jacob received a just retribution for having impersonated his brother, deceived his father Isaac, and stolen the blessing intended for Esau. There in the Bible, we recall, Isaac embraced Jacob and exclaimed (Genesis 27:22), "The voice is the voice of Jacob, yet the hands are the hands of Esau."

As we shall see, this rabbinic tradition adds nuance and depth to our understanding of Rachel of Mainz, who makes the most painful sacrifice that a mother possibly could. If the self-sacrificing character of Rachel evokes this episode in the relationship between Jacob and Esau, which one of these two brothers does Rachel of Mainz resemble? On the one hand, inasmuch as one identifies her with Rachel the matriarch in the midrashim we have just quoted, she assumes the role of Esau, the sibling that forfeits his or her rights as a result of impersonation; and, just as the Bible reports that Esau did (Genesis 27:34), so did Rachel of Mainz "burst into wild and bitter sobbing" (line 8).[23] On the other hand, as the "children's mother" (*em ha-banim* in Hebrew, line 8) suffering under the tyranny of Esau's Christian progeny, the chronicle also identifies Mistress Rachel with the

biblical Jacob, who, fearing that Esau would harm his family, divided his entourage into two camps, lest he "come and strike me down, *mothers together with their young [em 'al banim]*" (Genesis 32:11). And, as it repeatedly invoked this verse, rabbinic midrash intimated that the crusaders' attack upon Rachel and her children—like the attack of Esau that Jacob had feared—entailed the violation of two biblical commandments. The book of Leviticus (22:28) forbids sacrificing an animal and its offspring on the same day. And the book of Deuteronomy (22:6) commands one who chances upon a bird's nest not to take "the mother together with her young [*ha-em 'al ha-banim*]." In one source, these two precepts serve as a litmus test for distinguishing the righteous and the wicked.[24] Rabbinic homily allowed for yet another alternative: The prohibition against taking the mother bird together with her young reportedly led the famed ancient apostate Elisha ben Abuya to abandon his faith.[25] Was Rachel of Mainz truly righteous or wicked? Might not her character also hint at those who left one religious community and joined another?

In the Jewish imagination, Esau loomed large as the archrival of Israel, as a flagrant violator of God's law, and as a symbol of Edom, Rome, and Christianity.[26] To whose camp, then, did Rachel of Mainz truly belong, to that of Jacob and Israel, or to that of Esau and Christianity, or, somehow, to both? We shall return to this interesting question presently.

"As the Righteous Woman Died with Her Seven Sons . . ."

The chronicles themselves compare the selfless sacrifice of Rachel of Mainz with that of an earlier Jewish heroine (lines *xxix–xxx*, 37–38), referring explicitly to the mother of the seven sons who submitted to martyrdom rather than submit to the wicked Gentile ruler and worship an idol. Discussed in Chapter 1, this story first appeared in the biblical Apocrypha in the Second Book of the Maccabees, in the context of the persecution of the Jews by the wicked King Antiochus. The Talmud and several collections of rabbinic midrash relate the occurrence to Roman rule over the Jews, while the tenth-century Italian-Jewish history book *Josippon* returned it to Maccabean times. In 2 Maccabees and the Talmud the mother is nameless; midrashic versions of the story identify her as Miriam bat Tanchum; and in the editions of *Josippon* available to eleventh- and twelfth-century Ashkenazic Jews she remains unnamed, while other versions named her Hannah. Thus has the tale lived on in Jewish memory, as that of Hannah and her seven sons.[27]

A thorough analysis of this tradition would require a detailed review of all of the surviving texts, but we quote simply from the version of the story in the midrashic collection *Lamentations Rabbah* in order to allow for a meaningful comparison with our tale of Rachel of Mainz.

It happened that Miriam bat Tanchum was taken captive along with her seven sons, and the ruler imprisoned all of them separately. He brought the first of them and said to him, "Bow down to the idol, just as your brothers bowed." He said, "Heaven forbid, my brothers did not bow, nor shall I bow down to it . . . , because it is written in our Torah, 'I am the Lord your God.'" He commanded to execute him. He brought out the second one and said to him, "Bow down to the idol, just as your brothers bowed." He said, "Heaven forbid, my brothers did not bow nor shall I bow down . . . , because it is written in our Torah, 'You shall have no other gods besides me.'" At once he commanded to execute him. . . . [And so with the third, fourth, fifth, and sixth sons.] He brought out the seventh, the youngest of them all, and said, "My son, bow down to the idol, just as your brothers bowed." He said, "Heaven forbid . . . , for we have sworn to our God that we shall not give him up for another god . . . ; and just as we have sworn to him, so has he sworn to us that he will not give us up for another people. . . ." The emperor said to him, "Here, I shall throw this ring down in front of the idol; just go and fetch it, so that people will see and say [presume] that you have obeyed the emperor's command." Said he, "Woe unto you, Caesar. Should I be fearful of you, a mere mortal, and not be fearful of the king of kings of kings, God of the world . . . ?!" At once he commanded to execute him. His mother said to him, "By your life, Caesar, let me embrace and kiss my son." They gave him to her, and she took out her breasts and nursed him with her milk. She said to him, "By your life, Caesar, put the sword to my neck and his at the same time." Caesar said to her, "Heaven forbid, I shall do nothing of the sort. . . ." They took him from her, and she said to him, "My son, do not waver or have any fear. You are going to your brothers, and you will be placed in the bosom of Abraham our father; tell him for me, 'You built one altar and did not sacrifice your son; but I built seven altars and sacrificed my sons upon them in a single day. . . .'" They said that within several days that woman lost her senses, went up to the roof, and threw herself to her death. And they said of her, "a happy mother of children."[28]

The chronicles, to be sure, invoke the memory of the mother of seven, but they highlight the striking contrast between her and Mistress Rachel. Accentuating details that help in solving the riddles of our tale, the various differences between the two women and their stories deserve our attention.

- Our heroine of 1096 is Rachel; the only name that Ashkenazic martyrs and survivors of 1096 might have associated with the mother of seven was Miriam (not Hannah).[29]

- Miriam has seven sons, whose names we never learn, and we know nothing of her husband. Our Rachel has two sons and two daughters—Aaron and Isaac, Bella and Madrona—and the Solomon bar Samson narrative identifies her husband as Judah, who killed himself after viewing the slaughtered corpses of his wife and children.
- Miriam's seven sons zealously accept their fate, even the youngest, who dies while nursing at his mother's breast; yet Rachel's Aaron attempts to flee from his mother and escape death.
- Unlike the seven brothers, Rachel's children have no direct encounter with the Gentile oppressors of their people. The narrative does not present them as direct targets of persecution or of rampant anti-Jewish violence, but as the victims of the deliberate decision of their mother Rachel, who controls precisely what transpires in this scene.
- Mistress Rachel tends to the blood and the bodies of her slain children, catching the blood in her sleeves and sitting with the corpses on her lap. The mother of seven does nothing of the sort.
- Perhaps most revealing of all, Miriam bat Tanchum takes pride in the sacrifice of her children; she surely merits the psalmist's distinguished status of "a happy mother of children" that is conferred upon her. Rachel of Mainz bewails her fate and that of her offspring as the scene in the chronicles draws to a close. One can hardly label her a happy mother of children; to the contrary, of her the prophet Hosea had written (lines *xxviii–xxix*, 36), "Mothers and babes were dashed to death together."[30]

Let us review the distance we have traveled. Bearing the name of the biblical Rachel, Mistress Rachel of Mainz embodies the two sides to her forebear's character, heroic and yet profoundly tragic. Rachel of Mainz also recalls the mother of Israel in exile to whom the prophet called out (Jeremiah 31:20), "Return, virgin Israel, to these towns of yours"; as such, Rachel appears right alongside the crusader-like call of the watchers (*notzerim* in biblical Hebrew) to ascend to Zion and a messianic vision of a new covenant. As such Rachel exemplifies the grieving Jewish mother, the matriarch who represents all of the Jewish people. She laments over the suffering of her children, whom the chronicle suggestively compares to the lamb sacrificed on Passover, and she will, so the Bible promises, find consolation in their redemption. Rachel of Mainz recalls the Rachel among the barren women highlighted in the liturgy of the Jewish High Holy Days, and this liturgy links her especially to the biblical story of the Akedah, for which

Jeremiah's resonant prophecy serves as a fitting *Haftarah* on Rosh Hashanah. Her merit—like that of the bound Isaac—serves to offset Israel's guilt
in abandoning its God; she will be rewarded, her children shall return to
their land, and God will receive her descendant Efraim back into the fold
with love, past quarrels between them notwithstanding. Rachel sacrificed
her wedding, her husband, and even her grave for a greater good. Her
unrivaled kindness to Leah likens her to both Jacob and Esau; like Esau,
she sacrificed what was rightfully hers to her sibling, but, like Jacob, her
progeny suffered at the hands of Esau's Christian descendants. The chronicles compare Rachel of Mainz to the mother of the seven martyrs, whom
medieval Jews might well have known as Miriam. Yet the comparison also
underscores some telling differences between the two women. Rachel slew
her sons as martyrs against their will. According to the chronicles, she gathered the blood of her children, placed their corpses on her lap, and died in
her misery. One could not easily call her, as the tradition repeatedly described the mother of the seven sons, a "happy mother of children."

Rachel and Christianity

Who, then, was Rachel of Mainz? She, her children, and perhaps her husband, too, evidently died as martyrs when bands of crusaders attacked the
Jewish community in Mainz in May of 1096. But the stories of the Hebrew
Crusade chronicles present Rachel as more than that. Not only does the
behavior of Mistress Rachel take shape through the prism of many layers
of Jewish tradition concerning the biblical Rachel, but, in allowing for her
association with Esau as well as Jacob, it also betrays a vital Christian com-
ponent to her identity. Three important women from Christian tradition
seem to converge in our heroine.

First, corresponding to the Jewish mother par excellence, Rachel of
Mainz reminds us of the maternal personification of the church, whom
Christian writers often labeled *Sancta Mater Ecclesia*, or Holy Mother
Church.[31] In early medieval Christian art, this female figure of Ecclesia often
appeared in scenes of the crucifixion, standing underneath the crucified
Jesus' right arm—and set against the female personification of the Jewish
people, Synagoga, who generally stood under his left arm. Both women
commonly appeared together under the cross, because the crucifixion
marked the transition from Old Testament to New. In depicting the maternal figures representing the two covenants, artists thus dramatized the im-

portance of the event and characterized the two women accordingly: Ecclesia, representing the church and Jesus' covenant of grace, had displaced Synagoga, representing Israel and Moses' covenant of law, as God's chosen and beloved. Ecclesia has inherited the symbols of God's election. She acknowledges her savior and ministers to his wounds, frequently raising her arms up to Jesus and receiving his saving blood in a chalice, as in a typical scene on a mid-eleventh-century ivory tablet from the Rhineland (see Figure 1).[32] Amazingly, so does the Solomon bar Samson chronicle report of Rachel of Mainz (lines 14–16): "The mother stretched out her arms to receive their blood, and she received the blood in her sleeves instead of in the cultic chalice of blood [*temur mizrak ha-dam*]."[33]

I cannot help wondering if one of the Hebrew chronicles' recent translators recognized the Christian symbolism in our story but intentionally tried to obscure it, writing instead that Rachel "spread her sleeves to receive the blood, according to the practice in the ancient Temple sacrificial rite."[34] Granted that a chalice of blood figured prominently in the Jewish sacrificial cult, but a woman spreading her sleeves did not, and this translation removes the chalice completely. Perhaps this Jewish scholar, writing in the wake of the Holocaust and haunted by the memory of Jewish martyrs, felt threatened or offended by this Christian dimension to Rachel the Jewish heroine's identity.

Twelfth-century Ashkenazic Jews, however, should have had no trouble making the connection. Many Christian theologians of ancient and medieval times had identified the biblical Rachel—and the barren Sarah and Hannah, too—as "prefiguring" Mother Church, just as they beheld the displaced synagogue in the characters of their rival co-wives, Leah, Hagar, and Peninah.[35] (Similarly, in Christian understanding of the Bible, God's preference for younger brothers over their older brothers—Abel over Cain, Isaac over Ishmael, Jacob over Esau—foreshadowed the church's replacement of Israel as God's chosen people.) The association between Rachel, wife of Jacob, and Holy Mother Church was "in the air," most likely well known even to the rank and file of the Jewish minority.[36] And even if such Jews of the Rhineland had lacked direct knowledge of Christian theological sources, they could not have readily remained immune to the well-known motif of Synagoga and Ecclesia in the Christian majority's art, just as minorities in our own day cannot avoid exposure to the culture of the majority. In the case of our story, I believe the Rachel-Ecclesia connection unavoidable; only its implications remain to be hammered out.

The story of the mother and her seven sons was also in the air. Chris-

Figure 1. The crucifixion of Jesus: Synagoga and Ecclesia. Ivory. Cologne region, mid-eleventh century. Hessisches Landesmuseum, Darmstadt, KG 54:210b. Reproduced by permission of the Hessiches Landesmuseum, Darmstadt.

tian theologians of the age likewise viewed the mother of the seven Maccabean martyrs, as they called them, a symbol of Holy Mother Church and
her beloved, self-sacrificing children. As some biblical commentaries put it,
"What does the mother of the seven sons thus symbolize, if not the fertility
of Mother Church, who, through the grace of the Holy Spirit in its seven
different forms [that is, the seven Catholic sacraments], bears the adopted
sons of God the father?"[37] Perhaps the most respected churchman of the
early twelfth century, Abbot Bernard of Clairvaux, wrote that of all God's
martyrs who preceded Jesus, only these seven Maccabean martyrs deserved
a separate commemoration of their own in the liturgy of the church. Even
the martyrdom of John the Baptist fell short of the quality of their self-
sacrifice.[38] And, according to some traditions, Bishop Rainald of Cologne
brought the relics of the Maccabean martyrs to his cathedral in the Rhineland in 1164, not long after the Hebrew chronicles of the 1096 persecutions
had taken shape in the very same region.[39]

As we have seen, rabbinic midrash identified the mother of seven as
Miriam, which was the Hebrew name for Mary; and indeed, the second
Christian woman within the composite identity of Rachel of Mainz is none
other than the Virgin Mary, the mother of Jesus herself. The opening words
of our story buttress this association between Rachel of Mainz and the
mother of the Christian savior. In Hebrew, the phrase "the young Mistress
Rachel" (*marat Rachel ha-baḥurah,* lines *i*, 2–3) is somewhat self-contradic-
tory; for while the word for mistress (*marat*) clearly denotes a married
woman, the word for young (*baḥur/ah*) appears repeatedly in the Bible as
a synonym for an unmarried, presumably virginal man or woman, often in
juxtaposition with *betulah*.[40] A more accurate translation might be "Mistress Rachel the maiden," which hardly suits a typical married mother of
four.[41] In one chronicle, "the maiden" Mistress Rachel's husband never
appears, while in the other he appears, rather ineffectually, only after his
wife and children have died, simply to kill himself in grief. The narrative
paints an unseemly picture of Judah's death—"his entrails came out, and
he lay in the middle of the road, drenched in blood" (lines 41–42)—that
contrasts sharply with Rachel's stately composure as she meets her end. In
a word, Judah fails to perform as one would expect of a medieval husband
and father, unless, of course, he was not really a husband and father, like the
Virgin Mary's husband Joseph. If not with reference to a "father-ineffective
family" how can one explain why the chronicle labels Rachel's two daughters—but not her sons—"daughters of her husband R. Judah" (line 19)?[42]
Associating the sacrifice of her children to the Akedah of Isaac and the

sacrificial lamb of the Passover—two key symbols of Christ on the cross in Christian tradition—the chronicle adds to the equation between Mistress Rachel and the Virgin Mary, especially in view of the shared Jewish and Christian tradition that the Akedah took place on the Passover, when the crucifixion occurred as well.[43] And the closing picture in our story, that of Rachel lamenting her slain children on her lap (lines *xxv*, 32), evokes the motifs of Mary as the mother grieving over her slain offspring, the *mater dolorosa*, and the Madonna sitting with Jesus on her lap, which became increasingly popular in high medieval Europe.[44]

Eventually, these two motifs blended in that of the pietà, Mary sitting and holding the body of her crucified son (see Figure 2), and one naturally wonders if the gruesome picture of Rachel with her slaughtered children does not recall such an image. The pietà, however, did not appear in Europe until a century or two after our chronicles took shape, and one must look elsewhere for a more timely parallel in Christian art, perhaps in the common location of Jesus' birthplace, which had special attraction for crusaders, and the matriarch Rachel's tomb in Bethlehem.[45] This direction leads to the third persona in the "Christian" identity of Rachel of Mainz.

An eleventh-century work of ivory from the Rhine valley depicts a woman sitting, surrounded by her female companions, bewailing a slain child who lies in her lap (see Figure 3); in the background stands the city of Jerusalem.[46] Who is this grieving mother? We find the answer in the opening pages of the New Testament (Matthew 2:16–18), where we read that King Herod, after hearing that the king of the Jews had been born, ordered the slaughter of Jewish boys in Bethlehem.

> Then Herod, when he saw that he had been tricked by the wise men, was in a furious rage, and he sent and killed all the male children in Bethlehem and in all that region who were two years old or under. . . . Then was fulfilled what was spoken by the prophet Jeremiah: "A voice was heard in Ramah, wailing and loud lamentation, Rachel weeping for her children; she refused to be consoled, because they were no more."

At the center of this ivory, as in other portrayals of the "Slaughter of the Innocents" in medieval art,[47] stands—or, more correctly, sits—none other than Rachel the matriarch herself. For Christianity claimed the Rachel of Jeremiah's prophecy for itself no less than Judaism did. Buried in Bethlehem, the voice of the biblical matriarch bewailed the deaths of the innocent children of Judea; their deaths heralded the birth of the messiah in Bethle-

Figure 2. Pietà. Wood. Germany, ca. 1370. Rheinisches Landesmuseum, Bonn. Reproduced by permission of the Rheinisches Landesmuseum, Bonn.

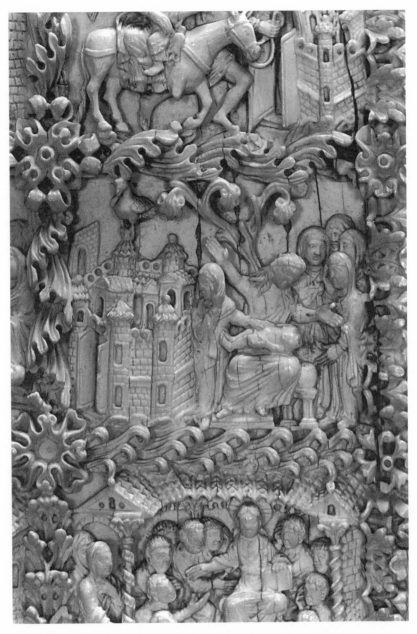

Figure 3. The Slaughter of the Innocents: Rachel weeping over her children. Ivory. Lower Rhine Valley, eleventh century. Victoria and Albert Museum, London, 379–1871. Reproduced by permission of the Victoria and Albert Museum, London.

hem, his death in Jerusalem, and the suffering and salvation in the history of the church that would follow.[48]

Like the veneration of the Virgin Mary and the cult of the Maccabean martyrs, Rachel and the martyred children of Herod's Bethlehem received renewed attention in eleventh- and twelfth-century Christian culture, as Latin dramas depicting the slaughter made their way into the liturgy of the church. The best known of these plays was entitled *Ordo Rachelis*, or "The Rite of Rachel," which, Lee Patterson has argued, originated in Germany in the wake of the first Crusades and the violent martyr's death that some Ashkenazic Jews inflicted on their innocent children.[49] The bereaved mother at the Slaughter of the Innocents, Christianity's biblical Rachel thus joins Holy Mother Church and the Virgin Mary in informing the character of Rachel of Mainz in Hebrew narratives of 1096. Curiously, Christian biblical commentators had wondered why Rachel should have mourned the innocents of Bethlehem, born to the tribe of Leah's son Judah, when Rachel's descendants belonged to the tribes of her son Benjamin and grandson Efraim.[50] Recalling that the Mainz Anonymous makes no mention of the husband of our Mistress Rachel, we cannot help but wonder: Might this very question that troubled Christian interpreters have moved the storyteller in the Solomon bar Samson chronicle to identify Rachel's husband as Judah (line 3) and at least some of her offspring as children of Judah (line 19) so that the allusion to the Slaughter of the Innocents would work?[51]

Between Judaism and Christianity

How, then, must we read the character of Rachel of Mainz? In what guise do our sources cast her? Which tradition's baggage does she bear, that of Judaism or that of Christianity? I hope the reader will agree that she reflects the traditions of each religion, both as they overlap and as they differ. The story of Mistress Rachel demonstrates well just how immersed medieval Jews were in the culture of the Christian majority surrounding them, even in northern Europe and even at times of violent conflict. But most of all, I believe that the composite identity of Rachel of Mainz testifies to the quandary of the Jewish survivors of 1096 in the aftermath of the persecutions.

We reiterate that Rachel reminds us of both Jacob and Esau—both by association with the midrash elaborating her self-sacrifice on her wedding night and in the direct biblical allusions of the chronicles before us. Rachel,

as we have indicated, "burst into wild and bitter sobbing" (lines *vi–vii*, 8); the only character concerning whom the Bible uses precisely the same language was Esau (Genesis 27:34), the forefather of Christianity in the medieval Jewish imagination. As my colleague Ivan Marcus has pointed out, however, the Hebrew chronicles repeatedly link Rachel to Jacob as well. The Mainz Anonymous relates (lines *viii–ix*) that Rachel took "her younger son," Isaac, just as the biblical matriarch Rebecca first dressed and then summoned "her younger son," Jacob (Genesis 27:15, 42), during the plot that provoked Esau's tears. And, in charging her companions not to slay Isaac "in front of" or "before" (the Hebrew *lifne* can mean either one) his older brother Aaron (lines *xi*, 11), Rachel echoes Laban's statement to Jacob (Genesis 29:26), that he could not marry off his younger daughter *before* the older one.[52] This, of course, brings us full circle, back to the fateful scene of Jacob's wedding night underlying the colorful midrash that likens Rachel to both Jacob and Esau.

In elaborating such tension in the identity of Rachel of Mainz, what might our story be telling us? I would propose a twofold response to this question. First, whereas Rachel, the exemplary Jewish heroine of 1096, excels as Esau (the archetype of evil in Jewish eyes) and whereas she assumes the character of the Virgin Mary and of Holy Mother Church as well, she allowed Jews who survived the First Crusade to respond to the oppressive challenge of crusading ideology in kind. The blood of genuine martyrdom is ours, proclaims the Hebrew narrative; so is the salvation that this blood will yield. Mistress Rachel's story reminds us how from the early Christian centuries, Jews and Christians had competed for the legacy of Jacob, projecting kinship with Esau onto their rivals; so, too, had each side come to claim Rachel, as well as the mother of the seven Maccabean-day martyrs, for itself.[53] As we explained in Chapter 3, the dangers of the Crusades prompted Jews to vie against Christians with renewed vigor for title to Isaac's Akedah and to the merit of those who believed in its message. Perhaps in Rachel of Mainz we encounter a new degree of aggressiveness in this Jewish response to crusading. Not only does Rachel the Jewess bind her son Isaac and slaughter her children like the paschal lamb[54]—just as Christians deemed their Christ the son sacrificed by his father and the lamb of God (*agnus Dei*)—but she boldly lays claim to the status of Christianity's two most important women-martyrs of all: none other than the Virgin and Holy Mother Church.

Second, caught between Jacob and Esau, between Judaism and Christianity, Rachel the martyr of 1096 mirrors the Jewish survivors of 1096 who

told and preserved her story. Unprepared for the onslaught of the crusaders, they floundered, not knowing whether to accept death in the tents of Jacob, in the synagogue of Judaism, or to seek life and refuge, however temporary, with Holy Mother Church, in the house of Esau. And Rachel, in some sense, did both. To be sure, she martyred her children and willingly submitted to martyrdom herself. Nevertheless, in doing so she assumed the telltale characteristics of the church in which many Jews who escaped death in 1096 found temporary refuge. As such, Rachel of Mainz blurs the boundary between martyr and survivor, between the events reported in our story and the text of the chronicles that contain it. Her tale bespeaks the absurdity, the world of limbo in which Ashkenazic Jews of the First Crusade must have thought that they lived.

Chapter 7
Kalonymos in Limbo

The chronicles describe the death and suffering of the martyrs in graphic detail. As we have seen, they also make room for those who opted for survival over death, referring to them at times explicitly and at times implicitly, in the "play," the symbols, and the allusions of the tales of the martyrs.

How did the Jews of the Rhineland make their fateful decision when the crusaders attacked them in 1096? Some historians have used our Hebrew chronicles to argue that their ideals of *kiddush ha-Shem*, of Jewish martyrdom, must have already been ingrained in Ashkenazic Jewish communities by the time of the First Crusade. When disaster struck, it remained for these Jews simply to translate what they had learned from theory into practice, perhaps after consulting with a local rabbi.[1] Such an understanding of what transpired leaves little room for skepticism when reading the narratives preserved in our chronicles. One presumes that they provide a factually accurate account of the persecutions, because their portrayal of the martyrs confirms what the reader already expects.

Our rereading of these narratives, however, has led us to think otherwise. We have tried to demonstrate that the stories of the martyrs preserved in the chronicles give expression to the survivors no less than to the martyrs and that their memories of Jews sanctifying God's name are riddled with complexity, irony, and ambivalence. If correct, such an approach to our sources demands that we avoid overly simplistic notions as to the ideals of martyrdom that may—or may not—have held sway among Ashkenazic Jews on the eve of the persecutions. In a word, the picture of Jews lining up outside the house of a respected rabbi to ask how they should react to the onslaught of the crusaders—and proceeding to submit to martyrdom simply because they were told to do so—strikes me as improbable. How can we simply assume that the memories of those who decided not to martyr themselves can reconstruct the thought process of those who did, without any question or hesitation?

If the chronicles do not reflect the Ashkenazic Jewish mentality before 1096 with total accuracy, perhaps they cannot explain conclusively what led the Jewish martyrs to reach their fateful decision, especially when many of them, those who killed themselves, violated the letter of Jewish law in doing so. But, inasmuch as these tales of martyrdom were told and then written down by those who survived the persecutions, they might shed more light on those who chose differently. What made some Jews attacked by the crusaders opt for baptism over death? The story of Isaac the *parnas* of Mainz discussed in Chapter 5 portrays a community leader running wildly back and forth in opposite directions, choosing one course of action and then another. Perhaps, we suggested, the story contains an element of parody; underscoring the ridiculousness of the scenario, the storytellers somehow found a release for the frustration and anxiety plaguing their own memories of what occurred.

Can we penetrate further into the experience of the Jew attacked in 1096? Granted that the chronicles testify to the quandary of the Jews in the Rhineland, do they illuminate the process of having to decide—between life as a Christian or death as a Jew? In this chapter, briefer than the previous ones, we consider one story that might help us along these lines.

"There They Remained in Desperate Straits . . ."

Only the chronicle attributed to Solomon bar Samson relates the tale of Kalonymos ben Meshulam, also a *parnas* or warden of the Jewish community, which brings the account of the massacre in Mainz to a close.

On the day [the third of Sivan] when the Lord said to his people [at Mount	1
Sinai], "Be ready for the third day," on that day [the Jews of Mainz]	2
prepared themselves and extended their necks and offered their sacrifice as	3
a pleasing odor to the Lord. On that day eleven hundred holy souls were killed on	4
behalf of his great name . . . , except for Rabbi Kalonymos the righteous	5
parnas and a few of the young people of Israel, fifty-three souls in all. On	6
that day they were saved, when they fled by way of the bishop's quarters	7
and came into the wardrobe in the church, a storage room for	8
treasures that they call the sacristy. There they remained in desperate	9
straits because of the sword that hung over their necks. Now the entry to	10
the wardrobe was narrow, and it was dark; no one of the enemy	11
sensed their presence, for they were utterly silent. The sun set and it	12
was very dark; they cried out, and their tongues stuck to their palates	13
because of thirst. So they approached the window to speak to the priest in	14

charge of the sacristy, so that he might pass water to them and restore   15
them. Yet he did not want to until they gave him ten silver coins for a   16
small bottle of water, fulfilling what is written in Scripture [Deuteronomy   17
28:44], "You shall have to serve your enemies in hunger and thirst, etc."   18
When the jar reached the window, the water could not make its way through   19
the narrow opening, until they took a lead tube and passed the water through it. 20
They drank, but not enough to quench their thirst.   21
Now I shall relate how it happened that these righteous people were killed.   22
In the middle of the night the bishop sent someone to the window of the   23
wardrobe to speak with Rabbi Kalonymos the *parnas*. He called to him,   24
saying: "Listen to me, O Kalonymos. The bishop has sent me to you to   25
determine if you are still alive, and he has ordered me to rescue you and all 26
those with you; come out to me. For he has with him three hundred   27
armored fighters, their swords drawn, and we pledge to protect you with   28
our lives. If you do not believe me, behold, I swear to you, for thus has   29
my lord the bishop commanded me. . . ." They did not believe him until he   30
swore to them, and then Rabbi Kalonymos and his party went out to him.   31
The officer put them in boats, took them across the Rhine, and brought   32
them by night to the village of Rüdesheim and to the bishop. The bishop   33
rejoiced that Rabbi Kalonymos was still alive and instructed to save him   34
and the others with him. Yet the sword of the enemy was bared against   35
them, and the Lord did not turn from his blazing anger at them. Rather, he   36
in whose hand the mind of the king and his officers is like channeled water   37
moved the heart of the bishop in our favor at first; but then he went back   38
on his word and summoned Rabbi Kalonymos to tell him: "I cannot save   39
you. For your God has turned away from you, having no desire to leave   40
any survivors among you; I therefore have no power to save you or help   41
you any more. Know, then, what you and those with you must do. Either   42
you must accept our religion or you must pay for the sin of your   43
ancestors." Rabbi Kalonymos answered him, crying out bitterly, "It is   44
true, our God does not desire to save us; it is therefore most certain, as you 45
said, that you no longer have the power to help. Give us until tomorrow to   46
respond to you." Rabbi Kalonymos returned to his pious companions and   47
told them what the bishop had said. All of them then arose together and   48
recited a blessing over their self-sacrifice; of one voice and mind, they   49
affirmed God's justice and accepted the burden of their religion. Before   50
he returned to the bishop, Rabbi Kalonymos the pious first took his son   51
Master Joseph, kissed him, and slaughtered him. When the bishop heard   52
that he had slaughtered his son, he grew incensed at him and said, "Now   53
surely I have no desire to help you any more." When the villagers heard   54
what the bishop had said, they as well as the crusaders gathered to kill the   55
Jews. In any event, on that same day Rabbi Kalonymos returned to the   56
bishop and on the way heard and appreciated what the bishop had said.   57
Having made his way back to him, he took a knife and approached him,   58
wanting to kill him. But the bishop's men—as well as the bishop   59
himself—sensed this. He ordered to remove him from his presence; and   60

the bishop's men attacked him and killed him with a wooden pole. Some   61
said that he never returned to the bishop, but, upon slaughtering his son, he   62
immediately took his sword, drove it into the ground, fell upon it, and drove   63
it into his stomach. Still others say that the enemy killed him en route. In   64
any event, the leader was slain for the unity of the name of the king of   65
kings of kings, the holy one, blessed be he; he was wholehearted and   66
perfect before the Lord, God of Israel. There the righteous one fell and   67
was slain together with his followers.[2]   68

The Narrative and the Events

The careful reader of this exciting and tragic story should find several of its details revealing. Bishops of the Rhineland functioned as rulers of their towns as well as the ranking clergymen of the area; Archbishop Ruthard of Mainz, our narrative informs us, had three hundred armed knights at his disposal (lines 27–28). It therefore should not surprise us that the Jews of Mainz sought refuge with "their" bishop, both as a representative of the Catholic Church, which was committed to preserving the Jews in Christendom, and as the local political and military leader. This same chronicle reports earlier that when news of the attacks on the Jewries of Speyer and Worms first reached Mainz, its Jews bribed the bishop handsomely, depositing their money in his treasury for safekeeping, and taking refuge in his palace.[3]

For his part, Ruthard at first appeared committed to aiding the Jews, assembling his courtiers to help in protecting them and agreeing not to leave Mainz as long as the Jews stood in imminent danger. When attacked, armed Jews actually offered resistance to the crusaders from within the bishop's compound. Like other bishops, however, Ruthard eventually could not withstand the crusaders, who found enthusiastic support among the local population (as in lines 54–56), and he fled his palace—and the city of Mainz—for his life. Our tale finds him across the Rhine River, from where he still extends himself, rather amiably, to the leadership of the Jewish community, in this case to its warden Kalonymos. The outcome of the story might leave us in doubt as to the bishop's underlying sincerity, but we read that Kalonymos and his followers agreed to exit their refuge in the sacristy upon receiving the bishop's pledge for their safe-conduct. Indeed, one does not sense deception in the chronicle's observation that the bishop rejoiced (line 34) to learn that Kalonymos was still alive, and one feels a measure of

genuine regret in his declaration that he can no longer provide for the Jews' security. Neither the bishop nor the Jews of Mainz looked favorably on the violence that devastated their town.

No less interesting, the chronicle's report that a leader of the Mainz Jewish community along with some fifty of its young adults—the Hebrew for "young people of Israel" (line 6, *baḥurei Yisra'el*) rings with a note of bravery and valor—fled the violence of the crusaders deserves our consideration. Actually, Kalonymos's decision to flee marks the end of a concerted attempt to resist the violence in a variety of ways. When the Jews of Mainz first appreciated the danger of the Crusade—that its leaders had sworn not to proceed before "avenging the blood of the crucified one with the blood of the Jews, leaving not a sole survivor"—Kalonymos the *parnas* rose to the occasion. The chronicle labels him the one who undertook to control the imminent damage, "God-fearing exemplar of his generation" as he was. What did Kalonymos do? He sent urgent letters to King Henry IV of Germany, who had promised to protect the Jews, apprising him of what lay in store.[4] Later, when the Jews of Mainz took up arms to fight against their attackers, Kalonymos stood at their head.[5] In the same breath the chronicle reports that repeated fasts had weakened the Jewish fighters, and their resistance proved ineffectual.[6] Simply put, Kalonymos appears to have coordinated the different efforts of the Jewish community to preserve itself—by seeking refuge with the local authorities, through bribery, through soliciting the help of the king, by praying and fasting, and by taking up arms. When all else failed, why should one wonder if Kalonymos and his able followers sought to flee?

Perhaps, one might respond, because in stories supposedly told to glorify the martyrs who willingly met their deaths, one would not expect the "God-fearing exemplar of his generation" to run away at the same time as eleven hundred of his kinsmen and neighbors sacrificed themselves to sanctify the name of God. When Archbishop Ruthard declares (line 40) that he can no longer protect the Jews because "*your* God has turned away from you" and Kalonymos himself affirms (line 45) that "*our* God does not desire to save us," the chronicle clarifies that all of Kalonymos's methods of resistance were in vain. Higher authority had brought these Jews to their end. Why highlight the flight of this heroic community leader, unless, of course, the narrative serves some other purpose besides lavishing praise on those who seized the opportunity to die as martyrs, if not to kill themselves?

The Limbo of Indecisiveness

Once again, our story extols the Jews of Mainz for their heroism, for their resolve to die as martyrs without compromising their faith. And yet, again, a closer reading yields a more complicated, nuanced picture.

Kalonymos joins other community leaders in the chronicles—David the *gabbai* of Mainz and Shemariah of Mörs, whom we mentioned in Chapter 3, and, of course, Isaac the *parnas*, the subject of Chapter 5—who needed time to deliberate before choosing a martyr's death. Moreover, as was the case in Isaac's tale, the storyteller offers inconclusive, alternative reports of what happened at the end of the scene; and this may well suggest that the symbolic, deeper significance of the story for the community that told it outweighs its factual accuracy. In this instance, the concluding protestation (lines 65–67) that, no matter how Kalonymos may have died, he in fact was slain "for the unity of the name" of God, "wholehearted and perfect before the Lord," reinforces that surmise. For according to two of the three alternative accounts of the warden's death, in no way was he "slain together with his followers," as the chronicle (line 68) emphatically states. On the contrary, in the first, most detailed, and, evidently, preferred version of how the story ended, immediately after Kalonymos's followers resolved to sacrifice themselves, accepting "the burden of their religion" (line 50), the narrative continues (line 51): "Rabbi Kalonymos the pious first took . . ." The reader expects to find that Kalonymos took up his sword or his knife and led his band in their ritual of collective suicide; no doubt he should have included himself, perhaps being the very first to die. But what Kalonymos did instead was first was to kill his son, just as Isaac the *parnas* had done, and he then set out to return to the bishop, who still expected the warden to convert to Christianity and live. Exactly what did Kalonymos intend to do?

Beyond such question marks concerning the community leader, other elements of this unusual tale point even more intriguingly to the self-image of the Jews that survived 1096. Unlike the hundreds of their fellow Jews in Mainz who, according to the chronicle, heroically met their deaths on May 27, 1096, Kalonymos and company fled in order to save their lives—which, for the record, is exactly what Jewish law prescribed that they do. Yet the refuge that they sought, the residence and dressing room of the bishop, proves to be no viable refuge at all. There Kalonymos and his group find the conditions unbearable: They are uncomfortable; they thirst for water;

the water given them proves inadequate and unsatisfying; their guardians among the Catholic clergy deceive them. These fifty-three Jews have sought to escape death and stay alive in a state of veritable limbo. Shrouded in thick darkness, they find neither the light of day nor the light of paradise, which the martyrs enjoyed immediately upon sacrificing their lives. There, in the church (literally, "in the idolatrous worship," *ba-'avodah zarah*, line 8), they lose their identity. They can neither see nor be seen. We read (lines 12–13) that "they cried out" in distress, but yet "they were utterly silent."

Symbolically, the haven where Kalonymos and his followers suffered in dire thirst for a time—just like the survivors who told their story—was clearly that of Christianity, which promised the Jews salvation. The church offered the Jews its water of baptism, but it did not quench their spiritual thirst; and, in the eyes of the Jews, the Christian clergy ultimately betrayed them. The chronicle's Hebrew term for this refuge, *meltahah* (line 8), appears only once in the Hebrew Bible, where, in the Book of Kings, it refers to the wardrobe for the distinctive clothing of those who worshipped the idol Baal. Suggestively, the Bible there recounts a trick devised by the Judean king Jehu for identifying—and punishing—the unfaithful among the Israelites.

Jehu assembled all the people and said to them . . . , "Summon to me all the prophets of Baal, all his worshippers, and all his priests. Let no one fail to come, for I am going to hold a great sacrifice for Baal. Whoever fails to come shall forfeit his life." Jehu was acting with guile in order to exterminate the worshippers of Baal. . . . Jehu sent word throughout Israel, and all the worshippers of Baal came; not a single one remained behind. They came into the temple of Baal, and the temple of Baal was filled from end to end. He said to the man in charge of the wardrobe [*meltahah*], "Bring out the vestments for all the worshippers of Baal," and he brought vestments out for them. Then Jehu and Jehonadab son of Rechab came into the temple of Baal, and they said to the worshippers of Baal, "Search and make sure that there are no worshippers of the Lord among you, only worshippers of Baal. . . ." When Jehu had finished presenting the burnt offering, he said to the guards and to the officers, "Come in and strike them down; let no man get away!" (2 Kings 10:18–25)

Not only do Kalonymos and his company excel as martyrs, but they also personify the survivors of 1096 remembering them in this narrative. For these fifty-three Jews sought refuge in the wardrobe of the church, wearing the clothes and assuming the appearance of Christians, even if they did not find fulfillment there. And just as King Jehu (spelled *yhw'* in Hebrew) punished those who identified with idolatry by entering the *meltahah*, so does

our story in the chronicle wrestle with what the survivors have done. For Kalonymos readily accepts the judgment of the bishop that the Lord (spelled *yhwh* in Hebrew) has sealed their fate following their brief stay in the church's *meltaḥah*. Can one help but hear an admission of guilt by those who hid out in that which our medieval Jewish storyteller called "the idolatrous worship"?

One should not dismiss this possibility too hastily. The Hebrew words describing "the desperate straits" (*be-tzar uve-matzok*) of these Jews in the church recall several biblical texts, all of which speak directly to their dilemma, trapped between martyrdom and baptism, the conflicting demands of two hostile religious communities. Among the curses promised those Israelites who would betray their God, Deuteronomy 28:53–57 uses nearly the identical phrase three times in succession: "You shall eat your own issue, the flesh of your sons and daughters that the Lord your God has given you, because of the desperate straits [*be-matzor uve-matzok*] to which your enemy shall reduce you. . . ." Kalonymos and company surely suffered from hunger and thirst, and we know that eventually they took the lives of their children. But might not the consumption of the flesh of the beloved child as a means of salvation refer to the sacrament—and sacrifice—of the Eucharist offered during the mass on the altar of the church? The vestry with its door and window so narrow that water had to be passed in through a lead pipe conjures up a picture of a bottle. Most interestingly, with these verses from Deuteronomy apparently in mind, Jeremiah employs that same image of a bottle or jug, which the prophet procures in order to convey a similar warning, no less relevant to those Jews who chose not to martyr themselves:

For they have forsaken me . . . to put their children to the fire as burnt offerings to Baal—which I never commanded, never decreed, and which never came to my mind. . . . I will cause them to fall by the sword before their enemies . . . , and I will cause them to eat the flesh of their sons and the flesh of their daughters, and they shall devour one another's flesh—because of the desperate straits [*be-matzor uve-matzok*] to which they will be reduced by their enemies, who seek their life. (Jeremiah 19:4–9)

After having relayed this message to the errant, Jeremiah is instructed "to smash the jug in the sight of the men who go with you and say to them: 'Thus said the Lord . . . , "So I will smash this people"'" (Jeremiah 19:10–11). Again, a telling constellation of motifs: Jews who offer sacrifice—and a sacrifice of the child above all—to a foreign god, for which God will reduce

them to desperate straits, oppressed by those who seek to take their lives and souls.

The threats of Deuteronomy and Jeremiah, however, speak only to one horn of the dilemma facing Kalonymos and his troop. Psalm 119:143 employs similar language to represent the path that perhaps, as one looked back at 1096 with guilt and still in doubt, they should have followed. "Though anguish and distress [*be-tzar uve-matzok*] come upon me, your commandments," declares the psalmist to God, "are my delight." Kalonymos and company faltered, unsure of which way to turn. Does the reader remember them for having worn the guise of Christians or for having died as martyrs—or both?

The list of suggestive allusions and details in our narrative goes on. Describing the silence that lingered over the vestry, the chronicle's words (" they were utterly silent," *va-yehi ke-maharish*, line 12) refer to the biblical report of how the newly anointed King Saul remained silent when the men of Belial mocked him (1 Samuel 10:27). Like Kalonymos, Saul wavered between ineffectual passivity at the outset of his reign, for which the Talmud notes that he and his children forfeited their kingship, and the voluntary death of a hero and martyr in his final battle against God's idolatrous enemies, the Philistines.[7] We read of Kalonymos and company that "their tongues stuck to their palates because of thirst" (lines 13–14). In this fashion they fulfilled the Bible's famed curse of infidelity (Psalm 137:5) uttered by those exiled after the destruction of Jerusalem, whose holiness the Jews of Mainz claimed to have replicated: "If I forget you, O Jerusalem . . . , let my tongue stick to my palate." If, as we saw in Chapter 3, the Jews of Mainz likened their own city to that of Jerusalem, the psalmist's curse proved most appropriate for those hiding out in the sacristy of the church—and, perhaps, for those who had difficulty in looking back and recounting their story.

Noting further that the Jews in the *meltahah* would not believe the promise of the bishop (*lo he'eminu*, line 30) until his messenger took an oath to them, the narrative may highlight the crisis of faith (*emunah*) that the Jews there underwent. Their very insistence that a Christian swear an oath to them may well have violated the halakhah in the eyes of some prominent Ashkenazic rabbis, because it caused him to call upon the Trinity and Jesus when he swore to God—which, in Jewish terms, bordered on idolatry.[8] As a result, when Kalonymos repeatedly affirmed the truth in the words of the bishop—"it is true" and "it is therefore most certain" (lines

44–45)—to what, exactly, did he refer? Strictly to the hopelessness of the situation? Or to something more fundamental in what the bishop preached?

Lingering Doubts

Reporting that "the sun set and it was very dark" (lines 12–13), our story recalls the same words in the biblical account of the "Covenant of the Pieces" (Genesis 15:17), in which God revealed to Abraham the destiny of his Israelite descendants. This was a moment of cosmic importance. But while Abraham overcame the doubts arising from his childlessness and "put his trust in the Lord," how did Kalonymos react? Would his heirs look back at his behavior and conclude with self-assurance, just as the Bible did in Abraham's case, that God "reckoned it to his merit" (Genesis 15:6)?

We have seen how indecisiveness in the face of death and conversion plagued Kalonymos and his troop on their way into the church, just as self-doubt and guilt followed them on their way out, even, perhaps, as they proceeded to die as martyrs. Remembering that our story derives from the memories of the survivors, I believe that this comprises a more reasonable reading of what Ashkenazic Jews, faced with the ultimate decision, experienced—and told about what they had experienced—in 1096. Attacked with a ferocity that they could not have expected, they had to decide on the spur of the moment between life and death, with all that each of these options entailed. How could they not have had hesitations, second thoughts, and misgivings?

The reader of this book may already have wondered, or even objected vehemently, and with good cause: Doesn't this picture of the events of 1096, though more critical and more complex than the standard one, still indulge in speculation? After all that we have argued, how can we begin to know the reactions of Ashkenazic Jews to the violence against them? In a certain, more limited measure, I admit, this picture does indeed speculate, insofar as it seeks to narrow the distance between the *event of the compilation of the chronicle* and the *event of the persecution*. Nevertheless, I would argue that it does so more responsibly, allowing for different and ambivalent reactions among the Jews who were attacked and understanding those reactions in their proper context. On the one hand, we must hear the heart and soul of the survivor crying out to us from the narrative, even as it ostensibly relates the suffering of the martyr; these stories took shape and circulated and became a part of Jewish culture among the living, not the dead. On the

other hand, we must understand that Jewish behavior during the First Crusade did not result simply from the unleashing of long dormant idealism, giving Jews an opportunity to prove their religious commitment. Rather, it derived from a broader cultural context that included crusading and Christianity as well as *kiddush ha-Shem* and traditional Judaism. Historian Ivan Marcus has recently argued that the newly refined Jewish ideals of *kiddush ha-Shem* as expressed in the Hebrew Crusade chronicles and other twelfth-century sources parallel or constitute a "Jewish equivalent" to the cry of *Deus vult*, "God wills it," with which the crusaders reportedly charged into battle.[9] So too, I submit, the doubt that we perceive in tales like that of Kalonymos echoes a similar phenomenon in contemporary Christian civilization.

In Chapter 6 we noted that the cult of the Virgin Mary was in the air at the time that our Hebrew chronicles took shape, and much the same can be said about doubt as an issue in religious life and thought. Historians have long recognized the powerful impact of dissent and disbelief on Christian thinkers of this period, from the dissenters themselves to the "orthodox" theologians who responded to them. Anselm of Canterbury, for instance, who has been termed "the summit" of Christian genius at this critical junction in medieval European history, completed his reply to skepticism and doubt concerning essential Christian belief, *Why Did God Become Human?*, during the years of the First Crusade. The famed philosopher and lover Peter Abelard authored his critically minded works during the two decades that led up to the Second Crusade, and he was condemned for some of his overly skeptical conclusions by a council of bishops in 1140. Recently, scholars have investigated an array of more subtle phenomena that characterized this period: the rise of individualism in twelfth-century European culture, the search for the self as traditional boundaries in society fluctuated, and a new emphasis on human intention in theology and philosophy. All of these were nourished by a growing tendency to question, to hesitate, and to agonize concerning long-hallowed behavioral norms in Christian thought.[10]

Against this backdrop, doubt from within Jewish communities that reportedly rallied enthusiastically to sanctify God's name in martyrdom should not surprise us, even if it requires *us* to read the tales of the Jewish martyrs more skeptically. In their doubts, too, Ashkenazic Jews during and after the First Crusade appear to have participated in the culture of the non-Jewish majority surrounding them. As we have noted repeatedly, although Jewish historians have commonly attributed such participation in

general and such religious skepticism in particular to Sefardic Jews as opposed to Ashkenazic ones, the Hebrew Crusade chronicles have led us to reevaluate those traditional assumptions.

Kalonymos and his followers in the limbo of the bishop's wardrobe remind us of Isaac the *parnas*, running wildly this way and that, unsure of what to do or where to turn next. Yet unlike Isaac's tale that we analyzed in Chapter 5, Kalonymos's story lacks any hint of parody, of the ridiculous. With its three alternative endings, this story has no clear ending at all. Expressing the doubts of its heroes, it leaves us, as its readers, in doubt as well—in doubt as to what Kalonymos and company did, and in doubt as to what they should have done.

Chapter 8
The Rape of Sarit

As the Jews of Germany looked back on the persecutions of 1096 and celebrated the heroism of their martyrs, they also recoiled in horror at the violence inflicted upon Jew by non-Jew and that inflicted upon Jew by Jew. Understandably, they could not rise up and clamor in protest against those Jewish heroes who had killed their loved ones before submitting to martyrdom themselves. That would have defeated one of the two primary purposes of their storytelling, to establish the grandeur and superiority of Jewish martyrdom in the face of the hostile challenge of crusading. But the other purpose of their narratives, to grapple with the post-traumatic anxiety, doubt, and guilt that plagued their survival, depended on their airing such misgivings nonetheless. Many scenes in the chronicles extol the virtues of the martyrs without hesitation. Others, as we have seen, strike an ambivalent note, demonstrating the tension between eulogy and protest. As we saw in the story of Mistress Rachel of Mainz, for example, the heroine matches—or perhaps even surpasses—the zeal of the Virgin Mary and Holy Mother Church in the sacrifice of her children. Still, at least one of those children seeks to flee her sword, and one naturally wonders how a mother could have done what she did to the fruit of her own womb. Finally, in a few instances, we can see how horror might actually overshadow esteem in the survivors' memories of the martyrs. Contemporary Christian reports of the First Crusade express their aversion to the self-slaughter of the Jews in the Rhineland;[1] why should similar voices among the Jews themselves surprise us?

We find such a voice in the story of the virgin-bride Sarit and her father-in-law Master Judah, who fled their homes along with most of Cologne's Jewish community when the crusaders first arrived, only to meet their end in the surrounding villages during the weeks that followed. Their tale appears in the Solomon bar Samson chronicle, in the account of what

transpired to the Jews in the village of Altenahr (or Eller—the Hebrew is unclear).

On Thursday, the fourth of Tammuz, the enemy amassed against the saints	1
of Altenahr,[2] set on inflicting cruel, extensive tortures on them until	2
they would consent to be polluted. The pious ones learned of this; they	3
confessed to their creator and willingly selected five pious,	4
righteous, valiant, God-fearing men to slaughter all of the others. There	5
were some three hundred souls there, the most noble of the	6
communities of Cologne, and they were all slaughtered. Not one	7
survived, for all of them died in purity for the sanctity of the exclusive	8
name of God.	9
The *parnas* there, chief spokesman, most noble, and leader of them all	10
was Master Judah ben Rabbi Abraham, a wise, distinguished	11
counselor. When all the communities would gather in Cologne for the	12
markets, three times a year, he would address them all in the	13
synagogue; they would be silent in his presence and appreciate what he	14
had to say. When the [other] leaders of the communities would begin	15
to speak, they would all rebuke them and chide them to listen to his	16
words. "What he says is true, sincere, and correct." He was of the	17
tribe of Dan, a man of good faith and the exemplar of his generation,	18
one who would sacrifice himself were someone else in distress.	19
Throughout his life no harm ever came to anyone on his account. He	20
was loved by God and kind to all souls; concerning him did David	21
recite his entire Psalm, "Lord, who may reside in your dwelling?"	22
Likewise did the women greatly sanctify God's name for all to see.	23
When Sarit the virgin-bride, beautiful, lovely, and most pleasant in the	24
eyes of her beholders, saw how they killed themselves with their	25
swords, one slaughtering the next, she wished to escape for fear of	26
what she observed outside through the window. But when her	27
father-in-law, Master Judah ben Rabbi Abraham the pious saw that	28
such was his daughter-in-law's intention, he called to her, "My	29
daughter, since you did not have the privilege of wedding my son	30
Abraham, you will not marry any Gentile either." He caught hold of	31
her, took her out through the window, kissed her on the mouth, and	32
raised his voice, wailing together with the maiden. He cried out in a	33
loud voice, bitterly, to all those present, "Behold, all of you, this is the	34
wedding ceremony [literally, canopy, *huppah*] of my daughter, my	35
kallah, that I am performing today." They all cried, sobbing and	36
wailing, mourning and moaning.	37
The pious Master Judah said to her, "Come and lie in the bosom of	38
Abraham our father, for in an instant you will acquire your place in the	39
next world and enter into the company of the righteous and pious." He	40
took her and laid her upon the bosom of his son Abraham her	41

betrothed, and, with his sharpened sword, he cut her up the middle   42
into two parts; then he also slaughtered his son. Over this do I cry and   43
does my heart grieve.[3]   44

Slaughter, Sex, and Dismemberment

This passage does not read like a typical martyr's tale. Sarit herself seeks to
flee rather than die, and, for all of the lavish praise that the narrative heaps
upon Master Judah ben Abraham, one has difficulty sympathizing with him
in the way one might extend one's heart to Rachel of Mainz. Though she
kills her children, one of them against his will, she sacrifices them in terms
that strike the Jewish reader as noble, even exemplary; for the narrative
associates her sacrifices with the paschal lamb and with the bound Isaac of
the biblical Akedah. Master Judah, however, cuts a different image.
Granted, we read (line 20) that "throughout his life no harm ever came to
anyone on his account," but the scene that follows renders such praise
virtually ridiculous. Sarit the bride, "beautiful, lovely, and most pleasant in
the eyes of her beholders" (lines 24–25) as she was, probably had sufficient
maturity to decide her course of action for herself.[4] The chronicle makes
no pretense that she, like the children of Isaac the *parnas* in Chapter 5,
"cannot distinguish between right and wrong." When Judah slaughters her,
then, he does not offer sacrifice but perpetrates an act of homicide. Her
violent death hardly resembles the Akedah or slaughter of the paschal lamb.
One might well conclude that it smacks more of rape than of sanctifying
the name of God.

Indeed, Sarit's story adds a potent sexual dimension to the violence of
1096. The comparison of her execution to a wedding canopy, or *ḥuppah*
(line 35), which in itself represents the bedsheet on which bride and groom
consummate their marriage and leave evidence of her virginity, is striking.
Judah kisses Sarit in a very nonpaternal fashion, "on the mouth" (line 32).
He calls her "my *kallah*" (lines 35–36), a telling, ambiguous term that means
both daughter-in-law and bride. Having called upon those present to witness his ritual act, as at a wedding, he lays her down together with his son,
her intended husband, presumably on their marital bed. But then Judah,
not his son Abraham, consummates their union by baring his sharpened
weapon, penetrating her and cutting her up the middle, and, finally, bringing about her death. No wonder that the heart of the narrator grieves (line
44)!

Sarit's story contains more than meets the eye at first glance, and we must try to understand what makes it so powerful. Arguing that twelfth-century Hebrew texts borrowed from the style and techniques of French literary romance, Susan Einbinder has called upon Sarit's story as a case in point.

The scene is portrayed with vivid confusion—the "beautiful and comely young" woman trying to flee, her father-in-law seizing her and holding her up to the window, then seating her in her betrothed's lap and hewing her in two. The narrator ensures that the bride's death takes place before witnesses, as would have her marriage; the symbolism of slaughter and sexual consummation converge in her graphic dismemberment. . . . Sarit's martyrdom is cast ambivalently. But the energy and breathlessness with which the characters are depicted, the urgency and emotion of the father's dialogue, the girl's panic and iconic death, owe much to romance style. Sarit's martyrdom, too, is exemplary; it integrates her into an ideal as it immortalizes her struggle. Her story still reinforces the moral emphasis of the narrative, ambivalences and all.[5]

Searching further, perhaps one could also find Sarit and her story a place in a long line of virginal figures, whose violent deaths magicians, writers, and artists depicted in blatantly sexual imagery. Numerous ancient sources represent the sword as a phallic symbol. In her fascinating book *Tragic Ways of Killing a Woman*, Nicole Loraux has shown how classical Greek tradition frequently likened the death or slaughter of a virgin by the sword to her marriage or her rape. On the stage in the Greek theater, "the sacrificed virgin, the bride of Hades, is simply one embodiment of the equivalence of death and marriage."[6] Even the wedding ceremony bore striking similarities to rape and to the rites of death.[7] The Louvre Museum houses a late ancient Egyptian curse tablet, which calls upon gods and spirits to guarantee its author sexual control over his beloved, and which accompanies a clay figurine of a woman pierced by thirteen nails, in her sexual organs and elsewhere (see Figure 4).[8] And suggestions of rape and sexual violation abound in early Christian accounts of virgin martyrs. As one scholar has recently commented, "the condemned woman, on her knees, her hands tied behind her back and sword placed to throat, was to suffer not just the obliteration of her body, but simultaneously to enact a violent sexual metaphor. The man who held his sword at her throat threatened her identity to assert his, ended her being to further his."[9]

These parallels might well help to broaden our appreciation of Sarit's story, but I believe that to a certain extent they miss their mark, for they

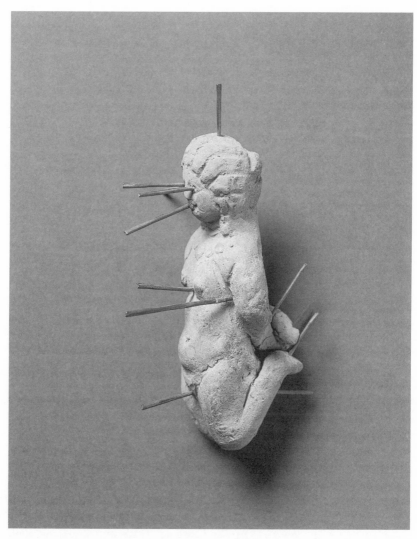

Figure 4. Ancient Egyptian statuette of bewitchment. Louvre, Paris. Reproduced by permission. © Photo RMN.

divert attention away from our story's main character. Unlike the virgins sacrificed in Greek tragedies or glorified in the acts of Christian martyrs,[10] Sarit does not give up her life either nobly or willingly; rather, she dies a casualty of sexual violence, not a saintly martyr. At the center of our story stands not Sarit, the victim of a horrendous attack, but her father-in-law Master Judah, its perpetrator.

Sarit seeks to flee, she resists, and, in the end, she succumbs to physical force. This renders her violation an act of rape, to be sure, but not a totally wanton act of sexual violence. For even at the height of his passion, Master Judah transforms his attack on Sarit into an act of ritual. He calls upon all those in the vicinity to witness and thereby, as it were, to participate in the ritual. They, in turn, proceed to join him in his lament. He confers upon his act the status of a *huppah*, a wedding ceremony, in which he substitutes for his son as his daughter-in-law's sexual partner; his *kallah*/daughter-in-law becomes his *kallah*/bride. And, in identifying "the bosom of his son Abraham" (line 41) with "the bosom of Abraham our father" (lines 38–39), he equates Sarit's defloration and murder with a sacrificial act that produces salvation for its victims.

Does the equation work? How shall we understand the ritualized rape that Master Judah commits in this narrative? More than the conventions of medieval literary romance, the imagery of Greek tragedy, or the tales told of early Christian martyrs, I believe that Sarit's story assumes clarity with reference to what medieval Europeans called *ius primae noctis*, the lord's right of the first night. Well known in Jewish as well as non-Jewish folk traditions, this convention entitled the local lord to sleep with all of the virgin-brides in his domain on the first night of their marriages.[11] Although scholars have questioned whether this right was ever exercised in practice or remained within the realm of myth and popular tradition, the historical basis for the tradition need not concern us at present. Medieval Jews and Christians *believed* that such ritualized rapes did occur, and they dreaded them.[12]

One can consider Master Judah's act more terrible still. While the lord's right of the first night derived, at least in theory, from a well-defined hierarchy of relationships and network of social boundaries, the violation of Sarit by her father-in-law threatened even those, undercutting the little social order and sense of security that the traditional lord-rapist left intact. For, like the biblical Judah who bedded and wedded his daughter-in-law Tamar instead of giving her to his son as he should have (see Genesis 38), our Judah blurs family boundaries and relationships. Twice does he call

Sarit his daughter (lines 30, 35); once he calls her his *kallah*, his daughter-in-law or his bride. No matter how one works out the ambiguity, one may not disregard the overtones of incest.

Moreover, as he beckons Sarit to lie in the bosom of "Abraham our father" and places—and then violates—her on the body of "his son Abraham her betrothed," not only does Judah destroy the fabric of the earthly family, but he also upsets the order of God's creation in a more cosmic sense. By the beginning of the twelfth century, the bosom of Abraham, a symbol well attested in Jewish tradition too,[13] had taken on new meaning in Christian art and religious literature. What once had represented a sort of way station or rest area for souls after their death now became the heavenly gathering point for the brotherhood of the righteous after their resurrection. But as French cultural historian Jérôme Baschet has demonstrated, this symbol also served as a metaphor for the elaborate network of relationships that underlay the conceptual integrity and self-image of Western Christian society, especially between the eleventh and thirteenth centuries. "The Bosom of Abraham, in so far as it shows heavenly reward in terms of a reunion with the father, should be considered not in isolation, but as part of the medieval system of kinship . . . : fleshly, spiritual, and divine."[14] In identifying a marital bed in this world with the joys of paradise in the next, Master Judah thus obscured the lines of demarcation between body and spirit, earthly and heavenly.

In the sixth chapter of Genesis, such blurring of cosmic boundaries between the heavenly sons of the gods and the earthly daughters of men—a violation of world order that the Bible, too, portrays in sexual terms—moves God to undo his creation, to destroy the world with the flood. Where would Judah ben Abraham's actions lead? As we shall see, the world of Sarit's story is a world of chaos, a world of symbolic distortions that undermine assumptions at the bedrock of the Jewish community in the wake of the persecutions of 1096.

Heroes and Hesitations

Beyond his resemblance to the biblical Judah, our story portrays Judah ben Abraham as bearing similarities to at least four other famous personages in Jewish popular tradition. Yet a careful analysis of these similarities reveals that comparisons which might first appear complimentary ultimately prove

equivocal, if not disparaging, both for Master Judah and, in some instances, for those in whose likeness the narrative presents him.

Abraham and the Covenant of the Pieces

Reporting that Judah, son of Abraham, took his daughter-in-law and "cut her up the middle into two parts [*gezarim*]," Sarit's story—like that of Kalonymos in Chapter 7—reminds us of the biblical covenant in which God guarantees that Abraham's descendants will inherit the promised land. After noting (Genesis 15:6) how Abraham "put his trust in the Lord, and he reckoned it to his merit," Scripture records God's promise of the land, to which Abraham responds,

"O Lord God, how shall I know that I am to possess it?" He answered, "Bring me a three-year-old heifer, a three-year-old she-goat, a three-year-old ram, and a young bird." He brought him all these and cut them in two, placing each half opposite the other. . . . When the sun set and it was very dark, there appeared a smoking oven and a flaming torch which passed between those pieces [*gezarim*]. On that day the Lord made a covenant with Abram, saying, "To your offspring I assign this land." (Genesis 15:8–18)

In the patriarch Abraham's case, this sacrifice of a young heifer—a cow ripe for impregnation but still intact—elicits God's promise of redemption and inheritance for his offspring following their enslavement and suffering in Egypt. And, as rabbinic midrash observed, when the biblical poet thanks God (Psalm 136:13) for his kindness during the exodus when he "split the Sea of Reeds into parts [*gezarim*]"—the only other instance of this word in the Bible—he acknowledges that the Covenant of the Pieces bore fruit.[15]

Does Judah's sacrifice of the virginal, heiferlike Sarit compare with Abraham's offering and have similar salutary effects? If not, perhaps our medieval narrative has another biblical comparison in mind, an alternative "covenant of pieces," in which the prophet Jeremiah conveys God's promise of punishment for those who have violated his trust in them.

I will make the men who violated my covenant, who did not fulfill the terms of the covenant which they made before me, like the calf which they cut into two so as to pass between the halves. The officers of Judah and Jerusalem, the officials, the priests, and all the people of the land who passed between the halves of the calf shall be handed over to their enemies, to those who seek to kill him. Their carcasses shall become food for the birds of the sky and the beasts of the earth. (Jeremiah 34:18–20)

In this prophecy, those who have violated God's covenant will suffer the same fate as the animals they have hewn into two—a far cry from the salvation that God in his grace promised Abraham and delivered to his descendants in Egypt. Curiously, in addition to specifying that such was the punishment for those who rebelled against God, replacing his covenant with another, rabbinic tradition linked the verse to those who sacrificed their children in an idolatrous rite.[16]

Whom does Sarit resemble more, Abraham's young heifer in Genesis or the calf cut into two by those who then violated God's covenant in Jeremiah? Perhaps Scripture itself suggested the answer to those medieval Jews who told our story. Without stretching the imagination too far, one might find an allusion to our hero and heroine in the prophecy of Jeremiah. "*The officers of Judah . . .* who passed between the halves of the calf [and] shall be handed over to their enemies" are labeled in Hebrew *Sarei* (spelled s-r-i) *Yehudah*, an almost exact duplication of the names Sarit (spelled *s-r-i-t*) and Judah (*Yehudah*). More straightforwardly, our Hebrew chronicle connects Sarit's story to Jeremiah's prophecy in the lines immediately following the maiden's death. We read that, in the wake of Sarit's slaughter, the Jews hiding in Altenahr fast for three days, at which point they proceed to martyr themselves. And then, "after three days, when the enemies of the Lord had gone, the forcibly converted Jews whom the enemy had spared came and wished to bury them, because they had become *food for the birds of the sky and the beasts of the earth*."[17] These are Jeremiah's words exactly! Our story links the fate of Master Judah and his followers directly to those whom the prophet rebuked for betraying the Lord. Their covenant of pieces, it would seem, did not prove acceptable in the eyes of God.

Phineas the Priest and the Midianite Kozbi

One might contend that Sarit's story depicts Master Judah in the image of an exemplary hero and zealot in Jewish tradition: Phineas, son of Eleazar and grandson of Aaron the priest. And, in fact, the Bible itself justifies the leap between Abraham's Covenant of the Pieces and the zeal of Phineas. For just as Abraham had "put his trust in the Lord, and he [God] *reckoned it to his merit*," so do we later read that "Phineas stepped forth and intervened, and the plague ceased; *it was reckoned to his merit* for all generations" (Psalm 106:30–31).

What did Phineas do to earn such praise? Scripture reports how during their years of wandering in the wilderness the Israelites strayed from

the proper path, worshipping the pagan god of Midian and consorting with Midianite women, for which God sent a plague to punish the people. One Hebrew nobleman named Zimri shamelessly dared to bring Kozbi, a Midianite princess, into the Israelite camp, consorting with her before the eyes of Moses himself: "When Phineas, son of Eleazar son of Aaron the priest, saw this, he left the assembly and, taking a spear in his hand, he followed the Israelite into the chamber and stabbed both of them, the Israelite and the woman, through the belly. Then the plague against the Israelites was checked" (Numbers 25:7–8). Rabbinic midrash elaborates in graphic detail what the biblical text only hints at. Phineas barged in on Zimri and Kozbi during their coupling, and he killed them by plunging his spear into their genitals.[18] Our Master Judah does virtually the same to his son Abraham and his bride Sarit, attacking them as they lie together and killing them in similar fashion. The parallel between Judah and Phineas assumes greater clarity, when the same midrash reports that Phineas felt impelled to take the initiative himself because the tribes of Judah and Dan, which should have reacted aggressively to Zimri's shameful behavior, did not. "Is there no one here," he reflected, "ready to kill him [Zimri] and be killed himself? Where are the lions—for [Scripture teaches that] 'Judah is a lion's whelp' and 'Dan is a lion's whelp'?"[19] Most appropriately, then, the hero of Sarit's story who acts on the model of Phineas bears the name of Judah and reportedly stems from the "tribe of Dan" (line 18), even though no medieval European Jew could reliably claim descent from this tribe.

Yet Phineas also came under criticism in Jewish tradition—most curiously with regard to the sacrificial slaughter of a young virgin by her father, which prevented her from marrying and raising a family.[20] In exchange for victory over his Ammonite enemies, the biblical judge Jephthah had vowed to sacrifice the first creature that he would encounter upon his return from battle; when this turned out to be his daughter, he claimed to have no choice and fulfilled his vow (Judges 11). The outcome of the story, however, did not sit well with the rabbis of the Talmud. Phineas, they learned from the biblical story of "the concubine at Gibeah" (still another instance of the sexual slaughter of a young woman perhaps not unlike Sarit), served as chief priest at the time (Judges 20:28). Albeit long after the fact, some talmudic sages rebuked both Phineas and Jephthah over the death of Jephthah's daughter, subjecting their leadership to scathing criticism. Had Jephthah felt sufficiently contrite so as to seek a means to annul his vow, or had Phineas, who as priest had responsibility for the annulment of vows, taken the initiative to devise and propose such a means, they might have

averted this terrible tragedy. But as the events took their course, neither one deigned to make the first move and thereby, perhaps, acknowledge the superiority of the other. From this perspective, not a militant's zeal but pride, a lack of creativity at a moment of crisis, and ineffectual leadership resulted in the slaughter of Jephthah's daughter by her father. (According to one midrash, Phineas also bore responsibility for the ensuing civil war among the Israelite tribes, in which many thousands perished.)[21] Projecting from Phineas onto our Master Judah, can one draw a similar conclusion concerning the death of Sarit at the hands of her father-in-law?

Judah the Maccabee and His Sister

Ancient sources indicate that Jewish priests of the Second Temple period drew considerable inspiration from the biblical character of Phineas.[22] The First Book of the Maccabees, for example, as it relates the events underlying the Jewish holiday of Chanukkah, describes how Mattathias reacted to the persecution of Judaism by the wicked King Antiochus. "Thus he burned with zeal for the law, as Phineas did against Zimri" (1 Maccabees 2:26). Later in the same chapter, as he rallied his son Judah and his brothers the Maccabees to rise in rebellion, Mattathias recalled various heroes of Jewish tradition, including "Phineas our father [who], because he was deeply zealous, received the covenant of everlasting priesthood" (verse 52).[23]

From Abraham and Phineas, then, we move on to Judah the Maccabee, a third Jewish hero who seems to have contributed to the character of our Judah ben Abraham. Both drew inspiration from Phineas; both had the same name; and we remember both—not entirely favorably—in connection with the lord's right of the first night.

Late ancient and medieval rabbinic sources preserve a folktale that proves suggestive for our story.

At the time of the wicked Greek empire, they decreed against Israel . . . that whenever people should marry, the king would sleep with the woman first and only then would she return to her husband. This was the practice for three years and three months; and, in view of this, many in Israel refrained from [marrying and engaging in] family life.

In order to maintain the regimen of family life that was the bedrock of Jewish survival, the sages then devised ways to celebrate marriages and births in secret.

God the exalted performed a miracle, and not one daughter of Israel was defiled, until it was the turn of the daughter of the Hasmonean [Mattathias] to get married, and they could not keep it secret, because her father had close connections

with the authorities. . . . When she heard that the king had sent for her, she reflected: "If I go now to that heathen and he defiles me, the daughters of Israel will wonder, 'Are we better than the daughter of the Hasmonean whom the lord defiled [so that we must resist]?' God's name would thus be desecrated on my account. Rather, it is better that I die and that God's name not be desecrated on my account." She gave herself up to be executed, arose, and took off her clothes and jewels; having put on rags, she took a cup and jug of wine in her hand and served drinks throughout the city. When her kinsmen saw her, they were embarrassed because she appeared in such a manner in public. But she quickly picked up her head and, sobbing, cried out to them [in sarcasm]: "O righteous, pious folk, children of righteous, pious folk, why are you ashamed of me? Because I have dressed in rags? And yet you have no shame before the exalted God, as you are willing to surrender me to the heathen so that he can defile me!"

When Judah and his companions heard this, they conspired to kill their oppressor.

Having dressed their sister in festive clothes and decorated the road from the house of Mattathias to the palace of the governor, they feigned compliance with his decree. The governor then wished to honor Judah and his brothers, who entered his chambers, cut off his head, and plundered his possessions.[24]

We have no reason to think that twelfth-century Ashkenazic Jews were unfamiliar with this popular tradition, and we must focus on some critical differences between it and our narrative of 1096. In the case of Judah the Maccabee and his sister, the young bride-to-be zealously challenges the established authorities that facilitate and tolerate her downfall. She willingly endangers herself, prepares to die the death of a martyr, voices her desire to sanctify the name of God, and rallies the men of her family to join her in actively resisting the oppressor. Sarit, however, does none of these. Moreover, while Judah the Maccabee heeds his sister's wishes and strikes out successfully at her Gentile oppressor, Judah ben Abraham, *parnas* of Cologne, strikes his mortal blows at his son the groom and his bride against their will—or at least against hers. *He* assumes the role of the wicked oppressor. He usurps the right of the first night from the legitimate husband, raping the newlywed wife and slaying them both, just as heifer, ram, and calf were sacrificed in the biblical covenants of the pieces and just as Kozbi and Zimri were pierced by Phineas and his spear.

Master Judah ben Abraham has displaced the victim as the central character in our story. He emerges as an antihero, a blatant distortion of Abraham, Phineas, and Judah the Maccabee, molded as he is in perversions of their images. And yet, as if this did not suffice to vent our survivor-storytellers' horror at things that occurred during the persecutions of 1096, our narrative ventures further. For it models Master Judah after still an-

other legendary hero, well known to medieval Jews and Christians alike and far more pernicious than any of the preceding ones.

The Jewish Antichrist

Phineas, we recall, slew Kozbi and Zimri because the tribes of Judah and Dan did not rise to the occasion as those whom the Torah compares to lions should have. Furthermore, we have noted that our story links Master Judah to the tribe of Dan, even though no one could have understood that affiliation literally, since Dan numbered among the ten "lost tribes" of Israel. Beyond the association with Phineas, what might we learn from the convergence of Judah and Dan in our story's central character?

Rabbinic midrash linked the messiah to both Judah and Dan. The messiah, "son" of David, some reasoned, would descend from two tribes: Judah (and thus David) on his father's side and Dan's on his mother's, since the Torah compares both to the kingly lion, as the midrash on Phineas took note.[25] Yet the messiah still awaited by the Jews could only strike Christians as a fiendish impostor, since the real savior from the house of David had already appeared in the person of Jesus Christ. Late in the second century, the church father Irenaeus of Lyons wrote that the Antichrist, the cosmic villain who would appear at the end of days to dominate the world, persecute the wicked, and test the faithful before succumbing to the power of Christ, would be a Jew from the tribe of Dan.[26] Perhaps Irenaeus knew of Jewish traditions that linked the messiah to Dan as well as to Judah; perhaps Christian preachers before him had already made the association. Regardless of its origins, the notion of a Jewish Antichrist quickly caught on and by the twelfth century had become commonplace in Christian expectations of the end of time. As a French monk named Adso of Montier-en-Der, author of the most popular medieval "biography" of Antichrist, wrote in the middle of the tenth century,

Now let us see about Antichrist's origin. What I say is not thought out or made up on my own, but in my attentive reading I find it all written down in books. As our authors say, the Antichrist will be born from the Jewish people, that is, from the tribe of Dan, as the Prophet says, "Let Dan be a snake in the wayside, an adder in the path." He will sit in the wayside like a serpent and will be on the path in order to wound those who walk in the paths of justice and kill them with the poison of his wickedness.[27]

Underlying this belief that Antichrist would come from the tribe of Dan—who, though lionlike, also behaved like a snake—was the view of

Figure 5. Antichrist and his Jewish followers. Herrad of Hohenburg, *Hortus Deliciarum*, ed. Rosalie Green et al. (Leiden, 1979), vol. 2, pl. 134. Germany, late twelfth century. Reproduced by permission of the Warburg Institute, London.

Antichrist as the ultimate impostor and deceiver, who would purport to be the genuine redeemer, saintly, learned, and altogether worthy of supreme leadership. Antichrist would gain support, among the Jews especially, by appearing pious, wise, and heroic. (See Figure 5.) He would rebuild God's sanctuary in Jerusalem and hold court there, passing judgment to promote his image as rightful lord of the world and tolerating no opposition. Once ensconced in power, however, his true character would shine through, as he would begin to persecute the righteous and shamelessly serve his own evil interests in all that he did.[28] Curiously, twelfth-century German writers began to depict Antichrist's evil in sexual terms as well. Thus has Antichrist's modern biographer Bernard McGinn written of the portrayal of the impostor and his wretched birth by the famed German mystic and abbess Hildegard of Bingen: "Hildegard goes out of her way to emphasize that Antichrist's false teaching consists primarily in his attack on the Christian doctrine of virginity. . . . Antichrist is a sexual criminal, one whose very birth from his typological mother, the Church, is so violent and bloody . . . that it can be seen as a kind of reverse rape."[29] (See Figure 6.)

Our chronicles took shape a generation or two before Hildegard put her ideas in writing, but one wonders if this image of Antichrist as sexual criminal might not already have been circulating, "in the air" as we have suggested, during the first decades of the century. Curiously, by the end of the Middle Ages, such traditions had developed to the point of depicting

Figure 6. Vision of the Last Days: birth of Antichrist (lower panel). Hildegard of Bingen, *Scivias* 3.11 (CCCM 43A:576–577). Germany, twelfth century. Reproduced by permission of Brepols Publishers, Turnhout.

Antichrist's conception within an incestuous union of a Jewish father and daughter (see Figure 7).[30] Whether or not those who told Sarit's story so conceived of Antichrist, it is difficult to ignore the sexual dimension of the violence that Judah ben Abraham inflicted on his daughter-in-law-to-be. More important, their story depicts Master Judah as one who *appeared* to be the ideal leader. Deemed a righteous, venerable sage—like the Christians' Jewish Antichrist—he enjoys the attention and the acclaim of all

Figure 7. The conception of Antichrist: the impregnation of his mother by her father. *Der Antichrist*, Strasbourg, ca. 1480. Reproduced by permission of the Staats- und Universitätsbibliothek, Hamburg.

those who hear him speak in the synagogue. Considered gentle, harmless, and willing to suffer in place of his fellow Jew, he uses his station to control his followers in their response to the hostile threat of the crusaders. And with what end?

The reader of the Solomon bar Samson chronicle might choose to evaluate Master Judah's character without considering Antichrist and still paint a critical picture of the *parnas*; various rabbinic sources linked the tribe of Dan with idolatry, such that descent from Dan might not prove complimentary.[31] Nevertheless, throughout this book we have noted how the Ashkenazic martyrs' tales preserved in the chronicles make use of motifs, symbols, and traditions that Jews shared with and/or borrowed from Christians, as they convey their distinctive messages within the Jewish community. Earlier in this chapter, for example, we saw how the "bosom of Abraham," a motif well known in Jewish and Christian traditions, contributes to the story of Sarit in its own special way. Medieval Jews characterizing their community leader as Christians characterized the Antichrist might strike us as particularly harsh. But that in itself should not rule out the possibility, if such an association served the purpose of the narrative as it gave expression to the survivors of the 1096 persecutions.

What was this purpose? Considering the piyyutim (liturgical poems) of lamentation that medieval Jews wrote in the wake of tragedies like the persecutions of 1096, scholars of Hebrew literature have noted the frequency of "the image of the martyrdom as a wedding, and of the martyrs as brides and grooms hurrying to their nuptials."[32] Or, in the words of another investigator,

> The image of the slaughter as wedding pervades the piyyutim. . . . As an emblem of consummation, as the unification of God and the faithful in eternity, the *ḥuppah*, "marriage canopy," draws into a rich conceptual knot the many thematic strands of the poem: the linkage between the generations, the free-will offering of love, the sacramental flow of blood, unification and sanctification.[33]

Surely there are martyrs' tales recorded in prose in the chronicles that can be read in similar fashion, and one frequently reads Sarit's story in just this way. I believe, however, that in the case of her story, the narrative also served to express the utter horror with which survivors of 1096 remembered what they had experienced, from the violent assault of the crusaders to the violence that Jews inflicted upon themselves.

When I first began to wrestle with Sarit's story several years ago, I showed it to an American colleague, a distinguished scholar of comparative mythology. Stunned and visibly horrified by the tale, she concluded without hesitation that the narrative unabashedly condemns Judah ben Abraham for the brutal slaughter of his son's young bride. My colleague was thus doubly astounded to learn that this martyr's tale ostensibly seeks to praise the saintly warden of Cologne's Jewry for his valorous sacrifice, more demanding, perhaps, than suicide itself. Yet I believe that my colleague's reaction would not have shocked the survivors of 1096 who told Sarit's story, had they reflected introspectively and critically over their storytelling. Much like myths, even historical memories allow for multiple, ostensibly contradictory interpretations, and my colleague's gut reaction to the demise of Sarit drove home the realization that these stories undoubtedly embody the conflicted perspective of the survivors who told them.

What, then, constituted the right answer to the dilemma in which the Jews of Ashkenaz found themselves in 1096? Understood as we have read it, the story of Sarit appears to defy the question. There was no right answer, which is precisely the answer that enabled the survivors to go on living with themselves at the same time as they glorified the martyrs. The words of Hillel the Elder recorded in the small talmudic tractate *Pirkei Avot* ring loud and true: "Do not pass judgment on someone else before you undergo his experience yourself."[34]

Afterword

Memories of the martyrs of 1096 persist, among religious and secular Jews alike. Four times each year, Jews gather in synagogue to remember their loved ones in the memorial service of *Yizkor Elohim,* "May God Remember." Synagogue attendance for these prayers is generally high, as many who might not otherwise participate in community worship turn out on these days for remembering the dead. After individuals recite the *Yizkor* prayer for those in their own immediate families, they typically join in communal prayers on behalf of souls with whom all feel some connection: deceased leaders of the congregation, Jews who perished during the Holocaust, perhaps those who died fighting for the State of Israel. Traditionally, the *Yizkor* service ends with the prayer of *Av ha-Raḥamim,* "The Merciful Father," beseeching God to remember and to avenge those Jews who died as martyrs, as they sanctified his holy name.

May the merciful father, who dwells in heaven, in his abundant mercies remember compassionately the pious and righteous and pure, the sacred communities, who sacrificed themselves for the sanctification of the divine name. Beloved and cherished in life, they were not parted in death. They were swifter than eagles and stronger than lions in doing the will of their creator and the desire of their protector. May God remember them beneficently along with the other righteous of history. May he avenge the blood of his servants which has been spilled.[1]

The prayer of *Av ha-Raḥamim* captures the spirit of our reading of *Gezerot Tatnu* in more ways than one. On the one hand, dating from the aftermath of the First Crusade, it memorializes the Jewish martyrs of 1096, as do a number of other rituals in traditional Jewish life: dirges for the Ninth of Av, *Tish'ah be-Av,* the national day of mourning each summer; prayers for the High Holy Days every fall; and customs of mourning observed every spring during *Sefirat ha-'Omer,* the period between Passover and Pentecost when the persecutions began.

On the other hand, the meaning and function of *Av ha-Raḥamim* have themselves undergone change and development. Having originated in a

specific set of circumstances in order to commemorate events in a specific cluster of Jewish communities in northwestern Germany, it was recited on the Sabbath morning before Shavuʿot (Pentecost), initiating the week late in the spring when the anti-Jewish violence of 1096 climaxed, and on the Sabbath before Tishʿah be-Av, when Jews recall all the major catastrophes in their history. As time passed, however, the prayer spread throughout medieval Ashkenaz. Nowadays, Jews whose ancestors hail from all over central and eastern Europe actually recite this prayer on most Sabbaths of the year, even when *Yizkor* is not said, having little or no appreciation of its original purpose. Ironically, most now omit the prayer on the Sabbath before Shavuʿot, because the days before the festival are deemed inappropriate for recalling tragedy, even though it was precisely for that Sabbath that the prayer took shape at the outset. Most Jews have long forgotten what precipitated *Av ha-Raḥamim*; this text evoking the memories of the 1096 persecutions now signifies something else in those communities that recite it.

Echoes of the persecutions and martyrs of the First Crusade have not confined themselves to Jewish religious life, but they have gained a foothold in modern secular Jewish culture as well. Even before mid-twentieth-century Jewish historians linked the martyrdom of Ashkenazic Jews in 1096 to the extermination of European Jewry during the Holocaust,[2] the great Hebrew poet Saul Tchernichowsky (1875–1943) responded both to the pogroms against Jews in Czarist Russia and to the 1893 publication of the Hebrew Crusade chronicles with his epic "Baruch of Mainz."[3] Clearly evoking the character of Isaac the *parnas* of Mainz,[4] Tchernichowsky's Baruch stands at the grave of his recently martyred wife and recounts the trauma of the violence that the crusaders inflicted upon him, his family, and his community in 1096.

The clanging brass's message rang,
    the countryside astounding:
"Down with the Jews!"—from tower to tower
    the dread alarm sounding.
And in the streets the crowds of farmers,
    craftsmen, men on horses,
groans of the dying, children weeping,
    women's pleading voices;
broken vessels, clothes in tatters,
    blood in the mud like water,
shouts that fill the soul with quaking:
    "Beat them! to the slaughter!"

On their cruel, twisted faces,
   living hatred glowing,
waves of anger, seas of wrath,
   aflame and overflowing.
Amidst it all, myself . . . and then—
   the flashing knife unsated;
the thronging mob around me stood,
   eagerly they waited. . . . [5]

Like Isaac, Baruch sacrificed two children in sanctification of God's name.

Our darling children, do you remember—
   those two that now are free?
I liberated both their souls . . .
   Miriam resisted me;
Zipporah, also, nestling close,
   her sister's hurt deploring,
looked upon me with those eyes
   of hers, imploring. . . .[6]

And, like Isaac, Baruch himself survived that fateful day by converting to Christianity, and the resulting guilt drove him to the brink of madness.

I cannot remember now those words
   I uttered in my plight—
But I remember: the cathedral,
   organ's tones and light,
Seas of voices rising, soaring,
   everywhere prevailing—
Sea of song! and impotent
   I stood, my spirits failing—
The gathered priests, the chanting monks,
   the altar's burning ember. . . .
I cried an answer . . . forgotten? No!
   Forever shall I remember!
For then did I damn my people, Israel,
   my mother's breasts, my nurse,
my God . . . and what my father sacred held
   I spat on with a curse.[7]

Reflecting on what had transpired, Baruch proceeded to set fire to the monastery and church where he had taken refuge.

Recalling the fate of *Av ha-Raḥamim*, Tchernichowsky's poem soon found "a central place in the secular liturgy of the Zionist movement,"[8]

perhaps because, as Alan Mintz has noted, it broke away from the typical medieval Jewish resolve to sanctify the name of God in times of crisis and trial. Mintz contrasts Baruch of Mainz and Isaac the *parnas*, avowing Isaac's unmitigated religious commitment while portraying Baruch as one who had no such idealism.

> As more and more of Baruch's behavior is revealed, we realize that his actions are motivated not by religious zeal—though this is their sanction and camouflage—but by a racking conviction of guilt that is inalienably his own. The price of his failure to take responsibility for his actions is exacted from others; a shame too deep to be borne is made to be borne by other lives. The bloodcurdling methods he employs resemble the acts described in the medieval chronicles, but they are not the same, and in this slight but yet telling dissimilarity lies the gathering subversive force of the text. . . . Tchernichowsky's text does not end in apocalypse. . . . The fiery consummation was not all-consuming; the speaking subject survives, survives ingloriously. In that persistence, so unlike the expiatory suicide by fire of the prototype Master Isaac, Baruch emerges as [a] new figure with its own prototypical force: the tainted survivor of modern literature.[9]

This sensitive psychological analysis of Baruch befits Isaac the *parnas* much more than its author intended, even as his treatment of the Tchernichowsky poem espouses the standard approach to the Hebrew Crusade chronicles that we have found in need of correction. I submit that Isaac the *parnas* and the other heroes of *Gezerot Tatnu* considered in this book reveal more complexity and ambivalence than many readers have seen fit to acknowledge. Why should wavering in the face of disaster, or a survivor's "racking conviction of guilt . . . , shame too deep to be borne" in its aftermath comprise options only for modern Jews, but not for medieval ones? Both constitute such natural human reactions to trauma that were they not to find expression in medieval Jewish texts—right alongside the very religious zeal we have long tended to underscore—I believe that one should rightly be astonished.

Simply put, indecisiveness and lack of resolution characterize Jewish reflection on the martyrs of the First Crusade throughout the centuries: among the guilt-ridden survivors of 1096 and their families, for Jews like Tchernichowsky who wished to break out of the ghetto while continuing to "medievalize" contemporary Jewish disaster,[10] and even in the work of the contemporary Israeli writer Amos Oz. To be sure, Oz's novella *'Ad Mavet* (translated as *Crusade*) ostensibly adopts the perspective of a Christian protagonist, as it relates the exploits of a French count who sought to mobilize his band of crusaders against the pernicious Jewish infidel while en route

to Jerusalem in 1096.[11] No doubt unwittingly, however, *'Ad Mavet* captures some of the distinct, enigmatic characteristics of the Hebrew Crusade narratives and their tales of martyrdom and self-sacrifice.

Curiously, Oz's story communicates through the quotation and paraphrase of a chronicle recorded by one of the crusaders in the group, and the reader quickly realizes how difficult it is to distinguish decisively between historical narrative and fiction.[12] The novella's focus centers increasingly on the chronicler's representation of the brooding, obsessive ruminations of the count concerning his quest, such that the historical reality of transpiring events recedes far into the background. Both Jerusalem and the Jew—the goal of the count's expedition and the major impediment to its attainment—emerge as symbolic constructs within the imagination of the count, chronicler, and, by extension, the reader. Their significance loses all connection with their corresponding historical referents. Of the count we read,

He surveyed his men, every single one of them, their expressions and gestures, eating, at play, in sleep, and on horseback. Is there any reason for looking for signs in the sensible sphere? And what is Jewish in a Jew—surely not an outward shape or form but some abstract quality. The contrast does not lie even in the affections of the soul. Simply this: a terrible, malignant presence. Is not this the essence of treachery: to penetrate, to be within, to interfuse, to put out roots, and to flourish in what is most delicate. Like love, like carnal union. There is a Jew in our midst. Perhaps he had divided himself up, and insinuated himself partly here, partly there, so that not a man of us has escaped contagion.[13]

Like our medieval chronicles, Oz's narrative presents Jewish identity as divided, and as somehow present within the company of Christians, at the same time as it resides in actual Jews. Moreover, *'Ad Mavet* questions the ideals, the goals, and the very viability of the self-sacrifice that violent realities of crusading demanded of their participants. As Oz's crusaders' journey wore on, they spiritualized Jerusalem in a manner reminiscent of the Jews of the Rhineland in 1096 no less than Bernard of Clairvaux several decades later. "Jerusalem ceased to be regarded as a destination, as the arena of glorious deeds. A change took place. . . . One man among them began to realize, with the gradual dawning of an inner illumination, that the Jerusalem they were seeking was not a city but the last hope of a guttering vitality."[14] And, in the story's closing sentences, following the death of the French count, we read that his crusaders did not turn homeward;

they had given up all thought of human habitation. Not even toward Jerusalem, which is not a place but disembodied love. Shedding their bodies, they made their

way, growing ever purer, into the heart of the music of the bells and beyond to the choirs of angels and yet farther, leaving behind their loathsome flesh and streaming onward, a jet of whiteness on white canvas, an abstract purpose, a fleeting vapor, perhaps peace.[15]

When I ask my students to help me distinguish categorically between the historical narratives of our Hebrew Crusade chronicle and the fictional chronicle in Oz's '*Ad Mavet*, we typically find it a difficult challenge indeed. For I believe that many a twelfth-century Ashkenazic Jew could have included something astoundingly similar in his tales of the martyrs of 1096. He, too, might well have concluded his ruminations on the traumatizing violence and haunting memories of *kiddush ha-Shem* on a similar note of doubt. Along with much else, there lingered that consuming realization that one could not make complete sense of what had happened, either to the dead or to the living.

Notes

Preface

1. For instance, Zfatman 1993, p. 14.
2. In gematria, the numerical value of *TaTN"U* corresponds to the date of [4]856 *anno mundi*, or 1096 C.E.
3. Robert Chazan has actually authored three such studies: Chazan 1987, 1996, and 2000.
4. Kagan 1988, p. 43.
5. Ibid.
6. Thucydides 1.22, 1:38–41.

Introduction

1. H, pp. 61–62; tr. in Carmi, p. 372. Cf. also Davidson 1970, vol. 1, no. 465, and Levine 1998, pp. 77–79.
2. Modern scholarship has yielded scores of investigations of the persecutions of 1096 in their various dimensions. Helpful starting points in any attempt to navigate this vast literature might include Chazan 1987 and 2000, Hiestand et al. 1996, Grossman 1999, Assis et al. 2000, and Roos 2003.
3. On the motivations and causes underlying the violence, see, among many others, Riley-Smith 1984 and 2002, Chazan 1987, pp. 64ff., Flori 1997, 1999, and 2001, Toch 1999, and Lotter 2000.
4. N/S, p. 1; H, p. 24. Cf. also N/S, p. 47; H, p. 93; and the text of Obadiah the Proselyte adduced by Marcus 2000, p. 95.
5. Guibert 2.5, pp. 246–49; tr. Benton, p. 134.
6. See Brundage 1969, p. 21 and nn. 78–79, Gilchrist 1988, Lotter 1999, and Stow 2001; and the rulings appearing in Linder 1997, esp. pp. 651–54, 660, 676–77.
7. Raymond of Aguilers, *Historia Francorum* 17, *RHC* 3:280; tr. in Raymond/Hill, p. 95. On the linkage between papal calls for armed expeditions against enemies of the church and anti-Jewish violence, see also Flori 2001, pp. 302ff.
8. See Cohen 1995 and 1999c, pp. 233ff., and the additional references cited therein.
9. Peter, *Letters*, 1:327–30. I have analyzed Peter's letter and his view of the Jews as seen through the prism of crusading in Cohen 1999c, pp. 246ff.

10. Peter, Sermons, p. 252; Cohen 1999c, pp. 250ff. On the importance of the Holy Sepulcher in the Crusades, see also Schein 1996.

11. Albert of Aachen, *Historia hierosolymitana* 1.28, *RHC* 4:293.

12. See the sources collected and discussed in Aronius 1902, pp. 93ff; Dinur 1958–72, vol. 2, 1:42–45, Lotter 1999, and Stow 2001. Cf. also Moore 1992, p. 36 and n. 16.

13. On Trier, see Chazan 1997 and E. Haverkamp 1999; on Regensburg, Hacker 1966, pp. 229–31.

14. See the opposing arguments of Malkiel 2001a, suggesting that the Jews' attackers sought above all to kill them and that the Hebrew martyrologists highlighted the choice between baptism and death so as to render their martyrdom more idealistic and praiseworthy. While theoretically possible and highly interesting, Malkiel's thesis remains unproven and strikes me as implausible.

15. N/S, p. 1; H, p. 24.

16. N/S, p. 18; H, p. 44. Throughout this book, quotations from the Hebrew Bible generally follow the new translation of the Jewish Publication Society, and quotations from the New Testament generally follow the Revised Standard Version.

17. Cf. the interesting comments of Yuval 2000b, pp. 188ff.

18. Albert of Aachen, *Historia hierosolymitana* 1.27, *RHC* 4:293; tr. Peters 1971, p. 103.

19. See the discussion that has ensued among Cohen 1967, Gross 1994, Grossman 1998, Yuval 2000b, ch. 3, esp. pp. 109–31, and Ben-Shalom 2001.

20. A list of liturgical poems on the persecutions of 1096 appears in David 2000, pp. 197–98; helpful discussions of these poetic laments include Mintz 1984, pp. 90ff., Levine 1998, pp. 72–85, Hollender 1996, and Einbinder 2002. See also below, at n. 25.

21. The texts of the chronicles now appear in N/S and H; a critical edition by Eva Haverkamp should soon be in print. English translations appear in Eidelberg 1977 and in Chazan 1987.

22. Pertinent references appear in the notes to Chapter 2, below.

23. See, among others: Sonne 1933, Sonne 1947, Baer 1953, Abulafia 1982, Chazan 1998, and Chazan 2000.

24. See, for example, Ben-Sasson 1984.

25. Yerushalmi 1982, pp. 38, 42–43.

26. Funkenstein 1993, pp. 10ff.

Chapter 1. To Sanctify the Name of God

1. N/S, pp. 7–8; H, pp. 32.

2. Proponents of such ideas include: Baer 1953, Katz 1961, ch. 7, Cohen 1967, Soloveitchik 1987, Grossman 1992, 1998, and 1999, Yuval 1993, Marcus 1992, Goldin 1997 and 2002, and Ta-Shma 2000 and 2003 (esp. p. 173 and n. 16). Cf. also the additional references cited above in nn. 2–3 to the Introduction.

3. See Baer 1953, Katz 1960, pp. 318ff., and 1961, ch. 7, Marcus 1982 and 2000, and Chazan 1987, ch. 4.

4. To date, see Van Henten 1989, Van Henten and Avemarie 2002, Gafni and Ravitzky 1992, and Goldin 2002—to which the reader may profitably refer as the ensuing discussion progresses—as well as additional references cited below.

5. *OTP* 2:562. On ancient Jewish matryrdom, see Van Henten 1997, with additional bibliography, Goldstein 1989, Droge and Tabor 1992, and Shepkaru 1999—in addition to the works cited in the previous note.

6. Philo, *De legatione* 233–35, 10:122–23.

7. Josephus, *Bellum iudaicum* 7.386–87, 3:612–13. See also the instructive essay of Stern 1982.

8. Josephus, *Bellum indaicum* 3.141–391, 2:618–87. Cf. however, *Contra Apionem* 2.233–34, 1:386–87, where Josephus lauds the Jews for their willingness to die on behalf of their law.

9. Both *aggadot* appear in TB *Gittin* 57ab and parallels. On the mother and her seven sons, see also the notes to our discussion of Rachel of Mainz below, Chapter 6.

10. Reeg 1985; Stern and Mirsky 1990, ch. 7. Among the pertinent scholarly discussions of this tradition, see Marcus 1992, pp. 101ff., and Shepkaru 1999, pp. 21ff.

11. Tosefta *Shabbat* 15(16).17, 2:74–75.

12. TB *Sanhedrin* 74ab; TJ *Sanhedrin* 3.6, p. 21b, and *Shevi'it* 4.2, p. 35ab.

13. TB *'Avodah Zarah* 18a.

14. See Reines 1960 and 1963, Goldstein 1989; Droge and Tabor 1992, and Murray 1998–2000, 2:513–23.

15. In addition to the studies already cited, see Luz 1968, Gruenwald 1968, Herr 1972, Safrai 1980, Oppenheimer 1992, Schweid 1994 and Goldin 2002, ch. 3.

16. *Sifra*, "Aḥare Mot," parsh. 9.14; see also "Emor," ch. 9.4.

17. TB *Pesaḥim* 53b and parallels.

18. *Genesis Rabbah* 34.13–14, pp. 324–25, and parallels.

19. *She'iltot* 42, 3:40–48.

20. See the sources reviewed in Grossman 1992, pp. 105–19, with extensive annotation; and cf. also Ta-Shma 2000.

21. See also Yuval 1994, pp. 386ff. with notes, and Goodblatt 1995.

22. *Josippon* 1:310–11, 320–21, 423–31; and see Bowman 1995, pp. 32–36, and Grossman 1999, pp. 81–83.

23. Mann 1972, 1:23–27; and cf. Grossman 1992, pp. 109–11.

24. See H, pp. 19–21; and cf. the various analyses of Chazan 1970, Stow 1984, and Landes 1996, who surveys the pertinent Christian source material as well.

25. Moses Maimonides, *Mishneh Torah*, "Yesode ha-Torah" 5.1–4.

26. Tosafot, *'Avodah Zarah* 27b, d.h. "Yakhol," which misquotes the passage from TJ *Shevi'it* cited above, n. 12. Most recently, see Kanarfogel 2003, pp. 201–16.

27. Tosafot, *'Avodah Zarah* 18a, d.h. "Ve-'al yeḥabbel 'atzmo"; *Gittin* 57b, d.h. "Ve-kafetzu."

28. Gellis, 1:262–63.

29. Interesting contemporary halakhic discussions of the commandment to

sanctify God's name and its applications include the articles appearing in *Torah shebbe-'al Peh* 14 (1971) and Rosenberg 1984.

30. See M. R. Cohen 1994, pp. 174–77, Grossman 1998, and above, Introduction, n. 19.

31. Among others, see Lieberman 1939–44, Frend 1965, ch. 2, Yuval 1994, 1998, and 2000b, esp. chs. 1–2, Boyarin 1999, Marcus 2000, and Goldin 2002, ch. 2.

32. Among many others see Malone 1950, Frend 1965, Horbury and McNeil 1981, Seeley 1990, Droge and Tabor 1992, Wood 1993, Bowersock 1995, and Lamberigts and Van Deun 1995.

33. See also Brown 1978, ch. 2, and Perkins 1995. More recently, see also the most thoughtful discussion in Straw 2000.

34. Tertullian, *Apologeticum* 50.1–4, CCSL 1:169; tr. FC 10:123.

35. See, for instance, Musurillo, pp. 26–29, and Eusebius, 6.41.7, 8.14.17, 2:102–3, 310–11.

36. De Ste. Croix 1963, esp. pp. 21ff.; Perkins 1995; Bowersock 1995, pp. 59–74.

37. Clement of Alexandria, *Stromata* 4.4, GCS 15:254–57, tr. ANF 2:412.

38. Cyprian of Carthage, *Epistolae* 81.1.4, CSEL 3,2:842; tr. ACW 47:106.

39. Cited in De Ste. Croix 1954, p. 83 and n. 41.

40. Augustine of Hippo, *Contra Gaudentium* 1.6.7, 1.30.34, 1.37.49, CSEL 53:204, 232, 248; Droge and Tabor 1992.

41. See below, Chapter 3, nn. 28–29.

42. *Sefer Ḥasidim* 1350, p. 375. See my previous discussion of this text in Cohen 1999a, p. 455.

43. Droge and Tabor 1992, p. 4.

44. See Bowersock 1995, p. 62.

45. Eulogius of Toledo, *Memorialis sanctorum*, PL 115; Paulus Alvarus of Cordoba, *Indiculus luminosus*, PL 121.

46. See the helpful studies of Franke 1958, Waltz 1970, Daniel 1979, ch. 2, Wolf 1988, ch. 8, Nelson 1993, and Coope 1995;

47. Paulus Alvarus, *Indiculus luminosus* 3–6, PL 121:517–20.

48. Eulogius, *Memorialis sanctorum* 1.21, PL 115:754.

49. Ibid., 1.18, col. 751.

50. Erdmann 1977.

51. Baer 1937, esp. pp. 3–4; and cf. below, Chapter 2.

52. An instructive array of responses to Erdmann might include Rousset 1955, Brundage 1969, Blake 1970, Robinson 1973 and 1990, Cowdrey 1976, Gilchrist 1985, France 1996, and Schein 1996. On the Cluniac connection in particular, see Cowdrey 1970a, Delaruelle 1973, Rosenwein 1982, Richter 1992, and Flori 1999 and 2001. See also the references in the following notes.

53. See Cowdrey 1970b and 1985, Morris 1978 and 1993, Riley-Smith 1986, McGinn 1989, Flori 1991b, Cole 1991, pp. 1–36, and Tyerman 1998.

54. Riley-Smith 1980.

55. Riley-Smith 1986 (quotation on p. 2); cf. also Malone 1950, Cowdrey 1985, p. 50, and Cole 1998, pp. 9–10.

56. Flori 1991a.

57. Shepkaru 1999, p. 43.

Chapter 2. The First Crusade and Its Historians

Earlier versions of portions of this chapter appear in Cohen 2000 and Cohen 2001.

1. See Kedar 1998a, as well as Mayer et al. 1989, p. 653, and Murray 1998, pp. 284, 303–4.

2. See Lotter 1988, among others. On the disproportionate appraisal of *Gezerot Tatnu*, see also Soloveitchik 1998.

3. N/S, p. 8; H, p. 32.

4. See, for example, Schwarzfuchs 1989, Cohen 1989, Grossman 1992, pp. 100–105, and Malkiel 2003.

5. Ben-Sasson 1976, p. 414.

6. Roth 1969 (1st ed. 1936), p. 185.

7. Geary 1994.

8. Schwarzfuchs 1989, pp. 266–67. See also Myers 1999.

9. Graetz 1861, ch. 4; Güdemann 1880–88, 1:127ff.; Dubnow 1925–30, 4:271ff.

10. Güdemann 1880–88, 1:127–28.

11. See above, n. 4.

12. Baron 1952–83, 4:89ff.

13. Painter 1953, p. 219.

14. Baer 1947, p. 122.

15. Baer 1937, pp. 3ff.; and see above, Chapter 1.

16. See also Katz 1961, pts. 1–2, and Ben-Sasson 1984, pp. 342–49.

17. Baer 1953.

18. Katz 1961, p. 90.

19. Baer 1953, p. 126.

20. Dinur, vol. 2, pt. 1, p. 4.

21. Ben-Sasson 1976, p. 414.

22. Chazan 1987, 1996, and 2000; and Goldin 2002.

23. *Zion* 59, nos. 2–3 (1994); Hiestand et al. 1996; *Jewish History* 13, no. 2 (1999); A. Haverkamp 1999; Assis et al. 2000; Signer and Van Engen 2001.

24. Myers 1995; see also Kepnes 1996.

25. Chazan 1987 and 1991; Grossman 1992. Cf. Breuer 1994, Fleischer 1994, Gross 2000, and Ta-Shma 2000. See also the more nuanced and compelling presentation of E. Haverkamp 1999.

26. Sonne 1933 and 1947, p. 76.

27. Marcus 1982, esp. p. 42 (now with the added proviso in Marcus 2002, p. 506 n. 45).

28. See, for example, J. Cohen 1994 and 1999b, Yuval 1999, and Marcus 1995 and 2002 (which, with additional references and bibliography, affords the persecutions of 1096 center stage in its exposition of the "Jewish-Christian symbiosis" at the heart of Jewish culture in medieval Ashkenaz).

29. Yuval 1993. For an overview of the Yuval thesis—its background, its issues, the debate that it provoked—see Walz 1999.

30. Breuer 1994; Fleischer 1994.

31. Yuval 1994, pp. 352, 395–96, 402.
32. Minty 1994; Patterson 2001.
33. Marcus 2000. Cf. the approach to medieval Jewish martyrological poetry developed in Einbinder 2002.
34. Alsop 1971 and 1973.
35. Ben-Yehuda 1995, pp. 294–95.
36. Zerubavel 1995, p. 19; cf. also the interesting analysis of Lipsker 2000.
37. The acts of self-inflicted martyrdom at Masada continue to captivate the Israeli imagination; over the course of less than three weeks in November 2002, nine articles and letters on the subject appeared in the Israeli daily newspaper *Ha'aretz*.
38. Among others, see, for example, Alter 1973 and Kedar 1982.
39. Baer 1953, p. 140.
40. See above, Introduction.
41. Chazan 1987, quotations on pp. 45–46.
42. Chazan 1991, p. 45.
43. Chazan 1994, p. 24.
44. Marcus 1989; but see the more moderated stance in Marcus 1999.
45. See Ibn Daud.
46. Bonfil 1987, 1989, and 1993.
47. Marcus 1990, p. 367.
48. Bonfil 1993, p. 246.
49. Marcus 1990, pp. 366–67.
50. See below, Afterword.
51. Yassif 1999a, esp. pp. 297–98; see also Lipsker 2000, pp. 443–44.
52. LaCapra 1983, ch. 1.
53. White 1981b, p. 2.
54. Ibid., p. 11.
55. Ibid., pp. 16–18.
56. Ibid., p. 13.
57. Ibid., p. 23; see also the additional comments in White 1981a.
58. Coleman 1992, p. 37.
59. Ibid., p. 155.
60. Ibid., pp. 269, 286.
61. Ibid., ch. 14 (quotations on pp. 276, 286).
62. Morrison 1990, p. 79.
63. Ibid., p. 90.
64. Ibid., p. 25.

Chapter 3. Points of Departure

1. See my earlier presentation of these ideas in J. Cohen 1994 and 1999c.
2. Spiegel 1990, p. 84.
3. See, for instance, the thought-provoking studies of Marcus 1996 and Yuval 2000b.

4. Culler 1981, p. 103; Yassif 1998, p. 304.

5. Weiner and Weiner 1990, p. 15.

6. Perkins 1995, p. 12; cf. also Fishbane 1994.

7. See above, Chapter 1, n. 55.

8. See the citations above, Introduction, n. 12.

9. N/S, p. 29; H, p. 57.

10. See Katz 1961, ch. 7, Ben-Sasson 1984, pp. 393ff., Grossman 1992, and Goldin 1997.

11. La Capra 1983, p. 42.

12. Above all, see Yuval 1993.

13. Cf. the similar conclusions of Marcus 2002, p. 467 and elsewhere.

14. See the studies and opinions surveyed in Chazan 2000, pp. 217–21.

15. Bernard, *Epistulae* 363, 8:311–17; and see Cohen 1995.

16. N/S, pp. 1, 36; H, pp. 24, 72.

17. N/S, p. 14; H, p. 40.

18. N/S, p. 17; H, p. 43.

19. N/S, p. 8; H, p. 32.

20. Yuval 2000b, chs. 2, 5.

21. N/S, p. 6; H, p. 29.

22. N/S, p. 12; H, p. 37.

23. Bernard, *Epistulae* 64, 7:157–58. Cf. Galatians 4:25–26; and see also Renna 1992, pp. 80ff.

24. N/S, p. 7; H, p. 31.

25. N/S, p. 6; H, p. 30.

26. N/S, p. 4; H, p. 28; and cf. Marcus 1992.

27. N/S, p. 7; H, p. 30; and see Shepkaru 1999 and 2002b.

28. Among others, see Hall 1993, Hinson 1993, Jones 1993, Perkins 1995, and Cooper 1998.

29. See Noble 1971, and, more recently, Gershenzon and Litman 1995, Einbinder 2000, Breuer 2000, Grossman 2001, ch. 9, and Goldin 2002, pp. 118–23, all with additional helpful bibliography. For an assessment of the historiography, see Malkiel 2002.

30. N/S, p. 3; H, p. 27; and see Cohen 1983 and Watt 1999, esp. pp. 56–68.

31. N/S, p. 17; H, p. 43. On the chronicles' attitude toward Christian beliefs and symbols, see Abulafia 1985, Yuval 1999 and 2000a, and Horowitz 2000.

32. On Jewish-Christian competition over the true Passover, see also Yuval 1995.

33. See, for instance, the claim of the second-century church father Melito, pp. 74–75, that "Christ suffered, whereas Isaac did not suffer."

34. N/S, p. 8; H, p. 32. See Spiegel 1967, esp. ch. 10; and, on late ancient Jewish and Christian interpretations of the binding of Isaac, Vermes 1973, pp. 193–227, Daly 1977, Davies and Chilton 1978, Gutmann 1987, Agus 1988, Levenson 1993, and Noort and Tigchelaar 2002. Cf. also the discussion of the darkening of the daytime skies at the moment of Jesus' crucifixion in Crossan 1995, pp. 1–4.

35. Pelikan 1971–89, 3, ch. 5; Little 1978, ch. 3; Langmuir 1990, chs. 5, 8, 11; Abulafia 1995; Marcus 1995, esp. pp. 209–17; and Cohen 1999a.

36. *Kinot*, pp. 118–19; Davidson 1970, vol. 1, no. 288; tr. Rosenfeld, pp. 148–49.

37. For example: Deuteronomy 32:5, 2 Samuel 22:27, Isaiah 59:8, Psalm 101:4, *Mid. Tehillim* 101.2, p. 214a, and *Mid. Mishle* 28.1 (MS variant), p. 177.

38. H, p. 62; tr. Carmi 1981, p. 373.

39. Gellis, 1:262.

40. Meir b. Baruch, pp. 346–47; and see Goldin 2002, pp. 228ff.

41. See below, ch. 5.

42. N/S, p. 11; H, pp. 35–36.

43. Eidelberg 1977, p. 38; and cf. N/S, p. 104, and Chazan 1987, p. 261.

44. On the proverbial, problematic story of Amnon's martyrdom, see Marcus 1992, Yuval 1998, Yassif 1999b, pp. 192–200, and Fraenkel 2002.

45. N/S, p. 24; H, p. 51. See the recent thoughtful discussion in Shepkaru 2002a.

46. N/S, p. 14; H, p. 39.

47. Herman 1992, p. 7.

48. Ibid., p. 68.

49. Ibid., pp. 70, p. 181. On trauma, collective memory, and narrative accounts of past events, see also Agger and Jensen 1990, Kirmayer 1996, Caruth 1996, and Baumeister and Hastings 1997. I am grateful to Zahava Solomon for her suggestions in this regard.

Chapter 4. Last Supper at Xanten

1. N/S, p. 42; H, p. 78.

2. N/S, pp. 21–22; H, pp. 48–49.

3. See above, Chapter 2, n. 14.

4. For example, Chazan 1987, pp. 124–26; Chazan 2000, pp. 96–98, and Goldin 2002, pp. 112ff., 151ff.

5. H, p. 48, "corrects" the date in the sole manuscript, reading "on the fourth of the month."

6. N/S, pp. 17ff., 40ff.; H, pp. 43ff., 76ff.

7. N/S, p. 23; H, p. 50.

8. See Katz 1970 and the comments of Yuval 2000a, pp. 102–3.

9. Mishnah, *Tamid* 7.4; TB *Rosh ha-Shanah* 31a; and parallels. On an interesting similar tradition in medieval Christianity, see Lerner 1992, with ample references and bibliography.

10. *ARN* A, 1, p. 3a.

11. See the comments of Rashi on Exodus 31:15: "*margo'a*, as opposed to temporary rest." See also Judah, *Diwan*, 1:92, and Ibn Ezra, 2:38.

12. *Ruth Rabbah* 3.3, 2:86–89.

13. TB *Sanhedrin* 97a.

14. Cf. the illuminating studies of Lerner 1985 and 1992.

15. *Numbers Rabbah* 2.23.

16. *Mid. Zuta*, Kohelet 7.8, p. 68a.

17. TB *Sanhedrin* 111a; *Exodus Rabbah* 6.4, p. 188; *Tanḥuma*, "Va-Era" 1.1. And cf. *Mid. Tehillim* 114.3, p. 236a.

18. TB *Shabbat* 32a.

19. For example, TB *'Avodah Zarah* 35b; *Mekhilta*, "Beshalaḥ-Shira" 3, p. 127; *Mekh. Rashbi* 15.2, p. 60; *Sifre* Deut. 343, p. 399.

20. *Lam. Rabbah* 1, p. 41b; cf. TB *Gittin* 57b.

21. *Song Rabbah* 1.22, 7.2, pp. 23, 151–52.

22. TB *Rosh ha-Shanah* 16b–17a.

23. Smolar and Aberbach 1968; Mandelbaum 1990; Waldman 1998.

24. TB *Ta'anit* 31a.

25. *Mid. Tehillim* 119.17, p. 248a.

26. TB *Pesaḥim* 113b.

27. *Mid. Tehillim* 14.3, p. 56b.

28. See below at nn. 40–41.

29. See TB *Gittin* 59b; I am grateful to my son Rafi for directing me to this passage.

30. *Lev. Rabbah* 25.6, 3:580; cf. Petuchowski 1957.

31. *Mid. Tehillim* 9.17, p. 46a.

32. *Mid. Tehillim* 22.7, p. 92b.

33. TB *Berakhot* 63a.

34. TB *Berakhot* 63a, *Temurah* 14b, *Gittin* 60a—with Rashi's comments ad loc.

35. On the status of the martyrs' suicidal deaths in rabbinic law, see esp. Soloveitchik 1987, Grossman 1992, and Ta-Shma 2000.

36. Rashi's commentary on Psalm 119:162.

37. TB *Berakhot* 34b, *Sanhedrin* 99a.

38. TB *Shabbat* 88b–89a.

39. See Katz 1961, ch. 7, and Abulafia 1985.

40. Cf. Mark 15:33, Matthew 27:45, Luke 23:44.

41. Hebrews 5–7; and see Petuchowski 1957, Horton 1976, Fitzmyer 2000, and Rooke 2000.

42. Riley-Smith 1986, pp. 2, 151; and see the references cited above, Chapter 1, nn. 52ff.

43. At n. 23.

44. Leclercq 1946, pp. 82–90, 1948, p. 207, 1952, and 1974, pp. 60–67. On Jewish notions of the Sabbath as a substitute for the temple cult, cf. Green 1980 and Ginsburg 1989, esp. pp. 62ff.

45. Romans 8:35–36.

46. Hermann, pp. 91–92; tr. Morrison 1992, p. 90. On Hermann, his conversion, and its setting against the background of the 1096 persecutions and their memories, see Cohen 1999c, ch. 7.

47. *Midrash Tanḥuma*, "Tetzaveh" 5.

48. *Song Rabbah* 1.63, p. 48. On the theme of atonement for the sins of the nations of the world in the polemical responses of Ashkenazic Jews to crusading ideology, see Rembaum 1982, pp. 294ff.

Chapter 5. Master Isaac the Parnas

1. See below, n. 6.

2. See Kedar 1998b, Lotter 1999, Stow 2001, and, most recently, Friedman 2002, p. 27.

3. N/S, p. 40; H, p. 75, biblical citation in Psalm 50:23.

4. Cf. the report of the Solomon bar Samson chronicle below (line 49) that Isaac had a son and a daughter; cf. also Saul Tchernichowsky's "Baruch of Mainz," quoted below in the Afterword.

5. N/S, pp. 11–13; H, pp. 36–38.

6. Chazan 1987, p. 105, Yuval 1993, pp. 68–69, and 1994, pp. 386–91, 409–11, and Fleischer 1994, pp. 297ff. See also Goldin 2002, pp. 126–27.

7. Yet see the fascinating discussion of this theme in Levenson 1993, as well as the other works cited above, Chapter 3, n. 31.

8. For example, the commentaries of Rashi and Rabbi David Kimchi (Radak) ad loc. See also the curiously similar report of events that transpired "one year beforehand"—within a discussion of the destruction of Jerusalem, the priests of the temple, and the festival of Shavu'ot in the month of Sivan—related in *Josippon* 1:413–14, and cited by Yuval 1994, p. 389 n. 94.

9. Morrison 1990, p. 90.

10. N/S, p. 13; H, p. 38.

11. On the night of the Jewish Pentecost and its customary vigil—*tikkun lel Shavu'ot*—see Wilhelm 1948–52, pp. 125–30, Liebes 1993, pp. 55–63, 74–82, Halamish 1993, and Bar-Ilan 1996.

12. While women martyrs assume prominence in the narratives of the 1096 persecutions, early Jewish sources present their valor as surpassing that of the men less than the acts of the early Christian martyrs tended to do. See Breuer 2000 and Einbinder 2000 on Jewish women martyrs; and, on Christian martyrological tradition, Hall 1993, Jones 1993, Hinson 1993, and Shaw 1996, among others.

13. See the Nürnberg *Memorbuch*, p. 6, which mentions a woman named Skolaster killed in 1096 in the massacre in Worms. In n. 29, however, the editor cites two manuscripts that identify her as the wife of R. Isaac—evidently the same woman, whom conflicting Jewish memories of the Crusade massacres placed in two different Rhineland communities.

14. TB, *Sotah* 10b.

15. See also *PDRE* 25, 9:166, where Lot's wife is "overcome with compassion" for her married daughters living in Sodom; she turned around to ascertain if they, in fact, followed her; and *Midrash Tanḥuma*, "Tzav" 13, where God is "overcome with compassion" for the bound Isaac.

16. *Midrash Tanḥuma*, "Va-Yeḥi" 3.

17. *Pesikta Rab.* 31, p. 182b.

18. On the importance of this motif in Isaac's story, and its eschatological overtones in particular, see the illuminating comments of Yuval 1994, pp. 389–91; and Flusser in *Josippon* 1:301 with n. 26.

19. At n. 11 above.

20. On the patristic and medieval Christian Pentecost, its liturgy, and evidence of its nocturnal vigils, see the descriptions and sources gathered in Kretschmar 1954–55, esp. pp. 238ff., Van Dijk and Walker 1960, pp. 512–14, Van Dijk 1963, 2:256–58, Pascher 1963, pp. 234–39, Cabié 1965, esp. pp. 118, 218–20, and Gunstone 1967.

21. *Genesis Rabbah* 83.1, pp. 996–97. Cf. the depiction of a ship's mast in a nearly contemporary work of ivory from the Rhineland in Goldschmidt 1972–75, 1:48, fig. 231.

22. Einbinder 2001, p. 223.

23. Ad loc.

24. See *Numbers Rabbah* 8.3.

25. TB *Sanhedrin* 43a.

26. Seeley 1990; Droge and Tabor 1992. Cf. also Bowersock 1995.

27. *Pesikta Rab.* 26, p. 131a. Cf. TJ *Shekalim* 50a; TB *Ta'anit* 29a; *ARN* A, 4, p. 12b; *Lev. Rabbah* 19.6, 2:436–37; and see also Goodblatt 1995, as well as the citation in the following note.

28. Yuval 1994, pp. 386–91, 409–11 (quotation on 411).

29. Roskies 1989, esp. p. 46.

Chapter 6. Mistress Rachel of Mainz

1. Marcus 1982; see also Bonfil 1987, 1989, and 1993.

2. *Poetics* 9.1–3, pp. 58–59.

3. N/S, pp. 54–55; H, pp. 101–2.

4. Following Marcus 1999, pp. 40–41.

5. See, for example, ibid., pp. 41–44, Gross 2000, pp. 187–91, and Chazan 2000, pp. 166ff., 183f.

6. N/S, pp. 9–10; H, p. 34.

7. Rosenfeld, pp. 140–41—with modifications of the English translation; cf. Davidson 1970, vol. 1, no. 5971.

8. See the references in n. 5 above, along with Sonne 1933 and 1947, Baer 1953, and Abulafia 1982. See also the reading of the story proposed in Malkiel 2001b.

9. On Jacob's curse and its ramifications, see the insightful reading of Tucker 1994.

10. See Sarason 1988.

11. See below, n. 44.

12. Sered 1986, p. 16.

13. Sered 1991, p. 139; and cf. also Sered 1989, 1995, and 1996.

14. See the helpful studies of Callaway 1986 and Brown-Gutoff 1991.

15. *Mid. Shemu'el* 6, p. 33a.

16. TB *Rosh ha-Shanah* 10b.

17. *Genesis Rabbah* 71.2, pp. 823–24.

18. On such fourfold groupings, see Kasher 1927–92, 9/10:107–16, Daube 1956, ch. 8, and Eismeijer 1978.

19. See Goldschmidt 1969, pp. 22ff., Francis 1974, and Shemesh 1998.

20. N/S, p. 9 (with n. d), where *takhosu* is corrected to read *taḥusu*.

21. See Tucker 1994, Sarason 1988, and n. 44 below.

22. *Lam. Rabbah*, prol. 24, p. 28; see the insightful discussion of this midrash in Hasan-Rokem 2000, pp. 125–29, and cf. also Doniger 2000, esp. pp. 160–67.

23. The biblical description of Esau's cry (*tze'akah gedolah u-marah*) inspired that of Mordecai's lament over the Jews' seemingly imminent destruction at the hands of Haman (Esther 4:1: *ze'akah gedolah u-marah*); according to *Genesis Rabbah* 64.4, pp. 757–58, only then, in the Persian capital of Susa, did the descendants of Esau obtain their revenge from the descendants of Jacob for the grief of their progenitor.

24. *Genesis Rabbah* 76.6, p. 904; *Lev. Rabbah* 27.1, 3:644.

25. *Ruth Rabbah* 6, 2:168–71.

26. On the contest between Jews and Christians over the typological identification of Jacob and Esau, see Cohen 1991, pp. 243–70, and Hadas-Lebel 1984.

27. On the story, its origins, and development, see Gutman 1949, Doran 1980, Cohen 1991, pp. 39–60, Young 1991, Schweid 1994, pp. 25–26, and Hasan-Rokem 2000, pp. 114–25.

28. *Lam. Rabbah* 1, pp. 42b–43a. For other versions see 2 Maccabees 7; 4 Maccabees; TB *Gittin* 57b; *Eliyahu Rabbah* 28, pp. 150–51; *Josippon*, 1:70–75, 2:276.

29. *Lam. Rabbah*, 1, pp. 42b–43a; *Eliyahu Rabbah* 28, pp. 150–51; *Pesikta Rab.* 43, p. 180; cf. also *Josippon*, 1:70, with note.

30. Similarly missing in Rachel's story is the mother of seven's declaration, "I shall rejoice with you as on your wedding day" that we find in *Josippon*, 1:74, with note.

31. For general background, see the still useful study of Plumpe 1943.

32. On the motif of Synagoga and Ecclesia, see Schlauch 1939, Blumenkranz 1966, pp. 50–70, passim, Seiferth 1970, and Schreckenberg 1996, ch. 3.

33. Cf. the similarly suggestive image of capturing the blood of the paschal lamb—it too is fraught with overtones of Jewish-Christian animosities and shared cultural traditions—in Malkiel 1993, p. 93, with pl. 9.

34. Eidelberg, pp. 35, 151 n. 91.

35. Works discussing these exegetical tendencies abound. Among numerous others, see the foundational studies of Daniélou 1950 and De Lubac 1998–2000, chs. 5, 8; and, most recently, see the various studies collected in Saebo et al. 1996–2000. With specific regard to Jewish-Christian polemics, see also also Ruether 1974, ch. 3, esp. pp. 131–37, and Dahan 1990, pp. 386–405

36. For example, see Hilary of Poitiers, *Commentarius in Evangelium Matthaei* 1.7, PL 9:923; Gregory the Great, *Moralia in Iob* 30.25.72, CCSL 143B:1540; Paschasius Radbertus, *In Matthaeum*, on 2:17, CCCM 56:175–76; Pseudo-Bede, *In Matthaei evangelium expositio*, PL 92:14; Rupert of Deutz, *Super Matthaeum* 2, CCCM 29:46–47; and *Bible mor. 2554*, pl. 6v, p. 60.

37. Rabanus Maurus, *In II Machabaeorum* 7, PL 109:1236; *Glossa* 4:469r. See also Abel 1949, pp. 381–84.

38. Bernard of Clairvaux, *Epistolae* 98, 7:249–53. On the prominence of the persecution of Judaism at the time of the Maccabees in twelfth-century Christian

liturgy, see also Linder 1995, and, on the Christian cult of the Maccabean martyrs, Vinson 1994.

39. Van Henten 2000.

40. Cf. Deuteronomy 32:25, Isaiah 23:4, 62:5; Jeremiah 51:22, Ezekiel 9:6, Zachariah 9:17, Psalm 148:12, Lamentations 1:18, 2:21, 2 Chronicles 36:17.

41. Ivan Marcus has correctly insisted to me that the phrase can simply denote a young married woman, as it does repeatedly the Nürnberg *Memorbuch*. Yet in the Hebrew Crusade chronicles I have found such usage only here, and the other indicators of similarity to the Virgin Mary seem to bolster at least the plausibility of such a reading.

42. On the importance of the "father-ineffective family" for the cult of the Virgin Mary, see Carroll 1986, esp. pp. 49–61, 83–84; and, on virgin martyrs in general, Winstead 1997, esp. introduction, ch. 1.

43. See Déaut 1963, ch. 3, Davies 1979, and above, Chapter 3.

44. See Beissel 1909, Warner 1976, esp. ch. 14, "Mater Dolorosa," and Pelikan 1996. On the "Marian" consciousness of the Hebrew Crusade chronicles, cf. the interesting comments in Marcus 2002, pp. 469ff.

45. See Pinder 1922, Gold 1985, ch. 2, and Klack-Eitzen 1985. In Jerome, *Epistolae* 108.10, CSEL 55:316, Jerome's friend and correspondent Paula explicitly linked these two holy sites in Bethlehem; I am grateful to Ora Limor for her reference to this source.

46. Heimann 1959. See also Swarzenski 1935 and Schäfer 1980; and cf. Barasch 1976, pp. 64f., 80.

47. For example: Jerphanion 1925, p. 273, pl. 66(2); Demus 1970, p. 432, pl. 189; Pelekanidis et al. 1974–75, v. 2, pl. 393.

48. Among others. see Hilary of Poitiers, *Commentarius in Evangelium Matthaei* 1.7, PL 9:923; Jerome, *In Hieremiam* 6.18–19, CCSL 74:306–8, *In Matthaeum* 2.18, CCSL 77:15; Rabanus Maurus, *Commentaria in Matthaeum* 2.3, PL 107:763; Paschasius Radbertus, *In Matthaeum*, on 2:17, CCCM 56:177; and the thirteenth-century French *Bible moralisée*, cited above, n. 36, and discussed in Lipton 1999, p. 59, with notes. See also the interesting discussion in Armstrong 1993, pp. 75–85.

49. See Young 1919 and 1933, 2:102–24, Dudley 1994, and Patterson 2001, pp. 534, 556 n. 112 (with additional references).

50. See above, nn. 35–36, 45.

51. In an unpublished seminar paper on "Ma'aseh Raḥel" (1992), my student Yuval Frankel ventured to suggest that the chronicles mention that Rachel's grandfather was named Asher might link her to the children of the biblical Asher, among whom numbered Yish*v*ah and Yish*v*i (Genesis 46:17), and thus to Jesus/Yesh*u*, all of whom shared the same three letters of their Hebrew names.

52. Marcus 1999, pp. 40–41.

53. The legacy of this exegetical competition in medieval literature is further explored in Adams 1995.

54. Rachel's tale thus undermines the claim of McCracken 2002, pp. 57–58, that medieval narratives of the slaughter of children by their mothers never present such killings as ritualized sacrifices.

Chapter 7. Kalonymos in Limbo

1. For example, see Baer 1953, Grossman 1992, esp. 105ff., and Breuer 1994.
2. N/S, pp. 14–16; H, pp. 40–41. I have discussed the tale of Kalonymos in Cohen 1999a, pp. 436ff., and 1999b, pp. 31ff. See also Shepkaru 2002a, pp. 242ff.
3. N/S, pp. 3, 5–6: H, pp. 26, 29–30.
4. N/S, p. 3; H, p. 26. On Kalonymos's status, see also Grossman 1981, p. 401.
5. See the piyyut *Adabberah be-Tzar Ruḥi*, by an otherwise unknown Rabbi Abraham, which laments over what transpired in Mainz (Davidson 1970, vol. 1, no. 465) in H, p. 61, tr. Carmi, p. 382: "Kalonymus leaped [into battle], and all the others followed."
6. N/S, p. 6; H, p. 30.
7. TB *Yoma* 22b. The importance of Saul's martyrdom in justifying the suicides of 1096 has been discussed in Gross 2000, pp. 198ff.
8. Katz 1961, pp. 34ff.; Urbach 1980, 1:65, 234–35; Grossman 1995, p. 143.
9. Marcus 2000.
10. Here, however, I part company with Marcus 1992, p. 109, who has concluded concerning the massacres of Jews during the First Crusade: "If . . . we read carefully the narratives about 1096, we never find any sign that a Jewish sage or the leaders or members of a Jewish community expressed any doubt about the absolute value of dying rather than thinking about converting and regretting it." See the more extensive discussion of doubt in twelfth-century Ashkenaz in Cohen 1999a, with references to literature on doubt, skepticism, and individualism during the Christian Middle Ages and Renaissance.

Chapter 8. The Rape of Sarit

1. See above, Introduction, n. 18.
2. On the name of the village, see Chazan 1987, pp. 347–48 n. 250; on the problematic dating, see above, Chapter 4, at n. 5.
3. N/S, pp. 20–21; H, pp. 46–47.
4. While extant sources evidently do attest to the contraction of marriages involving child brides in medieval Ashkenaz—see Grossman 2001, ch. 2—the text of the chronicle seems to hint otherwise in the case of Sarit: She appears independently, with no mention of her parents, and the sexual overtones of her slaughter intimate that she had already reached maturity.
5. Einbinder 2001, pp. 226–27. Cf. also Wolfson 2001, pp. 184ff., where the death of Sarit and her fiancé Abraham exemplifies the phenomenon whereby "the eros of martyrdom" is evident in "the unwavering love of a couple who proclaim their everlasting commitment to one another by accepting the fate of death together." Wolfson argues that "the sacrificial death is thus eroticized not only on account of the love the martyrs express for God in their willingness to die, but also because the love of man and woman is fully consummated in their shared death." Although I find Wolfson's thesis on the linkage between *eros* and *thanatos* charac-

teristic of both *kiddush ha-Shem* and pietism in high medieval Ashkenaz generally compelling, my ensuing discussion explains why I cannot accept his reading of this story. In a word, here one finds in those killed neither a willingness to die out of love for God nor any hint of erotic love for one another, but only a horrific act of sexual violence on the part of the killer.

6. Loraux 1987, p. 41.

7. Redfield 1982, pp. 187–201.

8. Du Bourguet 1975; Gager 1992, pp. 97–100.

9. Shaw 1996, p. 304.

10. See also Petruccione 1990, Winstead 1997, and the references cited above, Chapter 3, n. 28.

11. See Schmidt 1881, Westermarck 1921, 1:166–206, and Boureau 1998.

12. Among the Jewish traditions, see Tosefta, *Ketubot* 1.1, 3:56; TJ *Ketubot* 1.5, 25c; TB *Ketubot* 3b; *Genesis Rabbah* 26.5, p. 248 (quoted in the commentaries of Rashi and Rabbi David Kimchi on Genesis 6:2); *Soferim*, add. 1.4, pp. 370–71; Lieberman 1955–88, 6:186–87; the Pentateuchal commentaries of Rabbi Meir ben Baruch of Rothenburg on Genesis 24:16, and the Chizkuni on Genesis 24:53; and Herr 1972, p. 101, n. 56, Patai 1974, Levi 1895, Noam 1994—along with the citations in n. 24 below.

13. See TB *Kiddushin* 72b; *Lam. Rabbah* 1, p. 43a; *Pesikta Rav K.* 43, 1:44; Yuval 2000b, p. 104 n. 13. The phrase appears also in the Mainz Anonymous (N/S, p. 50; H, p. 96), and, as Yitzhak Baer has noted (Baer 1953, p. 148), even the Christian chronicle *Gesta Treverorum*, add. 17, MGH Scriptores 8:190, invokes it in quoting the rationale of Jews who martyred their children in 1096.

14. Baschet 1993, p. 741. See also Rosenthal 1945–46, Ntedika 1971, pp 137–49, Markow 1983, Sheingorn 1987, and, above all, the foundational study of Baschet 2000.

15. *Genesis Rabbah* 44.14ff. (esp. 44.21), pp. 436–44; *Yalkut Shim'oni*, Joshua 15. See also Zakovitch and Shinan 1996, pp. 15–21.

16. *Sifre* Deut. 171, p. 218; *Mid. Tana'im* 18.9, 1:109–10.

17. N/S, p. 21; H, p. 48.

18. *Sifre* Num. 131, pp. 172–73.

19. Ibid.

20. The sources have been amassed and discussed in Mack 1993. On the depiction of Phineas in postbiblical literature, see also Klassen 1986.

21. *Eliyahu Rabbah* 12, pp. 58–59; Mack 1993, p. 129.

22. See Klassen 1986.

23. Cf. also *Josippon* 1:79.

24. *She'iltot* 27, 1, 2:187–88. See also the variant versions in *Bet ha-Midrash* 1:133, 6:2–3, and *Otzar Mid.* 1:192; the piyyutim *Odekha ki anafta* and *Odekha ki 'anitani* in '*Avodat Yisra'el*, pp. 629ff., 636ff. (Davidson 1970, vol. 1, nos. 1651, 1653); and Noam 1994, esp. pp. 438–40. I thank Eyal Poleg for his advice.

25. *Genesis Rabbah* 97.9, p. 1218; and cf. above, n. 18.

26. On the origins and development of this tradition, see Hill 1995; and, on its impact on late medieval German literature and culture, Gow 1995.

27. Adso, *Tractatus de Antichristo*, CCCM 45:23; tr. McGinn, p. 90.

28. On the developing Christian notion of Antichrist, see, among many others, Rauh 1979, Emmerson 1979 and 1981, McGinn 2000, and Flanagan 2000—all with copious bibliography. On Adso's biography of Antichrist, see also Konrad 1964 and Verhelst 1973.

29. McGinn 2000, p. 131. Hildegard's portrayal of Antichrist appears in her *Scivias* 3.11, CCCM 43A:574ff.; see also Emmerson 2002.

30. Gow 1999, esp. p. 7 and fig. 2. I am grateful to Professor Gow for his assistance in this regard.

31. *Mid. Tehillim* 101.2; *Pesikta Rav K.* 1:49–50; and see Ginzberg 1909–38, 6:24 n. 141, 132 n. 776.

32. Einbinder 2000, p. 116. Cf. also Wolfson 2001.

33. Mintz 1984, p. 97.

34. Mishnah, *Avot* 2.4.

Afterword

1. Roskies 1989, pp. 44–45. For the original Hebrew text, see *'Avodat Yisra'el*, p. 233.

2. See above, Chapter 2.

3. Tchernichowsky, pp. 181–208.

4. See our analysis of Isaac's tale above, Chapter 5.

5. Tr. Sholom J. Kahn in Silberschlag 1968, pp. 114–15. Quotations are used by permission of the publisher, Cornell University Press; © Eisig Silderschlag.

6. Ibid., p. 117.

7. Ibid., p. 115.

8. Roskies 1989, pp. 82–83.

9. Mintz 1984, pp. 126, 129.

10. Ibid., p. 123.

11. Oz, *'Ad Mavet*.

12. See above, Chapter 2, at nn. 50.

13. Oz, *Crusade*, p. 30.

14. Ibid., p. 48.

15. Ibid., p. 81.

Bibliography of Secondary Sources

Abel, Felix-Marie. 1949. *Les Livres des Maccabées*. Paris.

Abulafia, Anna Sapir. 1982. "The Interrelationship between the Hebrew Chronicles of the First Crusade." *Journal of Semitic Studies* 27:221–39.

———. 1985. "Invectives against Christianity in the Hebrew Chronicles of the First Crusade." In *Crusade and Settlement*, pp. 66–72. Ed. Peter W. Edbury. Cardiff.

———. 1995. *Christians and Jews in the Twelfth-Century Renaissance*. London.

Adams, Robert. 1995. "Chaucer's 'New Rachel' and the Theological Roots of Medieval Anti-Semitism." *Bulletin of the John Rylands Library* 77:9–18.

Agger, Inger, and Soren Buus Jensen. 1990. "Testimony as Ritual and Evidence in Psychotherapy for Political Refugees." *Journal of Traumatic Stress* 3:115–30.

Agus, Aharon Ronald E. 1988. *The Binding of Isaac and Messiah: Law, Martyrdom, and Deliverance in Early Rabbinic Religiosity*. Albany, N.Y..

Alsop, Stewart. 1971. "The Masada Complex." *Newsweek*, July 12, 1971, p. 92.

———. 1973. "Again, the Masada Complex." *Newsweek*, March 19, 1973, p. 104.

Alter, Robert. 1973. "The Masada Complex." *Commentary* 56(1): 19–24.

Armstrong, Regis J. 1992. "Starting Points: Images of Women in the Letters of Clare." *Collectanea franciscana* 62:63–100.

Assis, Yom Tov, et al., eds. 2000. *Facing the Cross: The Persecutions of 1096 in History and Historiography* (in Hebrew). Jerusalem.

Bach, Dieter, and Hans-Joachim Barkenings, eds. 1996. *1096: Der erste Kreuzzug und die Verfolgung der Juden in deutschen Städten*. Mülheim an der Ruhr.

Baer, Yitzhak. 1937. "The Religious-Social Tendency of 'Sefer Ḥassidim'" (in Hebrew). *Zion* n.s. 3:1–50.

———. 1947. *Galut*. Tr. Robert Warshow. New York.

———. 1953. "Gezerat TaTN"U." In *Sefer Asaf*, pp. 126–40. Ed. M. D. Cassuto et al. Jerusalem.

Bar-Ilan, Meir. 1996. "Tikkun Lel Shavu'ot: Hithavut ve-Takdimim." *Meḥkare Ḥag* 8:28–48.

Barasch, Moshe. 1976. *Gestures of Despair in Medieval and Early Renaissance Art*. New York.

Baron, Salo Wittmayer. 1952–83. *A Social and Religious History of the Jews*. 2nd ed. 18 vols. New York.

Baschet, Jérôme. 1993. "Medieval Abraham: Between Fleshly Patriarch and Divine Father." *MLN* 108:738–58.

———. 2000. *Le sein du père: Abraham et la paternité dans l'Occident médiéval*. Paris.

Baumeister, Roy F., and Stephen Hastings. 1997. "Distortions of Collective Memory:

How Groups Flatter and Deceive Themselves." In *Collective Memory of Political Events: Social Psychological Perspectives*, p. 277–93. Ed. James W. Pennebaker, et al. Mahwah, N.J.

Beissel, Stephan. 1909. *Geschichte der Verehrung Marias in Deutschland während des Mittelalters*. Freiburg im Bresgau.

Ben-Sasson, Haim Hillel. 1984. *Continuity and Variety* (in Hebrew). Tel Aviv.

———, ed. 1976. *A History of the Jewish People*. Cambridge, Mass.

Ben-Shalom, Ram. 2001. "*Kidush ha-Shem* and Jewish Martyrdom in Aragon and Castile in 1391: Between Spain and Ashkenaz" (in Hebrew). *Tarbiz* 70:227–82.

Ben-Yehuda, Nachman. 1995. *The Masada Myth: Collective Memory and Mythmaking in Israel*. Madison, Wis.

Blake, E. O. 1970. "The Formation of the 'Crusade Idea.'" *Journal of Ecclesiastical History* 21:11–31.

Blumenkranz, Bernhard. 1966. *Le Juif médiéval au miroir de l'art chrétien*. Paris.

Bonfil, Robert. 1987. "Between Eretz Israel and Babylonia" (in Hebrew). *Shalem* 5:1–30.

———. 1989. "Myth, Rhetoric, History? A Study in the Chronicle of *Ahima'az*" (in Hebrew). In *Culture and Society in Medieval Jewry: Studies Dedicated to the Memory of Haim Hillel Ben-Sasson*, pp. 99–135. Ed. Menachem Ben-Sasson et al. Jerusalem.

———. 1993. "Can Medieval Storytelling Help Understanding Midrash? The Story of Paltiel: A Preliminary Study on History and Midrash." In *The Midrashic Imagination: Jewish Exegesis, Thought, and History*, pp. 228–54. Ed. Michael Fishbane. Albany, N.Y.

Boureau, Alain 1998. *The Lord's First Night: The Myth of the Droit de Cuissage*. Tr. Lydia G. Cochrane. Chicago.

Bowersock, G. W. 1995. *Martyrdom and Rome*. Cambridge, Eng.

Bowman, Steven B. 1995. "'Yosippon' and Jewish Nationalism." *Proceedings of the American Academy for Jewish Research* 61:23–51.

Boyarin, Daniel. 1999. *Dying for God: Martyrdom and the Making of Christianity and Judaism*. Stanford, Calif.

Breuer, Mordechai. 1994. "The Historian's Imagination and Historical Truth" (in Hebrew). *Zion* 59:317–24.

———. 2000. "Women in Jewish Martyrology" (in Hebrew). In *Facing the Cross: The Persecutions of 1096 in History and Historiography*, pp. 141–49. Ed. Yom Tov Assis et al. Jerusalem.

Brown, Peter. 1978. *The Making of Late Antiquity*. Cambridge, Mass.

Brown-Gutoff, Susan E. 1991. "The Voice of Rachel in Jeremiah 31: A Calling to 'Something New.'" *Union Seminary Quarterly Review* 45:177–90.

Brundage, James A. 1969. *Medieval Canon Law and the Crusader*. Madison, Wis.

Cabié, Robert. 1965. *La Pentecôte: L'évolution de la cinquantaine pascale au cours des cinq premiers siècles*. Tournai.

Callaway, Mary. 1986. *Sing, O Barren One: A Study in Comparative Midrash*. Society for Biblical Literature Dissertation Series 91. Atlanta.

Carroll, Michael P. 1986. *The Cult of the Virgin Mary: Psychological Origins*. Princeton, N.J.

Caruth, Cathy. 1996. *Unclaimed Experience: Trauma Narrative and History*. Baltimore.

Chazan, Robert. 1970. "1007–1012: Initial Crisis for Northern European Jewry." *Proceedings of the American Academy for Jewish Research* 38–39:101–17.

———. 1987. *European Jewry and the First Crusade*. Berkeley, Calif.

———. 1991. "The Facticity of Medieval Narrative: A Case Study of the Hebrew First Crusade Narratives." *Association for Jewish Studies Review* 16:31–56.

———. 1994. "The Timebound and the Timeless: Medieval Jewish Narration of Events." *History and Memory* 6:5–34.

———. 1996. *In the Year 1096: The First Crusade and the Jews*. Philadelphia.

———. 1997. "The Trier Unit of the Lengthy Hebrew First Crusade Narrative." In *Between History and Literature: Studies in Honor of Isaac Barzilay*, pp. 37–49. Ed. Stanley Nash. Tel Aviv.

———. 1998. "The Mainz Anonymous: Historiographic Perspectives." In *Jewish History and Jewish Memory: Essays in Honor of Yosef Hayim Yerushalmi*, pp. 54–69. Ed. Elisheva Carlebach et al. Hanover, N.H.

———. 2000. *God, Humanity, and History: The Hebrew First Crusade Narratives*. Berkeley, Calif.

Cohen, Gerson D. 1967. "Messianic Postures of Ashkenazim and Sephardim." In *Studies of the Leo Baeck Institute*, pp. 117–56. Ed. Max Kreutzberger. New York.

———. 1991. *Studies in the Variety of Rabbinic Cultures*. Philadelphia.

Cohen, Jeremy. 1983. "The Jews as the Killers of Christ in the Latin Tradition, from Augustine to the Friars." *Traditio* 39:1–27.

———. 1989. "Recent Historiography on the Medieval Church and the Decline of European Jewry." In *Popes, Teachers, and Canon Law in the Middle Ages: Essays in Honor of Brian Tierney*, pp. 251–62. Ed. James Ross Sweeney and Stanley Chodorow. Ithaca, N.Y.

———. 1994. "*Gezerot Tatnu*: Martyrdom and Martyrology in the Hebrew Chronicles of 1096" (in Hebrew). *Zion* 59:169–208.

———. 1995. "'Witnesses of Our Redemption': The Jews in the Crusading Theology of Bernard of Clairvaux." In *Medieval Studies in Honour of Avrom Saltman*, pp. 67–81. Ed. Bat-Sheva Albert et al. Bar-Ilan Studies in History 4. Ramat Gan.

———. 1999a. "Between Martyrdom and Apostasy: Doubt and Self-Definition in Twelfth-Century Ashkenaz." *Journal of Medieval and Early Modern Studies* 29:431–71.

———. 1999b. "The Hebrew Crusade Chronicles in Their Christian Cultural Context." In *Juden und Christen zur Zeit der Kreuzzüge*, pp. 17–34. Ed. Alfred Haverkamp. Vorträge und Forschungen (Konstanzer Arbeitskreis für mittelalterliche Geschichte) 47. Sigmaringen.

———. 1999c. *Living Letters of the Law: Ideas of the Jew in Medieval Christianity*. Berkeley, Calif.

———. 2000. "Between History and Historiography: On the Study of the Persecutions and the Determination of Their Significance" (in Hebrew). In *Facing the Cross: The Persecutions of 1096 in History and Historiography*, pp. 16–31. Ed. Yom Tov Assis et al. Jerusalem.

———. 2001. "A 1096 Complex? Constructing the First Crusade in Jewish Historical Memory, Medieval and Modern." In *Jews and Christians in Twelfth-Century Europe*, pp. 9–26. Ed. Michael A. Signer and John Van Engen. Notre
Dame, Ind.

Cohen, Mark R. 1994. *Under Crescent and Cross: The Jews in the Middle Ages.*
Princeton, N.J.

Cole, Penny J. 1991. *The Preaching of the Crusades to the Holy Land, 1095–1270.*
Cambridge, Mass.

———. 1998. "Christians, Muslims, and the 'Liberation' of the Holy Land." *Catholic Historical Review* 84:1–10.

Coleman, Janet. 1992. *Ancient and Medieval Memories: Studies in the Reconstruction
of the Past.* Cambridge, Eng.

Coope, Jessica A. 1995. *The Martyrs of Cordoba: Community and Family Conflict in
an Age of Mass Conversion.* Lincoln, Neb.

Cooper, Kate. 1998. "The Voice of the Victim: Gender, Representation and Early
Christian Martyrdom." *Bulletin of the John Rylands Library* 80:147–57.

Cowdrey, H. E. J. 1970a. *The Cluniacs and the Gregorian Reform.* Oxford.

———. 1970b. "The Peace and the Truce of God in the Eleventh Century." *Past
and Present* 46:42–67.

———. 1976. "The Genesis of the Crusades: The Springs of the Western Idea of
Holy War." In *The Holy War*, pp. 9–32. Ed. T. P. Murphy. Columbus, Ohio.

———. 1985. "Martyrdom and the First Crusade." In *Crusade and Settlement*, pp.
46–56. Ed. Peter W. Edbury. Cardiff.

Crossan, John Dominic. 1995. *Who Killed Jesus? Exposing the Roots of Anti-Semitism
in the Gospel Story of the Death of Jesus.* San Francisco.

Culler, Jonathan. 1981. *The Pursuit of Signs.* Ithaca, N.Y.

Dahan, Gilbert. 1990. *Les intellectuels chrétiens et les Juifs au Moyen Age.* Paris.

Daly, Robert J. 1977. "The Soteriological Significance of the Sacrifice of Isaac."
Catholic Biblical Quarterly 39:45–75.

Daniel, Norman. 1979. *The Arabs and Medieval Europe.* 2nd ed. London.

Daniélou, Jean. 1950. *Sacramentum futuri: Etudes sur les origines de la typologie
biblique.* Paris.

Daube, David. 1956. *The New Testament and Rabbinic Judaism.* London.

David, Abraham. 2000. "Historical Records of the Persecutions during the First
Crusade in Hebrew Printed Works and Hebrew Manuscripts" (in Hebrew).
In *Facing the Cross: The Persecutions of 1096 in History and Historiography*, pp.
193–205. Ed. Yom Tov Assis et al. Jerusalem.

Davidson, Israel. 1970. *Thesaurus of Medieval Hebrew Poetry.* Rev. ed. 4 vols. New
York.

Davies, Philip R., 1979. "Passover and the Dating of the Aqedah." *Journal of Jewish
Studies* 30:59–67.

Davies, Philip R. and Bruce D. Chilton. 1978. "The Aqedah: A Revised Tradition-
History." *Catholic Biblical Quarterly* 40:514–46.

Déaut, Roger. 1963. *La nuit pascale: Essai sur la signification de la Pâque juive à partir
du Targum d'Exode XII 42.* Analecta Biblica 22. Rome.

Delaruelle, E. 1973. "The Crusading Idea in Cluniac Literature of the Eleventh Cen-

tury." In *Cluniac Monasticism in the Central Middle Ages*, pp. 191–216. Hamden, Conn.

De Lubac, Henri. 1998–2000. *Medieval Exegesis: The Four Senses of Scripture*. Tr. Marc Sebanc, and E. M. Macierowski. 2 vols. Grand Rapids, Mich.

Demus, Otto. 1970. *Romanesque Mural Painting*. New York.

De Ste. Croix, Geoffrey E. M. 1954. "Aspects of the 'Great' Persecution." *Harvard Theological Review* 47:75–113.

———. 1963. "Why Were the Early Christians Persecuted?" *Past and Present* 26:6–38.

Doninger, Wendy. 2000. *The Bedtrick: Tales of Sex and Masquerade*. Chicago.

Doran, Robert. 1980. "The Martyr: A Synoptic View of the Mother and Her Seven Sons." In *Ideal Figures in Ancient Judaism: Profiles and Parallels*, pp. 189–221. Ed. John J. Collins and George W. E. Nickelsburg. Society of Biblical Literature Septuagint and Cognate Studies 12. Chico, Calif.

Droge, Arthur J., and James D. Tabor. 1992. *A Noble Death: Suicide and Martyrdom among Christians and Jews in Antiquity*. San Francisco.

Dubnow, Simon. 1925–30. *Weltgeschichte des judisches Volkes*. 10 vols. Berlin.

Du Bourguet, Pierre. 1975. "Ensemble magique de la période romaine en Egypte." *Revue du Louvre* 25:255–57.

Dudley, Martin. 1994. "Natalis Innocentum: The Holy Innocents in Liturgy and Drama." In *Church and Childhood*, pp. 233–42. Ed. Diana Wood. Studies in Church History 31. Oxford.

Edgington, Susan. 1997. "The First Crusade: Reviewing the Evidence." In *The First Crusade: Origins and Impact*, pp. 5–77. Ed. Jonathan Phillips. Manchester.

Einbinder, Susan L. 2000. "Jewish Women Martyrs: Changing Models of Representation." *Exemplaria: A Journal of Theory in Medieval and Renaissance Studies* 12:105–27.

———. 2001. "Signs of Romance: Hebrew Prose and the Twelfth-Century Renaissance." In *Jews and Christians in Twelfth-Century Europe*, pp. 221–33. Ed. Michael A. Signer and John Van Engen. Notre Dame, Ind.

———. 2002. *Beautiful Death: Jewish Poetry and Martyrdom in Medieval France*. Princeton, N.J.

Eismeijer, Anne C. 1978. *Divina Quaternitas: A Preliminary Study in the Method and Application of Visual Exegesis*. Assen.

Emmerson, Richard Kenneth. 1979. "Antichrist as Anti-Saint: The Significance of Abbot Adso's *Libellus de Antichristo*." *American Benedictine Review* 30:175–90.

———. 1981. *Antichrist in the Middle Ages: A Study of Medieval Apocalypticism, Art, and Literature*. Seattle.

———. 2002. "The Representation of Antichrist in Hildegard of Bingen's *Scivias*: Image, Word, Commentary, and Visionary Experience." *Gesta* 41:95–110.

Erdmann, Carl. 1977. *The Origin of the Idea of Crusade*. Tr. Marshall W. Baldwin and Walter Goffart. Princeton, N.J.

Fishbane, Michael. 1994. *The Kiss of God: Spiritual and Mystical Death in Judaism*. Seattle.

Fitzmyer, Joseph A. 2000. "Melchizedek in the MT, LXX, and the NT." *Biblica* 81:63–69.

Flanagan, Sabina. 2000. "Twelfth-Century Apocalyptic Imaginations and the Coming of Antichrist." *Journal of Religious History* 24:57–69.

Fleischer, Ezra. 1994. "Christian-Jewish Relations in the Middle Ages Distorted" (in Hebrew). *Zion* 59:267–313.

Fleischman, Suzanne. 1983. "On the Representation of History and Fiction in the Middle Ages." *History and Theory* 22:278–310.

Flori, Jean. 1991a. "Mort et martyre des guerriers vers 1100: L'exemple de la première croisade." *Cahiers de civilisation médiévale (xe–xiie siècles)* 34:121–39.

———. 1991b. "Une ou plusieurs 'première croisade'? Le message d'Urbain II et les plus anciens pogroms d'Occident." *Revue historique* 285:3–27.

———. 1997. *La première croisade: L'Occident chrétien contre l'Islam (Aux origines des idéologies occidentales).* 2nd ed. Brussels.

———. 1999. *Pierre l'Ermite et la première croisade.* Paris.

———. 2001. *La Guerre Sainte: La formation de l'idée de croisade dans l'Occident chrétien.* Paris.

Fraenkel, Avraham. 2002. "R. Amnon and the Penetration of 'U-Netanneh Tokef' into Italy, Ashkenaz, and France" (in Hebrew). *Zion* 67:125–38.

France, John. 1996. "Les origines de la première Croisade." In *Autour de la première Croisade*, pp. 43–56. Ed. Michael Balard. Paris.

Francis, Fred O. 1974. "The Baraita of the Four Sons." *Journal of the American Academy of Religion* 42:280–97.

Franke, F. R. 1958. "Die freiwilligen Märtyrer von Cordova und das Verhältnis der Mozaraber zum Islam." *Gesammelte Aufsätze zur Kulturgeschichte Spaniens* 13:1–170.

Frend, W. H. C. 1965. *Martyrdom and Persecution in the Early Church: A Study of a Conflict from the Maccabees to Donatus.* Oxford.

Friedman, Mordechai Akiva. 2002. *Maimonides: The Yemenite Messiah and Apostasy* (in Hebrew). Jerusalem.

Funkenstein, Amos. 1993. *Perceptions of Jewish History.* Berkeley, Calif.

Gafni, Isaiah M., and Aviezer Ravitzky, eds. 1992. *Sanctity of Life and Martyrdom: Studies in Memory of Amir Yekutiel* (in Hebrew). Jerusalem.

Gager, John G. 1992. *Curse Tablets and Binding Spells from the Ancient World.* New York.

Geary, Patrick J. 1994. *Phantoms of Remembrance: Memory and Oblivion at the End of the First Millennium.* Princeton N.J.

Gershenzon, Shoshana, and Jane Litman. 1995. "The Bloody 'Hands of Compassionate Women': Portrayals of Heroic Women in the Hebrew Crusade Chronicles." In *Crisis and Reaction: The Hero in Jewish History*, pp. 73–91. Ed. Menachem Mor. Studies in Jewish Civilization 6. Omaha.

Gilchrist, John T. 1985. "The Erdmann Thesis and the Canon Law, 1083–1141." In *Crusade and Settlement*, pp. 37–45. Ed. Peter W. Edbury. Cardiff.

———. 1988. "The Perception of Jews in the Canon Law in the Period of the First Two Crusades." *Jewish History* 3:9–24.

Ginsburg, Elliot K. 1989. *The Sabbath in the Classical Kabbalah.* Albany, N.Y.

Ginzberg, Louis. 1909–38. *The Legends of the Jews.* Tr. Henrietta Szold and Paul Radin. 7 vols. Philadelphia.

Gold, Penny S. 1985. *The Lady and the Virgin: Image, Attitude, and Experience in Twelfth-Century France*. Chicago.

Goldin, Simha. 1997. "The Socialisation for 'Kiddush ha-Shem' among Medieval Jews." *Journal of Medieval History* 23:117–38.

———. 2002. *The Ways of Jewish Martyrdom* (in Hebrew). Tel Aviv.

Goldschmidt, Adolph. 1972–75. *Die Elfenbeinskulpturen aus der romanischen Zeit, XI.–XIII. Jahrhundert*. Repr. of 1918–26 ed. 2 vols. Denkmäler der deutschen Kunst 3–4. Berlin.

Goldschmidt, E. D. 1969. *The Passover Haggadah: Its Sources and History* (in Hebrew). Jerusalem.

Goldstein, Sidney. 1989. *Suicide in Rabbinic Literature*. Hoboken, N.J.

Goodblatt, David. 1995. "Suicide in the Sanctuary: Traditions on Priestly Martyrdom." *Journal of Jewish Studies* 46:10–29.

Gow, Andrew Colin. 1995. *The Red Jews: Antisemitism in an Apocalyptic Age, 1200–1600*. Studies in Medieval and Reformation Thought 55. Leiden.

———. 1999. "(En)Gendering Evil: Sinful Conceptions of the Antichrist in the Middle Ages and the Renaissance." *Journal of Millennial Studies* 2(1):1–14.

Graetz, Heinrich. 1861. *Geschichte der Juden von den ältesten Zeiten bis auf die Gegenwart*. Leipzig.

Green, Arthur. 1980. "Sabbath as Temple: Some Thoughts on Time and Space in Judaism." In *Go and Study: Essays and Studies in Honor of Alfred Jospe*, pp. 287–305. Ed. Raphael Jospe and Samuel Z. Fishman. Washington, D.C.

Gross, Abraham. 1994. "On the Ashkenazi Syndrome of Martyrdom in Portugal in 1497" (in Hebrew). *Tarbiz* 64:83–114.

———. 2000. "Historical and Halakhic Aspects of the Mass Martyrdom in Mainz: An Integrative Approach" (in Hebrew). In *Facing the Cross: The Persecutions of 1096 in History and Historiography*, pp. 171–92. Ed. Yom Tov Assis et al. Jerusalem.

Grossman, Avraham. 1981. *The Early Sages of Ashkenaz: Their Lives, Leadership, and Works (900–1096)* (in Hebrew). Jerusalem.

———. 1992. "Shorashav shel Kiddush ha-Shem be-Ashkenaz ha-Kedumah." In *Sanctity of Life and Martyrdom: Studies in Memory of Amir Yekutiel* (in Hebrew), pp. 99–130. Ed. Isaiah M. Gafni and Aviezer Ravitzky. Jerusalem.

———. 1995. *The Early Sages of France: Their Lives, Leadership, and Works* (in Hebrew). Jerusalem.

———. 1998. "Martyrdom in the Eleventh and Twelfth Centuries: Between Ashkenaz and the Muslim World" (in Hebrew). *Pe'amim* 75:27–46.

———. 1999. "The Cultural and Social Background of Jewish Martyrdom in Germany in 1096." In *Juden und Christen zur Zeit der Kreuzzüge*, pp. 73–86. Ed. Alfred Haverkamp. Vorträge und Forschungen (Konstanzer Arbeitskreis für mittelalterliche Geschichte) 47. Sigmaringen.

———. 2001. *Pious and Rebellious: Jewish Women in Europe in the Middle Ages*. Jerusalem.

Gruenwald, Ithamar. 1968. "Kiddush ha-Shem: Berur shel Mussag." *Molad* 1:476–84.

Güdemann, Moritz. 1880–88. *Geschichte des Erziehungswesens und der Cultur der*

abendländischen Juden während des Mittelalters und der neueren Zeit. 3 vols. Vienna.

Gunstone, John. 1967. *The Feast of Pentecost: The Great Fifty Days in the Liturgy. Studies in Christian Worship 8.* London.

Gutman, Joshua. 1949. "Ha-Em ve-Shiv'at Baneha ba-Aggadah uve-Sifre Ḥashmona'im 2 ve-4." In *Commentationes iudaico-hellenisticae in memoriam Iohannis Lewy* (in Hebrew), pp. 25–37. Ed. Moshe Schwabe and Joshua Gutman. Jerusalem.

Gutmann, Joseph. 1987. "The Sacrifice of Isaac in Medieval Jewish Art." *Artibus et historiae* 16:67–89.

Hacker, Joseph. 1966. "About the Persecutions during the First Crusade" (in Hebrew). *Zion* 31:225–31.

Hadas-Lebel, Mireille. 1984. "Jacob et Esau ou Israel et Rome dans le Talmud et le Midrash." *Revue de l'histoire des religions* 201:369–92.

Halamish, Moshe. 1993. "Tikkun Lel Shavu'ot." *Mehkare Hag* 5:62–78.

Hall, Stuart G. 1993. "Women among the Early Martyrs." In *Martyrs and Martyrologies*, pp. 1–21. Studies in Church History 30. Oxford.

Hasan-Rokem, Galit. 2000. *Web of Life: Folklore and Midrash in Rabbinic Literature.* Tr. Batya Stein. Stanford, Calif.

Haverkamp, Alfred, ed. 1999. *Juden und Christen zur Zeit der Kreuzzüge.* Vorträge und Forschungen (Konstanzer Arbeitskreis für mittelalterliche Geschichte) 47. Sigmaringen.

Haverkamp, Eva. 1999. "'Persecutio' und 'Gezerah' in Trier während des Ersten Kreuzzugs." In *Juden und Christen zur Zeit der Kreuzzüge*, pp. 35–71. Ed. Alfred Haverkamp. Vorträge und Forschungen (Konstanzer Arbeitskreis für mittelalterliche Geschichte) 47. Sigmaringen.

Heimann, Adelheif. 1959. "An Ivory in the Victoria and Albert Museum: Its Iconography and Provenance." *Nederlands kunsthistorisch Jaarboek* 10:5–50.

Herman, Judith Lewis. 1992. *Trauma and Recovery.* New York.

Herr, Moshe David. 1972. "Persecutions and Martyrdom in Hadrian's Days." In *Studies in History*, pp. 85–125. Ed. David Asheri and Israel Shatzman. Scripta Hierosolymitana 23. Jerusalem.

Hiestand, Rudolf, et al. 1996. *Der erste Kreuzzug 1096 und seine Folgen: Die Verfolgung von Juden im Rheinland.* Düsseldorf.

Hill, C. E. 1995. "Antichrist from the Tribe of Dan." *Journal of Theological Studies* 46:99–117.

Hinson, E. Glenn. 1993. "Women among the Martyrs." *Studia Patristica* 25:423–28.

Hollender, Elisabeth. 1996. "Reaktionen auf die Kreuzzüge in hebräischen liturgischen Dichtungen." In *1096: Der erste Kreuzzug und die Verfolgung der Juden in deutschen Städten*, pp. 93–111. Ed. Dieter Bach and Hans-Joachim Barkenings. Mülheim an der Ruhr.

Horbury, William, and Brian McNeil, eds. 1981. *Suffering and Martyrdom in the New Testament: Studies Presented to G. M. Styler by the Cambridge New Testament Seminar.* Cambridge, Eng.

Horowitz, Elliott. 2000. "Medieval Jews Face the Cross" (in Hebrew). In *Facing the*

Cross: The Persecutions of 1096 in History and Historiography, pp. 118–40. Ed. Yom Tov Assis et al. Jerusalem.

Horton, Fred L., Jr. 1976. *The Melchizedek Tradition: A Critical Examination of the Sources to the Fifth Century A.D. and in the Epistle to the Hebrews.* Society for New Testament Studies Monograph Series 30. Cambridge, Eng.

Jerphanion, Guillume de. 1925. *Une nouvelle province de l'art byzantin: Les églises rupestres de Cappadoce.* Paris.

Jones, Chris. 1993. "Women, Death, and the Law during the Christian Persecutions." In *Martyrs and Martyrologies*, pp. 23–34. Studies in Church History 30. Oxford.

Kagan, Donald. 1988. "The First Revisionist Historian." *Commentary*, 85(5):43–49.

Kanarfogel, Ephraim. 2003. "Halakhah and Mezi'ut (Realia): Surveying the Parameters and Defining the Limits." *Jewish Law Annual* 14:193–224.

Kasher, Menahem M., ed. 1927–92. *Torah Shelemah: A Talmudic-Midrashic Encyclopedia of the Pentateuch* (in Hebrew). 43 vols. Jerusalem.

Katz, Jacob. 1960. "Martyrdom in the Middle Ages and in 1648–49" (in Hebrew). In *Yitzhak F. Baer Jubilee Volume*, pp. 318–37. Ed. Salo Wittmayer Baron et al. Jerusalem.

———. 1961. *Exclusiveness and Tolerance: Studies in Jewish-Gentile Relations in Medieval and Modern Times.* Oxford.

———. 1970. "'Alterations in the Time of the Evening Service': An Example of the Interrelationship between Religious Custom, Halacha, and Their Social Background" (in Hebrew). *Zion* 35:35–60.

Kedar, Benjamin Z. 1982. "Masada: The Myth and the Complex." *Jerusalem Quarterly* 24:57–76.

———. 1998a. "Crusade Historians and the Massacres of 1096." *Jewish History* 12:11–31.

———. 1998b. "The Forcible Baptisms of 1096: History and Historiography." In *Forschungen zur Reichs-, Papst-, und Landesgeschichte: Peter Herde zum 65. Geburtstag von Freunden, Schülern und Kollegen dargebracht*, 1:187–200. 2 vols. Stuttgart.

Kepnes, Steven, ed. 1996. *Interpreting Judaism in a Postmodern Age.* New York.

Kirmayer, Laurence J. 1996. "Landscapes of Memory: Trauma, Narrative, and Dissociation." In *Tense Past: Cultural Essays in Trauma and Memory*, pp. 173–98. New York.

Klack-Eitzen, Charlotte. 1985. *Die thronenden Madonnen des 13. Jahrhunderts in Westfalen.* Denkmalpflage und Forschung in Westfalen 6. Bonn.

Klapisch-Zuber, Christiane, ed. 1992. *Silences of the Middle Ages.* Vol. 2 of *A History of Women in the West.* Cambridge, Mass.

Klassen, William. 1986. "Jesus and Phineas: A Rejected Role Model." *Society of Biblical Literature Seminar Papers* 25:490–500.

Konrad, Robert. 1964. *De ortu et tempore Antichristi: Antichristvorstellung und Geschichtsbild des Abtes Adso von Montier-en-Der.* Lassleben.

Kretschmar, Georg. 1954–55. "Himmelfahrt und Pfingsten." *Zeitschrift für Kirchengeschichte* 66:209–53.

LaCapra, Dominick. 1983. *Rethinking Intellectual History: Texts, Contexts, Language.* Ithaca, N.Y.

Lamberigts, M., and P. Van Deun, eds. 1995. *Martyrium in Multidisciplinary Perspective: Memorial Louis Reekmans.* Bibliotheca Ephemeridum Theologicarum Lovaniensium 117. Leuven.

Landes, Richard. 1996. "The Massacres of 1010: On the Origins of Popular Anti-Jewish Violence in Western Europe." In *From Witness to Witchcraft: Jews and Judaism in Medieval Christian Thought,* pp. 79–112. Ed. Jeremy Cohen. Wolfenbütteler Mittelalter-Studien 11. Wiesbaden.

Langmuir, Gavin I. 1990. *Toward a Definition of Antisemitism.* Berkeley, Calif.

Lasker, Daniel J. 1999. "The Impact of the Crusades on the Jewish Christian Debate." *Jewish History* 13:23–36.

Leclercq, Jean. 1946. *La spiritualité de Pierre de Celle (1115–1183).* Etudes de théologie et d'histoire de la spiritualité 7. Paris.

———. 1948. "Les deux compilations de Thomas de Perseigne." *Mediaeval Studies* 10.

———. 1952. "Une élévation sur les gloires de Jérusalem." *Recherches de science religieuse* 40:326–34.

———. 1974. *The Love of Learning and the Desire for God: A Study of Monastic Culture.* Tr. Catherine Misrahi. New York.

Lerner, Robert E. 1985. "Antichrists and Antichrist in Joachim of Fiore." *Speculum* 60:553–70.

———. 1992. "The Medieval Return to the Thousand-Year Sabbath." In *The Apocalypse in the Middle Ages,* pp. 51–71. Ed. Richard K. Emmerson and Bernard McGinn. Ithaca, N.Y.

Levenson, Jon D. 1993. *The Death and Resurrection of the Beloved Son: The Transformation of Child Sacrifice in Judaism and Christianity.* New Haven, Conn.

Levi, Israel. 1895. "Hanouca et le *Jus primae noctis.*" *Revue des études juives* 30:220–31.

Levine, Israel. 1998. *Tannim ve-Khinor: Ḥurban, Galut, Nakam ve-Ge'ulah ba-Shirah ha-'Ivrit ha-Le'umit.* Tel Aviv.

Lieberman, Saul. 1939–44. "The Martyrs of Caesarea." *Annuaire de l'Institut de Philologie et d'Histoire Orientales et Slaves* 7:395–446.

———. 1955–88. *Tosefta ki-Fshutah: A Comprehensive Commentary on the Tosefta* (in Hebrew). 10 vols. New York.

Liebes, Yehuda. 1993. *Studies in the Zohar.* SUNY Series in Judaica: Hermeneutics, Mysticism, and Religion. Albany, N.Y.

Linder, Amnon. 1995. "*Deus venerunt gentes*: Psalm 78 (79) in the Liturgical Commemoration of the Destruction of Latin Jerusalem." In *Medieval Studies in Honour of Avrom Saltman,* pp. 145–72. Ed. Bat-Sheva Albert. Bar-Ilan Studies in History 4. Ramat Gan.

———, ed. 1997. *The Jews in the Legal Sources of the Early Middle Ages.* Detroit.

Lipsker, Avidov. 2000. "Kiddush ha-Shem ba-Aspaklaryah shel ha-Sifrut ha-'Ivrit le-Dorothea." In *Literature and Society in Modern Hebrew Culture: Papers in Honor of Geshon Shaked* (in Hebrew), pp. 440–54. Ed. Judith Bar-El et al. Tel Aviv.

Lipton, Sara. 1999. *Images of Intolerance: The Representation of Jews and Judaism in the* Bible moralisée. Berkeley, Calif.

Little, Lester K. 1978. *Religious Poverty and the Profit Economy in Medieval Europe.* Ithaca, N.Y.

Loraux, Nicole. 1987. *Tragic Ways of Killing a Woman.* Tr. Anthony Forster. Cambridge, Mass.

Lotter, Friedrich. 1988. "Hostienfrevelvorwurf und Blutwunderfälschung bei den Judenverfolgungen von 1298 ("Rintfleisch") und 1336–1338 ("Armleder")." *Fälschungen im Mittelalter* 5:533–83.

———. 1999. " 'Tod oder Taufe': Das Problem der Zwangstaufen während des ersten Kreuzzugs." In *Juden und Christen zur Zeit der Kreuzzüge,* pp. 107–52. Ed. Alfred Haverkamp. Vorträge und Forschungen (Konstanzer Arbeitskreis für mittelalterliche Geschichte) 47. Sigmaringen.

———. 2000. "Der Gerechte wird seine Hände im Blut des Gottlosen waschen: Die Reaktivierung des theologischen Antijudaismus im Psalmenkommentar des Bruno von Würzburg." *Aschkenas* 10:43–115.

Luz, Ehud. 1968. "Mekomo shel Kiddush ha-Shem be-Toledot Yisra'el." *Shedemot* 28:9–20.

Mack, Hanan'el. 1993. "Kana'uto shel Pinḥas ben El'azar ben Aharon ha-Kohen." *Maḥanayim* 5:122–29.

Malkiel, David. 1993. "Infanticide in Passover Iconography." *Journal of the Warburg and Courtauld Institutes* 56:85–99.

———. 2001a. "Destruction or Conversion: Intenion and Reaction, Crusaders and Jews, in 1096." *Jewish History* 15:257–80.

———. 2001b. "Vestiges of Conflict in the Hebrew Crusade Chronicle." *Journal of Jewish Studies* 52:323–40.

———. 2002. "The Underclass in the First Crusade: A Historiographical Trend." *Journal of Medieval History* 28:169–97.

———. 2003. "Jewish-Christian Relatins in Europe, 840–1096." *Journal of Medieval History* 29:55–83.

Malone, Edward E. 1950. *The Monk and the Martyr: The Monk as the Successor of the Martyr.* Catholic University of America Studies in Christian Antiquity 12. Washington, D.C.

Mandelbaum, Irving J. 1990. "Tannaitic Exegesis of the Golden Calf Episode." In *A Tribute to Geza Vermes: Essays on Jewish and Christian Literature and History,* pp. 207–23. Ed. Philip R. Davies and Richard T. White. *Journal for the Study of the Old Testament* Supplement Series 100. Sheffield.

Mann, Jacob. 1972. *Texts and Studies in Jewish History and Literature.* Repr. of 1931–35 original. 2 vols. New York.

Marcus, Ivan G. 1982. "From Politics to Martyrdom: Shifting Paradigms in the Hebrew Narratives of the 1096 Crusade Riots." *Prooftexts* 2:40–52.

———. 1989. Review of *European Jewry and the First Crusade,* by Robert Chazan. *Speculum* 64:685–88.

———. 1990. "History, Story, and Collective Memory: Narrativity in Early Ashkenazic Culture." *Prooftexts* 10:365–88.

———. 1992. "A Pious Community and Doubt: Qiddush ha-Shem in Ashkenaz

and the Story of Rabbi Amnon of Mainz." In *Studien zur jüdischen Geschichte und Soziologie: Festschrift Julius Carlebach*, pp. 97–113. Heidelberg.

———. 1995. "Jews and Christians Imagining the Other in Medieval Europe." *Prooftexts* 15:209–26.

———. 1996. *Rituals of Childhood: Jewish Acculturation in Medieval Europe*. New Haven, Conn.

———. 1999. "The Representation of Reality in the Narratives of 1096." *Jewish History* 13:37–48.

———. 2000. "From 'Deus Vult' to the 'Will of the Creator': Extremist Religious Ideologies and Historical Reality in 1096 and Hasidei Ashkenaz" (in Hebrew). In *Facing the Cross: The Persecutions of 1096 in History and Historiography*, pp. 92–100. Ed. Yom Tov Assis et al. Jerusalem.

———. 2002. "A Jewish-Christian Symbiosis: The Culture of Early Ashkenaz." In *Cultures of the Jews: A New History*, pp. 449–516. Ed. David Biale. New York.

Markow, Deborah. 1983. "The Soul in Ninth-Century Byzantine Art: Innovative Iconography and the Dilemma of Resurrection." *Rutgers Art Review* 4:2–11.

Mayer, Hans Eberhard et al. 1989. "Select Bibliography of the Crusades." In *A History of the Crusades*, vol. 6, *The Impact of the Crusades on Europe*, pp. 511–664. Ed. Kenneth M. Setton et al. Madison, Wis.

McCracken, Peggy. 2002. "Engendering Sacrifice: Blood, Lineage, and Infanticide in Old French Literature." *Speculum* 77:55–75.

McGinn, Bernard. 1989. "Violence and Spirituality: The Enigma of the First Crusade." *Journal of Religion* 69:375–79.

———. 2000. *Antichrist: Two Thousand Years of the Human Fascination with Evil*. New York.

Minty, Mary. 1994. "Kiddush ha-Shem in German Christian Eyes in the Middle Ages" (in Hebrew). *Zion* 59:209–66.

Mintz, Alan. 1984. *Ḥurban: Responses to Catastrophe in Hebrew Literature*. New York.

Moore, R. I. 1992. "Anti-Semitism and the Birth of Europe." In *Christianity and Judaism*, pp. 33–57. Ed. Diane Wood. Studies in Church History 29. Oxford.

Morris, Colin. 1978. "*Equestris ordo*: Chivalry as a Vocation in the Twelfth Century." In *Religious Motivation: Biological and Sociological Problems for the Church Historian*, pp. 87–96. Ed. Derek Baker. Studies in Church History 15. Oxford.

———. 1993. "Martyrs on the Field of Battle before and during the First Crusade." In *Martyrs and Martyrologies*, pp. 93–104. Studies in Church History 30. Oxford.

Morrison, Karl F. 1990. *History as a Visual Art in the Twelfth-Century Renaissance*. Princeton, N.J.

———. 1992. *Conversion and Text: The Cases of Augustine of Hippo, Herman-Judah, and Constantine Tsatsos*. Charlottesville, Va.

Murray, Alan V. 1998. "Bibliography of the First Crusade." In *From Clermont to Jerusalem: The Crusades and Crusader Societies, 1095–1500*, pp. 267–310. Ed. Alan V. Murray. International Medieval Research 3. Turnhout.

Murray, Alexander. 1998–2000. *Suicide in the Middle Ages*. Oxford.

Myers, David N. 1995. *Re-Inventing the Jewish Past: European Jewish Intellectuals and the Zionist Return to History.* New York.

———. 1999. "*Mehabevin et ha-tsarot*: Crusade Memories and Modern Jewish Martyrologies." *Jewish History* 13:49–64.

Nelson, Janet L. 1993. "The Franks, the Martyrology of Usuard, and the Martyrs of Cordoba." In *Martyrs and Martyrologies*, pp. 67–80. Studies in Church History 30. Oxford.

Noam, Vered. 1994. "The Seventeenth of Elul in Megillat Ta'anit" (in Hebrew). *Zion* 59:433–44.

Noble, Shlomo. 1971. "The Jewish Woman in Medieval Martyrology." In *Studies in Jewish Bibliography and Literature in Honor of I. Edward Kiev*, pp. 347–55. Ed. Charles Berlin. New York.

Noort, Ed, and Eibert Tigchelaar, eds. 2002. *The Sacrifice of Isaac: The Aqedah (Genesis 22) and Its Interpretations.* Themes in Biblical Narrative: Jewish and Christian Traditions 4. Leiden.

Ntedika, Joseph. 1971. *L'évocation de l'au-delà dans la prière pour les morts: Etude de patristique et de liturgies latines (IVe–VIIIe s.).* Recherches africaines de théologie 2. Louvain.

Oppenheimer, Aharon. 1992. "Kedushat ha-Hayyim ve-Heruf ha-Nefesh be-Ikvot Mered Bar-Kokhba." In *Sanctity of Life and Martyrdom: Studies in Memory of Amir Yekutiel* (in Hebrew), pp. 85–97. Ed. Isaiah M. Gafni and Aviezer Ravitzky. Jerusalem.

Painter, Sidney. 1953. *A History of the Middle Ages, 284–1500.* New York.

Pascher, Joseph. 1963. *Das liturgische Jahr.* Munich.

Patai, Raphael. 1974. "Jus Primae Noctis." In *Studies in Marriage Customs*, pp. 177–80. Ed. Issachar Ben-Ami and Dov Noy. Folklore Research Center Studies 4. Jerusalem.

Patterson, Lee. 2001. "'The Living Witnesses of Our Redemption': Martyrdom and Imitation in Chaucer's *Prioress's Tale.*" *Journal of Medieval and Early Modern Studies* 31:507–60.

Pelekanidis, S. M., et al. 1974–75. *The Treasures of Mount Athos: Illuminated Manuscripts, Miniatures, Headpieces, Initial Letters.* Athens.

Pelikan, Jaroslav. 1971–89. *The Christian Tradition: A History of the Development of Doctrine.* 5 vols. Chicago.

———. 1996. *Mary through the Centuries: Her Place in the History of Culture.* New Haven, Conn.

Perkins, Judith. 1995. *The Suffering Self: Pain and Narrative in the Early Christian Era.* London.

Peters, Edward, ed. 1971. *The First Crusade: The Chronicle of Fulcher of Chartres and Other Source Materials.* Philadelphia.

Petruccione, John. 1990. "The Portrait of St. Eulalia of Mérida in Prudentius' *Peristephanon 3.*" *Analecta Bollandiana* 108:81–104.

Petuchowski, Jakob J. 1957. "The Controversial Figure of Melchizedek." *Hebrew Union College Annual* 28:127–36.

Pinder, Wilhelm. 1922. *Die Pietà.* Bibliothek der Kunstgeschichte 6. Leipzig.

Plumpe, Joseph C. 1943. *Mater Ecclesia: An Inquiry into the Concept of Church as*

Mother in Early Christianity. Catholic University of America Studies in Christian Antiquity 6. Washington, D.C.

Rauh, Horst Dieter. 1979. *Das Bild des Antichrist im Mittelalter: Von Tyconius zum deutschem Symbolismus*. 2nd ed. Beiträge zur Geschichte der Philosophie und Theologie des Mittelalters, n.s. 9. Munster.

Redfield, James. 1982. "Notes on the Greek Wedding." *Arethusa* 15:181–201.

Reeg, Gottfried, ed. 1985. *Die Geschichte von Zehn Märtyrern*. Texte und Studien zum antiken Judentum 10. Tübingen.

Reines, Chaim W. 1960. "The Jewish Attitude toward Suicide." *Judaism* 10:160–70.

———. 1963. *Be-Ohale Shem: Masot u-Meḥkarim ba-Musar, ba-Mishpat uva-Sotziologiyah ha-Yisra'elit*. Jerusalem.

Rembaum, Joel E. 1982. "The Development of a Jewish Exegetical Tradition Regarding Isaiah 53." *Harvard Theological Review* 75:289–311.

Renna, Thomas. 1992. "Bernard of Clairvaux and the Temple of Solomon." In *Law, Custom, and the Social Fabric in Medieval Europe: Essays in Honor of Bryce Lyon*, pp. 73–88. Ed. Bernard S. Bachrach and David Nicholas. Studies in Medieval Culture 28. Kalamazoo, Mich.

Richlin, Amy. 1992. *The Garden of Priapus: Sexuality and Aggression in Roman Humor*. Rev. ed. New York.

Richter, Horst. 1992. "*Militia Dei*: A Central Concept for the Religious Ideas of the Early Crusades and the German *Rolandslied*." In *Journey toward God: Pilgrimage and Crusade*, pp. 107–26. Ed. Barbara N. Sargent-Baur. Kalamazoo, Mich.

Riley-Smith, Jonathan. 1980. "Crusading as an Act of Love." *History* 65:177–92.

———. 1984. "The First Crusade and the Persecution of the Jews." In *Persecution and Toleration*, pp. 51–72. Ed. W. J. Sheils. Studies in Church History 21. Oxford.

———. 1986. *The First Crusade and the Idea of Crusading*. London.

———. 2002. "Christian Violence and the Crusades." In *Religious Violence between Christians and Jews: Medieval Roots, Modern Perspectives*, pp. 3–20. Ed. Anna Sapir Abulafia. Hampshire, Eng.

Robinson, Ian S. 1973. "Gregory VII and the Soldiers to Christ." *History* 58:169–92.

———. 1990. *The Papacy, 1073–1198*. Cambridge, Eng.

Rooke, Deborah W. 2000. "Jesus as Royal Priest: Reflections on the Interpretation of the Melchizedek Tradition in Heb 7." *Biblica* 81:81–94.

Roos, Lena. 2003. "God Wants It! The Ideology of Martyrdom of the Hebrew Crusade Chronicles and Its Jewish and Christian Background." Ph.D. dissertation, Uppsala University.

Rosenberg, Henri, ed. 1984. *Kol Hakatuv l'Chaim: A Memorial Volume in Memory of Rabbi Chaim Tobias* (in Hebrew). Jerusalem.

Rosenthal, Erwin. 1945–46. "Abraham and Lazarus: Iconographical Considerations of a Medieval Book Painting." *Pacific Art Review* 4:7–23.

Rosenwein, Barbara H. 1982. *Rhinoceros Bound: Cluny in the Tenth Century*. Philadelphia.

Roskies, David G., ed. 1989. *The Literature of Destruction: Jewish Responses to Catastrophe*. Philadelphia.

Roth, Cecil. 1969. *A Short History of the Jewish People*. Rev. ed. London.

Rousset, P. 1955. "L'idée de croisade chez les chroniquers d'Occident." In *Relazione del X Congreso Internazionale di Scienze Storiche, III: Storia del Medioevo*, pp. 547–563. Florence.

Ruether, Rosemary R. 1974. *Faith and Fratricide: The Theological Roots of Anti-Semitism*. New York.

Saebo, Magne, et al., eds. 1996–2000. *Hebrew Bible, Old Testament: The History of Its Interpretation*. Vol. 1, *From the Beginnings to the Middle Ages (until 1300)*. 1 vol. in 2 pts. Gottingen.

Safrai, Samuel. 1980. "Kiddush ha-Shem in the Teachings of the Tannaim" (in Hebrew). In *Yitzhak F. Baer Memorial Volume*, pp. 28–42. Ed. Haim Beinart et al. Jerusalem.

Sarason, Richard S. 1988. "The Interpretation of Jeremiah 31:31–34 in Judaism." In *When Jews and Christians Meet*, pp. 99–123. Ed. Jakob J. Petuchowski. Albany, N.Y.

Schäfer, Jost. 1980. "Einleitende Bemerkungen zur Ikonographie des Vesperbildes." In *Gotische Vesperbilder: Diözesan Museum Paderborn–Sauerland-Museum Arnsberg*, pp. 9–17. Ed. Karl Josef Schmitz et al. Paderborn.

Schein, Sylvia. 1996. "Jérusalem: Objective originel de la première Croisade?" In *Autour de la première Croisade*, pp. 119–26. Ed. Michael Balard. Paris.

Schlauch, Margaret. 1939. "The Allegory of the Church and the Synagogue." *Speculum* 14:448–64.

Schmidt, Karl. 1881. *Jus primae noctis: Eine geschichtliche Untersuchung*. Freiburg im Breisgau.

Schreckenberg, Heinz. 1996. *The Jews in Christian Art: An Illustrated History*. Tr. John Bowden. New York.

Schwarzfuchs, Simon. 1989. "The Place of the Crusades in Jewish History" (in Hebrew). In *Culture and Society in Medieval Jewry: Studies Dedicated to the Memory of Haim Hillel Ben-Sasson*, pp. 251–67. Ed. Menachem Ben-Sasson et al. Jerusalem.

Schweid, Eliezer. 1994. "Hatzdakat Elohim be-Sippurei 'Edut 'al 'Kiddush ha-Shem': Ha-Mekorot ha-Rishonim." *Dimmui* 7:18–27.

Seeley, David. 1990. *The Noble Death: Greco-Roman Martyrology and Paul's Concept of Salvation. Journal for the Study of the New Testament* Supplement Series 28. Sheffield.

Seiferth, Wolfgang S. 1970. *Synagogue and Church in the Middle Ages: Two Symbols in Art and Literature*. Tr. Lee Chadeayne and Paul Gottwald. New York.

Sered, Susan Starr. 1986. "Rachel's Tomb and the Milk Grotto of the Virgin Mary: Two Women's Shrines in Bethlehem." *Journal of Feminist Studies in Religion* 2:7–22.

———. 1989. "Rachel's Tomb: Societal Liminality and the Revitalization of a Shrine." *Religion* 19:27–40.

———. 1991. "Rachel, Mary, and Fatima." *Cultural Anthropology* 6:131–46.

———. 1995. "Rachel's Tomb: The Development of a Cult." *Jewish Studies Quarterly* 2:103–48.

———. 1996. "Our Mother Rachel." *Annual Review of Women in World Religions* 4:1–56.

Shaw, Brent D. 1993. "The Passion of Perpetua." *Past and Present* 139:3–45.

————. 1996. "Body/Power/Identity: Passions of the Martyrs." *Journal of Early Christian Studies* 4:269–312.

Sheingorn, Pamela. 1987. "The Bosom of Abraham Trinity: A Late Medieval All Saints Image." In *England in the Fifteenth Century*, pp. 273–95. Ed. Daniel Williams. Woodbridge, Eng.

Shemesh, Aharon. 1998. "The *Baraita* of the Four Sons" (in Hebrew). *Sidra* 14:131–36.

Shepkaru, Shmuel. 1999. "From Death to Afterlife: Matryrdom and Its Recompense." *Association for Jewish Studies Review* 24:1–44.

————. 2002a. "Death Twice Over: Dualism of Metaphor and Realia in 12th-Century Hebrew Crusading Accounts." *Jewish Quarterly Review* 93:217–56.

————. 2002b. "To Die for God: Martyrs' Heaven in Hebrew and Latin Crusade Narratives." *Speculum* 77:311–41.

Signer, Michael A., and John Van Engen, eds. 2001. *Jews and Christians in Twelfth-Century Europe*. Notre Dame, Ind.

Silberschlag, Eisig. 1968. *Saul Tchernichowsky: Poet of Revolt*. Ithaca, N.Y.

Smolar, Leivy, and Moshe Aberbach. 1968. "The Golden Calf Episode in Postbiblical Literature." *Hebrew Union College Annual* 39:91–116.

Soloveitchik, Haym. 1987. "Religious Law and Social Change: The Medieval Ashkenazic Example." *Association for Jewish Studies Review* 12:205–21.

————. 1998. "Catastrophe and Halakhic Creativity: Ashkenaz—1096, 1242, 1306, and 1298." *Jewish History* 12:71–85.

Sonne, Isaiah. 1933. "Nouvel examen des trois rélations hebraïques sur les persécutions de 1096." *Revue des études juives* 96:137–52.

————. 1947. "Which Is the Earliest Account of the Persecutions during the First Crusade" (in Hebrew). *Zion* 12:74–81.

Spiegel, Gabrielle M. 1990. "History, Historicism, and the Social Logic of the Text in the Middle Ages." *Speculum* 65:59–86.

Spiegel, Shalom. 1967. *The Last Trial: On the Legends and Lore of the Command to Abraham to Offer Isaac as a Sacrific—The Akedah*. Tr. Judah Goldin. New York.

Stern, David, and Mark J. Mirsky, eds. 1990. *Rabbinic Fantasies: Imaginative Narratives from Classical Hebrew Literature*. New Haven, Conn.

Stern, Menachem. 1982. "The Suicide of Eleazar ben Jair and His Men at Masada, and the 'Fourth Philosophy'" (in Hebrew). *Zion* 47:367–98.

Stow, Kenneth R. 1984. *The "1007 Anonymous" and Papal Sovereignty: Jewish Perceptions of the Papacy and Papal Policy in the High Middle Ages. Hebrew Union College Annual* Supplement 4. Cincinnati.

————. 1987. "Ha-Kenesiyyah ve-Historiografyah Neutralit." In *Studies in Historiography: Collected Essays* (in Hebrew), pp. 101–15. Ed. Joseph Salmon. Jerusalem.

————. 2001. "Conversion, Apostasy, and Apprehensiveness: Emicho of Flonheim and the Fear of Jews in the Twelfth Century." *Speculum* 76:911–33.

Straw, Carole. 2000. "Settling Scores: Eschatology in the Church of the Martyrs."

In *Last Things: Death and Apocalypse in the Middle Ages*, pp. 21–40, 261–77. Ed. Caroline Walker Bynum and Paul Freedman. Philadelphia.

Swarzenski, Hanns. 1935. "Quellen zum deutschen Andachtsbild." *Zeitschrift für Kunstgeschichte* 4:141–44.

Ta-Shma, Israel. 2000. "The Attitude of Medieval German Halakhists to Aggadic Sources" (in Hebrew). In *Facing the Cross: The Persecutions of 1096 in History and Historiography*, pp. 150–56. Ed. Yom Tov Assis et al. Jerusalem.

———. 2003. "Rabbi Isaac of Dampierre's Responsum Concerning Informers: On the Halakhic Value Attributed to Aggadic Material by Ashkenazic Tradition" (in Hebrew). *Zion* 68:167–74.

Toch, Michael. 1999. "Wirtschaft und Verfolgung: Die Bedeutung der Ökonomie für die Kreuzzugspogrome des 11. und 12. Jarhunderts." In *Juden und Christen zur Zeit der Kreuzzüge*, pp. 253–85. Ed. Alfred Haverkamp. Vorträge und Forschungen (Konstanzer Arbeitskreis für mittelalterliche Geschichte) 47. Sigmaringen.

Tucker, Gordon. 1994. "Jacob's Terrible Burden: In the Shadow of the Text." *Bible Review* 10(3):20–28, 54.

Tyerman, Christopher. 1998. *The Invention of the Crusades*. Toronto.

Urbach, Ephraim E. 1980. *The Tosaphists: Their History, Writings, and Methods* (in Hebrew). 4th ed. 2 vols. Jerusalem.

Van Dijk, S. J. P. 1963. *Sources of the Modern Roman Liturgy: The Ordinals by Haymo of Faversham and Related Documents (1243–1307)*. 2 vols. Studia et Documenta Franciscana. Leiden.

Van Dijk, S. J. P., and J. Hazelden Walker. 1960. *The Origins of the Modern Roman Liturgy: The Liturgy of the Papal Court and the Franciscan Order in the Thirteenth Century*. Westminster, Md.

Van Henten, Jan Willem. 1997. *The Maccabean Martyrs as Saviours of the Jewish People: A Study of 2 and 4 Maccabees*. Supplements to *Journal for the Study of Judaism* 57. Leiden.

———. 2000. "Whose Blood Is It Anyway? The Christianization of the Maccabean Martyrs." Unpublished lecture.

———, ed. 1989. *Die Entstehung der jüdischen Martyrologie*. Studia Post-Biblica 38. Leiden.

Van Henten, Jan Willem, and Friedrich Avemarie, eds. 2002. *Martyrdom and Noble Death: Selected Texts from Graeco-Roman, Jewish, and Christian Antiquity*. London.

Van Houts, Elisabeth. 1999. *Memory and Gender in Medieval Europe, 900–1200*. Toronto.

Verhelst, D. 1973. "La préhistoire des conceptions d'Adson concernant l'Antichrist." *Recherches de théologie ancienne et médiéval* 40:52–103.

Vermes, Geza. 1973. *Scripture and Tradition in Judaism: Haggadic Studies*. 2nd ed. Studia Post-Biblica 4. Leiden.

Vinson, Martha. 1994. "Gregory Nazianzen's Homily 15 and the Genesis of the Christian Cult of the Maccabean Martyrs." *Byzantion* 64:166–92.

Waldman, Nahum M. 1998. "Interpretive Cover-ups: Whitewashing the Images of Aaron and the Israelite People in the Incident of the Golden Calf." In *Freedom*

and Responsibility: Exploring the Challenges of Jewish Continuity, pp. 51–64. Ed. Rela Mintz Geffen and Marsha Bryan Edelman. Hoboken, N.J.

Waltz, James. 1970. "The Significance of the Voluntary Martyrs of Ninth-Century Cordoba." *Muslim World* 60:226–36.

Walz, Rainer. 1999. "Die Verfolgung von 1096 und die Ritualmordlegende: Die Debatte über die Thesen Israel J. Yuvals." *Aschkenas* 9:189–232.

Warner, David A. 2001. "Ritual and Memory in the Ottonian *Reich*: The Ceremony of *Adventus*." *Speculum* 76:255–83.

Warner, Marina. 1976. *Alone of All Her Sex: The Myth and Cult of the Virgin Mary.* New York.

Watt, Jack. 1999. "Parisian Theologians and the Jews: Peter Lombard and Peter Cantor." In *The Medieval Church: Universities, Heresy, and the Religious Life: Essays in Honour of Gordon Leff*, pp. 55–76. Ed. Peter Biller and Barrie Dobson. Studies in Church History 11. Woodbridge, Eng.

Weiner, Eugene, and Anita Weiner. 1990. *The Martyr's Conviction: A Sociological Analysis.* Brown Judaic Studies 203. Atlanta.

Westermarck, Edward. 1921. *The History of Human Marriage.* 5th ed. New York.

White, Hayden. 1981a. "The Narrativization of Real Events." In *On Narrative*, pp. 249–54. Ed. W. J. T. Mitchell. Chicago.

———. 1981b. "The Value of Narrativity in the Representation of Reality." In *On Narrative*, pp. 1–23. Ed. W. J. T. Mitchell. Chicago.

Wilhelm, J. D. 1948–52. "Sidre Tikkunim." In *Alei Ayin: The Salman Schocken Jubilee Volume* (in Hebrew), pp. 125–45. Jerusalem.

Winstead, Karen A. 1997. *Virgin Martyrs: Legends of Sainthood in Late Medieval England.* Ithaca, N.Y.

Wolf, Kenneth Baxter. 1988. *Christian Martyrs in Muslim Spain.* Cambridge, Eng.

Wolfson, Elliot R. 2001. "Martyrdom, Eroticism, and Asceticism in Twelfth-Century Ashkenazic Piety." In *Jews and Christians in Twelfth-Century Europe*, pp. 171–220. Ed. Michael A. Signer and John Van Engen. Notre Dame, Ind.

Wood, Diana, ed. 1993. *Martyrs and Martyrologies.* Studies in Church History 30. Oxford.

Yassif, Eli. 1998. "Intertextuality in Folk Literature: Pagan Themes in Folktales of the Early Modern Period" (in Hebrew). *Jerusalem Studies in Jewish Folklore* 19–20:287–309.

———. 1999a. *The Hebrew Folktale: History, Genre, Meaning.* Bloomington, Ind.

———. 1999b. "Legends and History: Historians Reading Hebrew Legends of the Middle Ages" (in Hebrew). *Zion* 64:187–220.

Yerushalmi, Yosef Hayim. 1982. *Zakhor: Jewish History and Jewish Memory.* Seattle.

Young, Karl. 1919. *Ordo Rachelis.* University of Wisconsin Studies in Language and Literature 4. Madison, Wis.

———. 1933. *The Drama of the Medieval Church.* 2 vols. Oxford.

Young, Robin Darling. 1991. "The 'Woman with the Soul of Abraham': Traditions about the Mother of the Maccabean Martyrs." In *"Women Like This": New Perspectives on Jewish Women in the Greco-Roman World*, pp. 67–81. Ed. Amy Jill Levine. Society of Biblical Literature: Early Judaism and Its Literature 1. Atlanta.

Yuval, Israel Jacob. 1993. "Vengeance and Damnation, Blood and Defamation: From Jewish Martyrdom to Blood Libel Accusations" (in Hebrew). *Zion* 58:33–90.

———. 1994. "'The Lord Will Take Vengeance, Vengeance for His People'— Historia sine ira et studio" (in Hebrew). *Zion* 59:351–414.

———. 1995. "The Haggadah of Passover and Easter" (in Hebrew). *Tarbiz* 65:5–28.

———. 1998. "Shetikat ha-Historyon ve-Dimyon ha-Sofer: R. Amnon mi-Magentzah ve-Ester-Minah mi-Vermaiza." *Alpayim* 15:132–41.

———. 1999. "Christliche Symbolik und jüdische Martyrologie zur Zeit der Kreuzzüge." In *Juden und Christen zur Zeit der Kreuzzüge*, pp. 87–106. Ed. Alfred Haverkamp. Vorträge und Forschungen (Konstanzer Arbeitskreis für mittelalterliche Geschichte) 47. Sigmaringen.

———. 2000a. "The Language and Symbols of the Hebrew Chronicles of the Crusades" (in Hebrew). In *Facing the Cross: The Persecutions of 1096 in History and Historiography*, pp. 101–17. Ed. Yom Tov Assis et al. Jerusalem.

———. 2000b. *"Two Nations in Your Womb": Perceptions of Jews and Christians* (in Hebrew). Tel Aviv.

Zakovitch, Yair, and Avigdor Shinan. 1996. *Splitting Apart the Sea of Reeds* (in Hebrew). President's Study Group on the Bible and Sources of Judaism 10. Jerusalem.

Zerubavel, Yael. 1995. *Recovered Roots: Collective Memory in the Making of Israeli National Tradition.* Chicago.

Zfatman, Sara. 1993. *The Jewish Tale in the Middle Ages: Between Ashkenaz and Sepharad* (in Hebrew). Jerusalem.

Index